Eat to Beat

Arthritis, Diabetes, High Blood Pressure, High Cholesterol

and 51 Other Common Health Problems

By the Editors of
FC&A Medical Publishing

Publisher's Note

The editors of FC&A have taken careful measures to ensure the accuracy and usefulness of the information in this book. While every attempt has been made to assure accuracy, errors may occur. We advise readers to carefully review and understand the ideas and tips presented and to seek the advice of a qualified professional before attempting to use them. The publisher and editors disclaim all liability (including any injuries, damages or losses) resulting from the use of the information in this book.

The health information in this book is for information only and is not intended to be a medical guide for self-treatment. It does not constitute medical advice and should not be construed as such or used in place of your doctor's medical advice.

"Do not fear, for I am with you; do not anxiously look about you, for I am your God. I will strengthen you, surely I will help you, surely I will uphold you with My righteous right hand."

Isaiah 41:10

Table of Contents

Allergies

Watch out for hidden herbal allergies

Your echinacea pills may cause more sniffles than they cure if you're allergic to ragweed. That's because the two plants are related. Like medications, herbs and their essential oils can sometimes trigger unexpected allergic reactions.

If you find yourself with a rash or other unusual symptom, think about the herbs and oils you use — they could be responsible for your discomfort. Here are a few common culprits and their effects.

Echinacea. Like ragweed, this heal-all is a member of the daisy family. In fact, so are chamomile, yarrow, and feverfew. If you have ragweed allergies, you may want to walk wide of these herbs since they can set off an itchy rash and symptoms similar to hay fever.

One man had a different response to echinacea. He developed bruise-like bumps under the skin of his legs after he began taking supplements. Once he stopped, the bumps went away. Although the herb didn't seem to cause permanent damage, reactions like these may be serious and should be treated by a doctor.

St. John's wort. Sometimes called "herbal Prozac," this herb could have you burning for relief. That's because St. John's wort can be phototoxic, making your eyes and skin more sensitive to sunlight. You might sunburn easily, get hives, or develop a rash.

Not everyone has these reactions, but it's best to play it safe. If you take this supplement, stay out of the sun, even on cloudy days. Experts aren't sure whether sunscreen and sunglasses will help, but they certainly won't hurt.

Celery seeds. You can get a rash just from handling celery seeds, much less eating them. Although used to treat arthritis and rheumatism, they can cause contact dermatitis and other allergies, especially if you're allergic to birch pollen. Not only that, the chemical psoralen found in the seeds can be phototoxic, like St. John's wort. If you take celery seed, the same rules apply — avoid sunlight and wear protection.

Ginkgo biloba. Thirty-five children learned the hard way about the allergies this plant can cause. After stepping on fruit from a ginkgo tree, they each developed an itchy rash like that from poison ivy. Scientists aren't certain if the ginkgo extract sold in stores could have the same effect, but if you develop a rash while taking ginkgo, keep in mind it may be an allergic reaction.

Cinnamon. This favorite scent may bring back memories of mom's apple pie, but the oil may not be as safe as the spice. Cinnamon oil is high in phenols, chemicals that can irritate skin and cause a rash. So take care not to put it directly on your skin. If you're set on using cinnamon, mix it first with a carrier oil like sweet almond.

Bergamot. Although bergamot once was used widely in cosmetics, some countries now ban it in perfumes because of its side effects. This essential oil contains psoralen, the same phototoxic chemical found in celery seeds. Although you should avoid sunlight when using any phototoxic medicine, be aware of hidden dangers. It's actually the sun's invisible ultraviolet (UV) rays that trigger a reaction, not the light itself.

Dangerous UV rays can come from other sources, too. A woman in Austria went to a commercial spa that gave her bergamot oil and then put her in a tanning bed where she soaked up UV rays. In three days she had painful skin sores — without once setting foot in the sun.

Even professionals can make mistakes. That's why it's important to educate yourself on the do's and don'ts of natural remedies.

★ Buy oils from reliable sources. Some suppliers dilute expensive oils with cheaper ones, so you may not know exactly what you're paying for — or if you'll be allergic to it.

★ Dilute essential oils, especially those you plan to use on your skin. This goes for more than just cinnamon. Because they are so concentrated, even "safe" oils can irritate sensitive skin. To cut their strength, mix them with a carrier oil like sweet almond, olive, or hazelnut.

★ Keep oils away from your eyes. You wouldn't handle hot peppers and then rub your eyes, right? Treat oils with the same respect. Even the mildest of them can cause irritation.

★ Check the labels on your herbal supplements, and read up on the company who makes them. Some products are mislabeled and actually claim to pack more herbs than they really do. Or you could be allergic to other ingredients in the supplement. So read carefully, and do your homework before you buy.

★ Choose herbs and oils by their botanical name. Several different species may go by the same common name, and an herb's strength and healing power may vary from one species to another.

★ Tell your doctor about any herbs or essential oils you're using. He can help you watch for side effects and drug interactions.

If you have asthma, sensitive skin, or a history of allergies, you may want to think twice before using any herbs or oils. More importantly, if you think you are having an allergic reaction to your treatment, see your doctor right away. Play it safe and smart with nature's remedies, and you'll live a longer, healthier life.

What you should know about nasal sprays

You've been a slave to your sinuses for years, taking your nasal spray each day just like the doctor ordered. Well, here's something your doctor may not know — you may not have to use nasal sprays daily to get relief from your allergies. Recent research has found they work just as well if you take them only as needed.

Another thing you should know — some nasal sprays require special care as they can cause dangerous side effects. Others you can make at home for free, saving yourself the high cost of store-bought medications. If you want to protect both your health and your pocketbook, you need to learn the facts about nasal sprays.

Get the scoop on steroid sprays. Doctors usually recommend you use steroid sprays daily during allergy season to keep your nose and sinuses from swelling. But researchers at the University of Chicago suggest you may only have to use them when symptoms hit. In their study of 52 allergy sufferers, they found that those who used steroid sprays only on their "bad" days had fewer symptoms than those taking a placebo.

Talk to your doctor about whether you can benefit from these new findings. You could save yourself money and still stay healthy.

Beware the dangers of decongestants. These sprays work well at drying up your sinuses, but they can also cause two major problems.

★ **Rise in blood pressure.** Decongestants can raise your blood pressure. So if you have high blood pressure or heart disease, they may put a greater strain on your heart. You could also suffer a serious reaction if you have diabetes or a thyroid disease. Experts say two ingredients are a threat — pseudoephedrine and phenylpropanolamine. The Food and Drug Administration has proposed removing phenylpropanolamine from the market because it may cause bleeding in the brain. Read labels to make sure your decongestant doesn't contain these ingredients, and talk to your doctor before trying new medications.

★ **Rebound congestion.** Sometimes, when you stop using the spray, your allergy symptoms get worse than before. You end up depending on the spray to breathe comfortably all the time. For this reason, you should only use decongestant sprays when you really need them and never more than three days at a time.

If you feel like you can't live without your decongestant spray, it's time to break the habit. Try not to use it for six to eight hours. Breathe through your mouth if your nose gets stuffy, and run a vaporizer to keep your sinus and nasal membranes moist.

Try a soothing spray of saline. This saltwater solution gently cleans out your sinuses while soothing and moistening your nasal passages. You can also use it to wean yourself from decongestants. Just spray two puffs of saline in each nostril up to four times a day.

If you buy saline spray in a store, be careful. Some over-the-counter solutions contain a preservative, benzalkonium chloride (BKC), that actually kills the cells that fight off infections. As a result, you could have more infections in the long run. Instead, look for phosphate buffered saline solutions rather than those made with BKC.

Better yet, save yourself money by making your own saline solution at home. Just mix a half teaspoon of table salt with a cup of warm water. You can pour the solution into a rubber syringe, like the kind made to clean out children's noses, or use a small spray bottle. If the saline makes your nose burn, try using a little less salt in the mixture.

Whether your nasal spray comes in a pump bottle or a pressurized canister, follow these steps to get the best results:

★ Blow your nose before you use the spray, and make sure you can breathe through both nostrils. Otherwise, the medicine may not get deep enough into your nose and sinuses to relieve your symptoms.

★ Aim the spray toward the back of your head, not the top, and try not to sneeze or blow the medicine back out.

★ As with other medications, store your nasal spray away from sunlight.

If your nose starts to hurt, sting, or bleed after using any kind of nasal spray, stop, and talk to your doctor. With these tips in mind, you should have a more comfortable allergy season.

Top 7 ways to drive off dust mites

Dust mites are a nightmare if you suffer from allergies. Don't lose sleep over the bothersome bugs. These no-sweat solutions will soon have you sneeze-free.

Wash them away. Launder clothing and bedding weekly in water that's at least 77 degrees Fahrenheit to kill the most mites.

Turn on the heat. Fluffing your clothes in a hot dryer will get rid of both wrinkles and dust mites.

Take them to the cleaners. The chemicals kill the tiny bugs and seem to keep them from coming back.

Start packing. Store out-of-season clothes in a cool, dry place, then wash them when you bring them out.

Get a little steamed. Vacuum floors, rugs, and upholstered furniture regularly, preferably with steam heat.

Sleep light as a feather. Feather pillows trap fewer dust mite allergens than synthetic pillows.

Wrap it up. Slip plastic or vinyl covers over your mattresses and pillows to keep the bugs out.

Rx for household allergies

The next time you stay home sick with allergies, think about this — your home could be causing them. Step outside for a few minutes. If you notice any odors when you walk back in, your house could have poor ventilation, resulting in a case of sick building syndrome.

Today's climate-controlled buildings tend to recycle the same indoor air over and over. When that air becomes polluted, the building gets "sick" — and so could you. You may develop coughing, sneezing, headaches, and other allergy symptoms. Your environment could also dull your mental sharpness and leave you unable to concentrate.

The good news is you can "cure" sick building syndrome with a few simple steps.

★ Open your windows occasionally to bring in fresh air.

★ Change the filters in your heater and air conditioner every few months — more often if you find them dirty.

★ Clean your house regularly to cut down on airborne dust and dirt.

★ Make sure you have lots of ventilation when you use chemical cleaners. Better yet, stick with soap and water for everyday grime.

★ Add some plants to your home. Varieties such as the spider plant, aloe vera, and English ivy do a great job of cleaning and purifying the air.

Your home could harbor other allergy troublemakers as well. If you've been baffled by a rash, hair loss, or similar symptoms, take a look at some of these unexpected causes.

★ **A rash from cash.** A cashier in Germany developed eczema, a skin condition, on his hands from dyes in the paper money he handled. You might not break out at the sight of a $50 bill, but if you have an unexplainable rash, you could be sensitive to the dyes in other products like cloth, paper, wax, leather, or synthetic materials.

★ **The woes of yellow.** Yellow No. 5, a food coloring found in processed veggies, desserts, and drinks, can cause hives and itching in some people. For this reason, manufacturers must list it in the ingredients, so be sure to check labels.

★ **Balding blues.** The products meant to keep your hair healthy may actually trigger hair loss. Sodium lauryl, also known as laureth sulfate, is a common ingredient in shampoos, liquid soaps, mouthwashes, toothpastes, and other soapy stuff. And while it gets you clean, it can leave you with bald spots if you're allergic to it. Your hair will grow back, but you'll need to read labels carefully to avoid this chemical culprit.

Many things can set off allergies inside and out. If you have symptoms you just can't shake, talk to your doctor about the possible causes. She can work with you to find the culprit, and get your symptoms under control.

Master mold — indoors and out

Mold doesn't just lurk in caves like a monster in a horror movie. It hides in your basement, the yard, around leaky pipes, and even in your houseplants. Inside or out, it grows any place that's damp and warm. If you suffer from allergies or asthma, you know how troublesome mold can be.

But it doesn't have to wreak havoc with your health. You can take control of mold — and take back your life — with a few changes around your home.

Keep your house cool and dry. Low humidity and cool temperatures discourage mold growth. Run the air conditioner (AC) and a dehumidifier to keep the temperature under 70 degrees Fahrenheit and the humidity at less than 50 percent. Just remember to empty the AC's evaporation tray often.

Catch up on cleaning. Bleach and water work wonders on mold. Use them to clean those damp places under sinks, in showers, and around tubs, toilets, and washing machines. Clean your dehumidifier regularly with the bleach-water mixture.

Leave the light on. Hang low-watt light bulbs in damp closets and crawl spaces, and leave them turned on all the time. The heat from the bulb should help these places stay dry.

Don't over-water houseplants. Mold loves damp soil and standing water. So water your houseplants moderately, and drain any excess that collects in the pot's bottom. You can also buy products at your local plant nursery that slow the growth of mold.

Heat, don't hang, your laundry. Hanging your clothes outside to dry may save energy, but your allergies will pay since mold spores can cling to your clothing. You can hang delicate clothes on a drying rack indoors, but use the dryer for most things. Move wet laundry from the washer to the dryer as soon as possible to fend off mold. And make sure your dryer vents to the outside, not to an attic or side room.

Check basements and pipes. Dry out damp basements with a space heater and a dehumidifier. While you're down there, check your basement for leaks or damp areas. A mold-resistant paint on the floor and walls may help control mold. Remember to check the faucets and pipes in and under your house for leaks, too, and get them repaired.

Battle mold in the bathroom. Pick up wet clothing and towels instead of leaving them on the floor, and air out the shower so the extra moisture can dry. Running the fan for a while after you bathe will also lower the humidity in bathrooms.

Fix flooded carpets. If your carpet gets wet due to leaks or flooding, clean and dry it as soon as possible. Mold sets in fast. If you can't dry out the carpet, you may have to replace it.

Get out of yard work. Wet leaves and grass are some of mold's favorite hiding places. Try to avoid yard work when it's damp outside, or hire someone else for the job. If you decide to do it yourself, wear a dust mask to filter out some of the mold and other allergens. After working outdoors, change your clothes, shower, and rinse the mold spores out of your nose with a saline solution.

With a little creativity, you can manage your mold allergy year-round. But if allergies still bother you, work with your doctor to find other solutions for your symptoms.

6 ways to dodge the danger of latex

From gloves to pacifiers, rubber makes life simple. But if you're one of the 800,000 people allergic to rubber latex, this miracle material may stretch you to your limits.

You don't have to be born with a latex allergy. Constant exposure can sensitize you to it, especially in places like a hospital or care home. If you have a runny nose, itchy rash, hives, or trouble breathing, you could be allergic to latex.

Your doctor can test you to find out for sure. If you are allergic, or if you think you're at risk, follow these tips on where to find this common substance and what to do to protect yourself.

Know your enemy. In the last 15 years, latex allergies have become a serious problem, especially among health care workers and patients who use the material every day. It's in most disposable gloves, IV tubes, catheters, stethoscopes, syringes, bandages, dressings, medicine bottles, and other medical supplies. But it can show up around the home, too — in baby pacifiers and bottle nipples, rubber bands, waistbands, shoe soles, tires, balloons, and condoms.

Read labels. The best way to beat this allergy is to avoid the source, according to the American College of Allergy, Asthma, and Immunology. Start by reading labels. The U.S. Food and Drug Administration (FDA) requires most gloves and medical supplies to tell you if they contain natural rubber latex. Other products may also list it in their ingredients. If you're unsure about something, try to contact the company that makes it, and ask.

Look out for hidden latex. Labeled or not, latex can be sneaky. For instance, the powder in gloves can make the latex allergen airborne. So even if you don't wear rubber gloves, you could react to someone else wearing them near you. If you've stopped using them but are still having an allergic reaction, ask the people around you to wear non-latex gloves.

Another hidden source of latex can be the lids and droppers of prescription medicine bottles. The rubber can taint the medication inside, causing allergic reactions in some people. The FDA does not require bottles to carry warning labels about their latex content. Your pharmacist can ask the manufacturer if they use rubber, and he can put your medication in non-latex bottles.

Spread the word. Tell your doctor, nurse, dentist, pharmacist, and other health professionals about your allergy. They'll know not to use latex during surgery, checkups, in bottling your medicines, or during other procedures.

Label yourself. Even better, carry an ID card or bracelet to warn others of your allergy. This way, if you're in an accident, the people treating you will know to avoid using latex.

Be prepared. If your allergic reaction is severe, take a hint from people with bee sting allergies, and carry an emergency kit with you. Make sure it contains a syringe of adrenaline that you or someone near you can inject as soon as you start having a reaction.

Although this modern material can be hard to avoid, it's worth the added trouble. With a little care and know-how, you can deal success-fully with a latex allergy.

Change your diet to ditch dermatitis

Tomatoes are everywhere. They go on hamburgers and pizza, in soups and salads. Some people even eat them like apples. But if you suf-fer from contact dermatitis, some of your favorite foods — like tomatoes, ice cream, and even chocolate — could be the reason you're seeing red.

That's because certain foods may cause the same kind of rash you get from poison ivy or perfume. Called contact dermatitis, it usually results from touching something you're allergic to. Researchers have now found that eating certain foods also may trigger dermatitis. If you're allergic to what you eat, you could end up with red, scaly rashes on your hands, face, genitals, chest, or back, along with a constant itching that drives you crazy.

Discovering the cause of your allergy can be even more frustrating. But dermatologists at the University of Louisville in Kentucky seem to have found a common link among rash-raising foods. The tasty culprit — a plant extract called balsam of Peru (BOP) — is found in many everyday foods, such as citrus fruit, sodas, and, yes — tomatoes.

If BOP is so common, how do you avoid it? In the Louisville study, people who had contact dermatitis went on a strict diet, cutting out all food that contained balsam of Peru. After six weeks, almost half the participants saw serious improvement. Some even said their symptoms went away completely.

If you've failed to banish your rash by avoiding perfumes or other allergens, see your dermatologist to find out if you're allergic to balsam of Peru. A change in diet could do the trick for you, too. Work with your doctor to cut out all BOP foods for four weeks. Then slowly start eating them again, one every few days. This way, if you suddenly break out in a rash, you'll know what caused it.

Here are some foods you need to look out for:

★ Tomatoes and tomato products like ketchup, red sauces, chili, and pizza. Remember, this includes most Italian and Mexican meals, too.

★ Citrus fruits like oranges, lemons, grapefruit, and tangerines as well as anything made with them like fruit juice or baked goods.

★ Spices, especially cinnamon, vanilla, cloves, ginger, allspice, curry, and anise.

★ Spicy side items like pickles or pickled vegetables, barbecue sauce, and liver paste.

★ Sweets that may have added spices or flavorings, including chocolate, ice cream, gum, candy, and baked treats like Danish pastries.

★ Sodas and flavored teas.

★ Certain alcohols like beer, wine, gin, and vermouth.

★ Tobacco products like menthol cigarettes as well as some cough medicines and throat lozenges.

Chances are, you're only allergic to one or two foods. The challenge is to find out which ones. That's why, if you try the diet, it's important to put your willpower to the test and not eat any BOP foods for a while. You may have to skip your favorites, but you might finally scratch that itch for good.

Food labels: helpful guides or health risks?

Food labels are notoriously confusing. Yet if you have an allergy, your health — and maybe even your life — could depend on your ability to understand them.

Nine out of 10 allergic reactions are caused by eight foods — shellfish, eggs, fish, milk, soy, wheat, peanuts, and tree nuts — often because manufacturers don't list them in the ingredients. New food labeling guidelines may change that.

The Food Allergies Issues Alliance has asked manufacturers to use simple, clear words to label all the ingredients in their food, including what's in the spices, flavorings, and additives. That means new labels will not only be more accurate, they'll also be easier to read.

For now, these guidelines are voluntary and not required by the Food and Drug Administration. All manufacturers may not follow the new rules. So it's still up to you to understand labels and eat carefully. Here are a few tips to help you out.

Know the lingo. Labels may seem to speak in riddles, but many complicated words are just industry terms for common foods. For instance, "semolina" generally means wheat, and if your hot chocolate mix contains "casein," you're really drinking a milk product.

In fact, casein can show up where you'd least expect. It's often used to glue together processed foods like frozen or canned fish. If you're allergic to milk, you could have a reaction to eating even small amounts of casein. Products made in the U.S. must list it in their ingredients, but imported foods may not. So choose carefully, and check the label.

Look for the unexpected. At least one brand of barbecue sauce is made with pecans. And the snack-size version of your favorite candy bar may contain an allergen not found in the regular size. Although the labels may list these potential allergens, you may not think to check for them.

Manufacturers also tend to change their recipes without warning. Words like "new" or "improved" should send up red flags. But be sure to read all labels, not just those that sound suspicious.

Watch out for unlabeled allergens. The ingredients on the label look safe, but that may not protect you from another problem — cross-contamination. Food processing plants that make more than one product can end up with tainted food if the equipment isn't cleaned well between batches. As a result, a plain chocolate candy bar could contain traces of peanuts from another candy bar. Yet chances are the label won't list peanuts as an ingredient.

It's hard to protect yourself against cross-contamination. Just be aware of everything you eat so you can track down the source if you have a reaction.

What if there is no label? Street vendors and restaurants may not list all the ingredients in their dishes. Even the chef may not know exactly what's in some specialties like desserts and sauces.

Instead of taking a risk, ask about the ingredients. Tell the waiter or chef what you're allergic to and how severe your reaction could be. Once they understand, they should take your questions more seriously. They may even take a few extra precautions in the kitchen.

Don't become one of the 150 Americans who dies from food allergies each year. If you have doubts about any food, don't eat it. Should you have an allergic reaction, get to an emergency room immediately. Your life may not be in danger, but when it comes to your health, you're better off safe than sorry.

Alzheimer's Disease

Fight Alzheimer's with this 4-cent solution

Scientists may have found the real cause of Alzheimer's disease (AD) — brain inflammation. Better yet, they may have found a way to treat, and even prevent, AD for just pennies a day with the help of a simple anti-headache pill.

Nonsteroidal anti-inflammatory drugs (NSAIDs) like aspirin, ibuprofen, and naproxen are often used to reduce the swelling of arthritis. But they may ease brain inflammation as well.

Experts believe toxins slowly accumulate in your brain over a number of years. This buildup triggers inflammation that gradually damages brain cells and eventually leads to memory loss and Alzheimer's.

You can fight back against AD with a daily NSAID. A recent study published in the *New England Journal of Medicine* revealed that taking NSAIDs regularly for two or more years could cut your risk of Alzheimer's by up to 80 percent. NSAIDs even seem to focus your memory as they slow the disease's progress. That means people who already have AD can still reap the benefits of this low-cost medication.

Talk to your doctor before you decide to take NSAIDs regularly. They can lead to serious side effects like internal bleeding and stomach problems. You're more likely to have trouble if you use more than one kind of NSAID or take blood thinners.

Rule out Alzheimer's look-alikes

Alzheimer's disease is the most misdiagnosed mental health problem in older adults, according to the National Institute of Mental Health. That's because it mimics some symptoms of these other conditions:

★   heart disease   ★   stroke

★   depression   ★   loneliness or boredom

★   poor nutrition   ★   alcohol abuse

★   side effects of medication ★   head injuries

★   high fevers   ★   thyroid problems

These are all treatable conditions your doctor should rule out before considering Alzheimer's. A proper diagnosis means the right treatment — and that can make all the difference.

Knock out AD with nutritional know-how

Reach 90 without getting Alzheimer's disease, and chances are you never will. Experts think eating right is the key.

Researchers at Johns Hopkins University studied over 3,000 residents of Cache County, Utah. Those who made it into their 90's without developing AD had a dramatically lower risk for the disease later. Even people with a genetic risk for Alzheimer's reduced their chances just by living a long life.

You may think that's small beans, but the U.S. Census Bureau estimates that 1.8 million Americans will be in their 90's by the year 2005. And over 8 million will be 90-something by 2050. If the Cache County results hold true, many of these long-lived seniors may manage to dodge Alzheimer's.

You can be one of them. New studies show that the foods and vitamins you get every day can safeguard your brain against aging and

Alzheimer's. Start protecting yourself now, and soon you could be home free in your 90's.

Beef up your B's. Homocysteine — the same amino acid linked to heart disease and stroke — could also contribute to AD. The National Institute on Aging studied over 1,000 people for eight years. High blood levels of homocysteine nearly doubled their risk of developing AD. Researchers believe the higher the homocysteine levels and the longer they stay high, the greater your risk.

But there's good news. Doctors know B vitamins, like folate, B6, and B12, can slash homocysteine levels. It just makes sense that getting enough of these nutrients might also protect you from Alzheimer's.

Fortified cereals and grains are great sources of folate. But balance is important — too little B12 and too much folate could actually make your memory worse. Lean meats and low-fat dairy products are the best sources for B12, while bananas, potatoes, and leafy green vegetables load you up with B6.

Start counting calories. Watching what you eat may keep your body young and healthy. Now a lab study on "senior" mice suggests it might do the same for your brain.

Mice fed a low-cal diet showed fewer signs of aging in their brain cells than mice fed traditional diets. This doesn't mean eat less food. Just choose foods low in added sugars and saturated fat. Fill your plate with low-calorie vegetables, fruits, whole grains, and lean meat.

Cut back on fat. An even better strategy is to watch the fat content of your food choices. People who carry what's called the "Alzheimer's gene" — Apo E4 — are more likely to develop AD if they eat a high-fat diet.

Your body needs some fat to stay healthy, but skipping extras like butter and salad dressing, or choosing low-fat versions of these treats is simply a healthier way to eat.

Balanced nutrition is part of a smart treatment program for many illnesses. But see your doctor if you begin to notice serious memory lapses, mental confusion, or other signs of Alzheimer's. Today's medicine can help AD sufferers continue to lead rich, full lives.

Simple strategy sinks AD

You don't have to live in fear of Alzheimer's. Fight back with this daily plan designed to keep your mind sharp.

Kick off with folate and fiber. Start your day with a bowl of hot or cold fortified cereal. It's a great source of brain-saving folic acid. Plus, fiber is famous for lowering cholesterol and blood pressure, both linked to Alzheimer's disease.

Include a major mineral. Add low-fat milk to your cereal and drink calcium-enriched orange juice on the side. Calcium helps your brain and nerve cells work together.

Feast on a rainbow. Fill your meals with colorful fruits and vegetables for memory-boosting antioxidants. Foods like carrots and mangoes are the best sources of beta carotene. Green leafy veggies, on the other hand, provide lots of vitamins E and C, which experts think may lower your risk for Alzheimer's.

Keep your body fit. Take a walk in the early evening. Exercise supplies your brain with the fresh oxygen essential to a healthy mind.

Get out and about. Join friends for a movie or a game of cards. Socializing keeps you active, one of the secrets to fending off Alzheimer's.

Stop memories from going up in smoke

Smoke and you double — even quadruple — your risk of dementia. You shouldn't be surprised smoking puts you at risk for Alzheimer's disease (AD) and other types of mental decline. It's one of the most preventable causes of major disease and premature death in the U.S.

Every day, new studies provide more information on the dangers of smoking, and the benefits of quitting. So put out that last cigarette, and pick up the battle against Alzheimer's.

Asthma

7 ways to make your workout a success

You can improve your asthma symptoms while cutting back on your medication — all through the magic of exercise. When you burn calories on a jog or during a round of golf, you literally take a load off your lungs. Other exercises, like yoga, help calm your breathing and improve your posture. Working out is the key to boosting your heart and lung power.

Unfortunately, all that heart-pumping, lung-boosting activity could trigger an asthma attack. It's a frightening dilemma called exercise-induced asthma (EIA), and it affects up to 90 percent of all asthmatics. So it's crucial to take care when you exercise. Here are some proven ways to ease your breathing and guarantee a successful workout.

Tote a water bottle. The easiest way to prevent EIA is by drinking lots of water during your workout. Dehydration is a major spark for asthma attacks, and you could be dehydrated even if you don't feel thirsty. Drink at least six glasses of water every day — even more when you're exercising.

Load up on lycopene. New research says the antioxidant lycopene — well-known as a cancer fighter — may also combat EIA. In the study, wheezers who took a lycopene supplement every day for a week showed fewer asthma symptoms than those who didn't take it.

The supplement also contained other antioxidants such as vitamin E, so researchers aren't sure lycopene can take all the credit. Still, it's a good nutrient to add to your diet. Enjoy tomato-based sauces, soups, salsas, and ketchups, and eat fresh tomatoes, grapefruits, and watermelons — all potent sources of lycopene.

Cover up with a scarf. Wearing a scarf or a bandana over your mouth can really make a difference on brisk fall and winter days. Cold, dry air is one of your lungs' biggest enemies. Your scarf, however, will make the air you breathe warm, moist, and safe.

Dive into a swimming pool. Many asthmatic athletes find swimming is one of the safest ways to exercise. The humid air in the pool area is easy to breathe, and swimming naturally slows and steadies your breathing. If you're not a dolphin at heart, or even a tadpole, find other ways to exercise indoors on a wintry day. A heated, well-ventilated indoor track, gym, or even a mall can provide the perfect spot for some aerobic exercise.

Clean your plate of danger foods. Some experts claim foods like shrimp, peanuts, egg whites, and bananas can bring on an asthma attack even if you eat them two hours before your workout. Test this theory yourself by keeping a daily log of what you eat. If you notice a trend between your diet and your asthma symptoms, work with your doctor to cut out the suspicious foods one by one.

Take five (or 15). If you suffer an asthma attack during your workout even after following these precautions, rest may be the best remedy. In many cases, simply catching your breath for 15 minutes is enough to get the asthma to subside.

Consult a medical expert. Ask your doctor if she can prescribe a medicine that helps prevent EIA attacks. In fact, get her advice before you even start your program. Then you'll be less likely to let asthma sidetrack you later on.

Warning: Inhalers may be hazardous to your bones

Almost two-thirds of asthmatics may suffer from brittle bones because of their steroid inhalers. Research has found the corticosteroid medications deal a double whammy — they slow bone growth while speeding up bone loss. Check out these startling findings:

★   More than 61 percent of women on long-term asthma medication lost bone density in their spine and hip, according to a study published in *The Annals of Allergy, Asthma and Immunology*. Forty-three percent of those over age 65 had osteoporosis compared to just 30 percent of normal post-menopausal women.

★ Young women with asthma who follow a high-dosage program of steroids — 12 inhaler puffs per day, or 1,200 micrograms — may be twice as likely as non-asthmatic women to break their hip after age 65.

★ Men with lung disease are five times more likely to have a low score on a bone mineral density (BMD) test, a clear indication of bone loss. When men get steroid treatment for these conditions, they're nine times more likely to be at risk.

Does this mean you should stop your steroid treatment? No bones about it — the answer is no. Steroids are a breakthrough in asthma medicine and have saved countless lives. Instead, follow these suggestions to reap your medication's benefits while protecting your bones.

Take the BMD test. A bone density test will tell just how much your steroid medication has affected your bones. With this information, you and your doctor can come up with a plan to help stop your bone loss.

Ask about alternative medicine. Most experts agree you should take the lowest dose of steroids that works. So it's a smart idea to ask your doctor about lowering your dose and perhaps supplementing with a steroid-free drug.

Feed your bones two key nutrients. You need extra calcium and vitamin D when you're on steroid therapy, so talk to your doctor about the appropriate supplements. In addition, make sure you eat plenty of high-calcium foods like dairy products, broccoli, almonds, and fortified orange juice, and get a daily dose of sunshine.

Add a new weapon to your arsenal. Substances called bisphosphonates can help prevent steroid's bone-whittling effects. Most doctors recommend them if you're on steroids for less than three months. But long-term use can cause serious gastrointestinal problems so make sure you follow your doctor's advice.

Consider taking hormones. A hormone called calcitonin is an option for preventing bone loss if you haven't reached menopause. If you're postmenopausal, hormone replacement therapy will counter steroid side effects. Men should have their testosterone level checked and consider hormone replacement if it's low. Your doctor can help you decide if these options are right for you.

Strengthen your skeleton. Weight-bearing exercises could increase the thickness of your bones by 30 percent. So walk, jog, lift weights, dance, or do any exercise that puts pressure on your bones — just as long as you do it at least three times a week.

Pack away the cigarettes. If you need another reason to stop smoking and drinking alcohol, here's one. Both increase your risk of bone loss.

Top 5 'breathe-easy' breakfast foods

A balanced breakfast could be just what your lungs ordered. Packed with anti-asthma compounds, these five morning foods could help you breathe easier all day long. Just make sure they aren't among your asthma triggers, then sit down, relax, and enjoy!

Pour a glass of orange juice. Just one glass can punch up your vitamin C levels. This awesome antioxidant is a must for warding off asthma symptoms.

Grab a (pink) grapefruit. Lycopene, the carotenoid that gives foods their pink or red coloring, may be just what you need to boost your asthma defenses.

Top your cereal with wheat germ. It will give you an extra dose of fiber as well as lung-protecting vitamin E.

Scramble some eggs. Eating egg yolks could open up your lung passages — all thanks to their vitamin A.

Brew a cup of coffee. The same substance that perks you up could help you breathe easier by relaxing the muscles around your airways.

Steer clear of pollen-stirring storms

You may hold your breath when your local weatherman reports the day's pollen count. But it's also smart to be concerned when he forecasts a thunderstorm. Getting caught outdoors in the wrong storm could spell an asthma attack worthy of a hospital visit.

According to documented cases in Britain and Australia, certain types of thunderstorms can clog the air with up to 12 times more grass pollen than normal. That's a serious statistic if you have pollen allergies. After one London squall, for instance, more than 640 people — 10 times the normal number — poured into local emergency rooms suffering from asthma attacks.

The booming thunder and pounding rain aren't the asthma-causing culprits, say Australian researchers. A powerful kind of wind pattern called an outflow causes "thunderstorm-associated asthma." The outflow whips up pollen, pulls it into the clouds, and then blasts it back to earth. The pollen-polluted air then hovers near ground level, where you can easily breathe it in without knowing it.

You know, though, when the effects hit. The air passageways between your lungs and windpipe — the bronchi — overreact to the pollen and swell up. Your chest feels tight, and you start to wheeze and cough. Anxiety sets in. Breathing seems, or even becomes, impossible.

To protect yourself, you need more than an umbrella. Your safest bet is to stay indoors during any thunderstorm, especially in the allergy season from late spring to summer. Not all thunderstorms cause outflows, but you won't be able to tell a dangerous storm from a plain-Jane downpour until it's too late.

If you do take your chances and brave the elements, wear a surgical mask or dust mask over your mouth. You can find them at your local hardware store or pharmacy.

Atherosclerosis

Trim your tummy to save your arteries

If that little paunch you developed in your thirties has grown into a potbelly, your heart could be in big trouble.

Here's the connection: People with abdominal fat have more inflammation in their arteries. And inflamed arteries lead to atherosclerosis.

But take heart — this inflammation can be reversed. "Apple-shaped" women, who dieted and exercised to lose at least 10 percent of their weight, improved their waistlines and their arteries.

It's easier than you think to flatten your belly and avoid artery damage. Just follow these tummy-reducing and toning tips.

Cut back on calories. Don't get confused by all the hype. The bottom line is if you eat more calories than your body needs, the extra turns to fat. For many, that fat winds up front and center on your stomach.

So instead of eating until you're full, train yourself to stop before you reach that point. Sample different vegetables and fruits to satisfy your desire for variety. Fill up on whole grains like whole-wheat bread and brown rice. They're more nutritious and will stick with you longer, too.

You can slash hundreds — even thousands — of calories a week by eliminating fast food and by cooking more at home. Experiment with recipes from cultures that use a variety of fruits, vegetables, and whole grains. Fast food never tasted this good.

Work off the weight. Some studies have found that exercise is as effective as medication at increasing good cholesterol levels and reducing the bad. That means healthier arteries and lower blood pressure.

Find an exercise you enjoy, such as swimming, bicycling, or brisk walking. Even yard work counts. Rake leaves, hoe the garden, or trim shrubs. Exercise 45 minutes a day at least five days a week and soon you'll see results.

Tone up that tummy. Tightening a flabby stomach doesn't have to mean grueling crunches or sit-ups. Do these pelvic tilts daily to banish your belly and strengthen your back and stomach muscles. If you have any serious health problems, like osteoporosis, check with your doctor first.

★ Using a firm mattress or exercise mat, lie on your back with your knees bent.

★ Keep your feet and your upper body firmly planted on the mattress or mat.

★ Lift your hips and buttocks toward the ceiling and hold for several seconds.

★ Bring your hips back down and push the small of your back into the mattress or pad. If you're doing the exercise correctly, the space between the small of your back and the mat should disappear.

★ Hold the position for several seconds, then rest.

Breathe regularly throughout the exercise. Start with five pelvic tilts a day and work your way up to 15.

Before long, you'll notice your midsection tightening and toning up. You can be proud of your new look and, more importantly, your healthier heart.

A woman's guide to heart attack survival

Martha never hesitated when one of her five children needed emergency medical care. She bundled them into the car and went straight to the ER. She did the same when her husband of 30 years had chest pains and shortness of breath. Thanks to her quick action, he survived his heart attack.

Then one morning, Martha had nausea and dizziness after breakfast but refused to go to the hospital. She collapsed before lunch. Even her husband's frantic 911 call couldn't save her.

On average, women wait longer than men to get help for a heart attack. And like Martha, many die needlessly. Learn the warning signs and act fast to save your own life.

Know the symptoms. These can vary based on your sex. A man is more likely to have:

★ Squeezing chest pressure that lasts more than 10 minutes

★ Pain that spreads to the neck, jaw, shoulders, or arms — especially the left arm

★ Sweating, nausea, dizziness, or shortness of breath

But a woman is more likely to experience:

★ Mild chest pain

★ Breathlessness

★ Dizziness or lightheadedness

★ Nausea or heartburn

If you suffer any of these symptoms for more than 10 minutes, get immediate medical care. Once you recognize heart attack symptoms, focus on what to do instead of your fears.

Don't waste time. All too often, people spend valuable minutes in denial. Only by accepting the possibility that you're having a heart attack will you react in a way that will save your life.

★ Deal with the danger. Many people underestimate their risk for heart attack. In fact, most women don't know that heart disease is a greater health threat to them than cancer. Don't sit around thinking your symptoms will get better. Remember the 10-minute rule.

★ Don't wait for permission. Your friends, family, and even your doctor don't have to say it's okay for you to get emergency help or go to the hospital. Take responsibility for your own survival.

★ Trust the pros. Never drive yourself to the hospital. That would endanger your life and the lives of others on the road. Call 911 or your local emergency service. Emergency medical technicians are trained to deal with heart attacks. Should you lose consciousness, they'll know what to tell the emergency room doctors.

Pop an aspirin. Taking an aspirin at the first sign of a heart attack improves your odds of survival. The salicylic acid gets right to work preventing blood clots that can block the flow of blood to your heart. That buys precious time until you can get stronger medicine at the hospital. Talk to your doctor about carrying a 325-milligram aspirin with you at all times.

Assert yourself. Women are more likely to die after a heart attack than men — in part because they take longer to get to the hospital but also because, once there, they often get less intensive treatment than men.

One solution is for women to become more assertive about their medication. Ask at the hospital about clot-dissolving drugs. When you're discharged, inquire about medicine to prevent another attack, and ask if you should take a daily aspirin.

If you think you're having a heart attack, concentrate on following these tips. You'll have less time for fear and a better chance of survival.

Follow the 'Healthy Eating Pyramid' to better heart health

A new food pyramid by Harvard researcher Walter C. Willett, M.D., boldly goes where no USDA pyramid has gone before — recommending daily exercise and weight control as the foundation of a healthy diet.

In his book, *Eat, Drink, and Be Healthy*, Willett uses decades of painstaking research to design a food pyramid based on facts instead of

Healthy Eating Pyramid

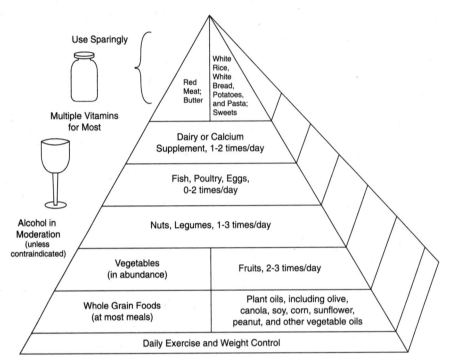

popular thinking or special interests. Called the Healthy Eating Pyramid, this new design only overlaps the old one in its emphasis on fruits and vegetables.

His eating strategy is all about making better dietary decisions. "Careful attention to the type of fat and carbohydrate," says Willett, "along with selection of healthy sources of protein, can greatly reduce the risk of heart disease and other serious conditions."

"In fact," he says, "not smoking, regular exercise, and a healthy diet can prevent over 80 percent of heart attacks."

Work it off. Without regular exercise, the best diet plan will do you little good. According to Willett, the biggest problem in a typical American diet is the number of calories compared to the level of activity. In other words, if you're an American, you probably eat too much and exercise too little.

USDA Pyramid

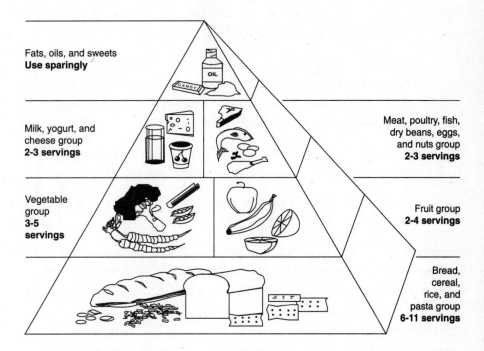

Fats, oils, and sweets
Use sparingly

Milk, yogurt, and cheese group
2-3 servings

Meat, poultry, fish, dry beans, eggs, and nuts group
2-3 servings

Vegetable group
3-5 servings

Fruit group
2-4 servings

Bread, cereal, rice, and pasta group
6-11 servings

Ask your doctor about starting a fitness program that includes aerobic exercise and strength training. Research shows you can improve your heart, lungs, and overall muscle strength by alternating these two kinds of exercise.

Aerobic exercise includes walking, swimming, bicycling, and even vigorous chores like vacuuming or raking leaves. Strength training involves building muscles with weights or specific exercises.

In a study of people with chronic heart disease, volunteers did three one-hour exercise sessions per week. These sessions stressed both aerobic exercise and strength training. Participants improved their hearts, lungs, and muscles after only eight weeks.

Opt for heart-healthy oils. Willett disagrees with using oils sparingly, as recommended by the USDA. "Unfortunately," he says, "current recommendations to replace fat with starch will have little benefit. And some people will be harmed." This switch can lead to weight gain and dangerous changes in your blood fats.

You have to watch calories, he warns, which add up fast in oils, so don't go crazy. But some oils, such as olive, canola, soybean, and other vegetable oils, are actually good for your heart. That's also true for the essential omega-3 fats found in seeds, grains, and fish.

And avoid the saturated, and trans fat found in fast food, processed food, baked goods, red meat, butter, and whole milk. Check labels for ingredients like "partially hydrogenated vegetable oils" or "vegetable shortening" (both trans fats) and steer clear of them.

The bottom line is, by switching to healthy oils, you can improve your cholesterol levels and keep your heart beating regularly.

Eat unrefined. This doesn't mean to start eating with your fingers, just switch to whole, unrefined grains.

Study the USDA pyramid, and you might think you should eat 11 servings of white bread a day. That, of course, is not healthy. Instead, Willett says to eat refined grains like white bread, white rice, and pasta sparingly. Because your body processes these refined grains quickly, your blood sugar and insulin levels rise to unhealthy levels. In addition, your blood fats take a turn for the worse.

Eat unrefined grains like brown rice, whole-wheat bread and pasta, and whole oats. Choose interesting grains from other cultures — quinoa, kasha, and bulgur are good for starters. They not only taste good, but also protect you from a variety of diseases.

Be picky about protein. When you think of protein, you probably picture a piece of meat at the center of your plate. That makes sense if you're used to the USDA pyramid.

It's true, protein is important for a healthy body, building stronger hair, skin, muscles, and blood. But Willett says to eat less animal protein (meat) and more protein from vegetables. You don't have to cut out meat entirely, but substitute legumes, nuts, and whole grains some of the time. You'll get the benefits of protein without the saturated fat. When you do eat meat, choose skinless chicken and turkey, and fish.

Supplement your coverage. Willett says not to sweat it if you don't drink milk. These days you can get calcium in fortified juices or supplements and bypass the extra calories and saturated fat. That's why he recommends fewer servings of dairy.

He also believes there's little proof that just boosting your calcium intake will prevent fractures. Instead, he says vitamin D looks promising as a defense against the brittle bones of osteoporosis. He suggests talking to your doctor about adding a daily multivitamin to cover all your bases.

About his Healthy Eating Pyramid, Willett says, "Best of all, these food choices can lead to a diet that is more enjoyable and varied."

Amazing ways to spot heart disease

Is it harder to make beds or unload groceries than it was six months ago? Your answer could indicate advancing heart disease.

Even though one of every two women in the United States dies from heart disease or stroke, many don't know the warning signs. That means senior women need a screening process that relates to their lifestyle. So, think about your daily chores and how you've had to change your routine — problems aren't always just a sign of aging. If you can no longer do the things you used to, talk to your doctor. And don't ignore chest pain or breathlessness.

Here are some unusual ways you can stay a step ahead of heart trouble.

Nail down your numbers — now. Even though you're more likely to develop heart disease after menopause, you should start tracking your blood pressure and cholesterol as early as possible. Readings before menopause can often predict whether you'll develop heart disease later in life.

Pay attention to both HDL, good, cholesterol and LDL, the bad kind. Experts say keep your total cholesterol below 200 ml/dL, LDL below 100 mg/dL, and HDL above 60 mg/dL. The American Heart Association defines normal blood pressure as 130/85 or somewhat lower.

If yours starts creeping up, your heart might be headed for trouble. Knowing your numbers early means you can take action sooner rather than later. Diet, exercise — and in some cases medicine — can push you out of the danger zone.

Check your C. There's a new blood test that can quickly and easily predict your risk of heart attack. The test checks for a substance in your blood called C-reactive protein, which shows up if your arteries are inflamed. Inflammation can be a silent symptom of heart disease.

Since half of all heart attack victims don't have high cholesterol, this test could identify many who might otherwise fall through the cracks. Ask your doctor if you would benefit from a C-reactive protein test.

Look out for a low-performing thyroid. You could suffer from a sluggish thyroid and never know it. Most people with hypothyroidism experience weight gain, dry skin, brittle nails, and fatigue. But many older women have a low-performing thyroid without any symptoms. Doctors call it subclinical hypothyroidism.

If your thyroid is on the blitz, you may have high cholesterol and high blood pressure — and a higher risk of heart disease. A blood test can give you the news and your doctor can get you help.

Pay attention to PCOS. Women over 45 who have polycystic ovary syndrome (PCOS) may be at risk for premature hardening of the arteries. Some symptoms of PCOS include a tendency to be overweight, problems with blood sugar that can lead to diabetes, excess facial and body hair, and a deepening voice. If you think you might have PCOS, see your doctor for testing. And if you're told that you have the syndrome, keep an eye on your heart.

Treat a troubled marriage. A woman in a difficult relationship may describe her heart as "breaking." Experts now say an unhappy marriage truly can harm a woman's heart — by increasing her risk of heart disease.

Don't delay in getting help for a troubled marriage. Ask your spouse to attend counseling with you. If he refuses, go alone. A trained counselor can give you practical suggestions for coping with your stressful relationship. That could make a difference in your heart health.

But don't stop there. Spend time with good friends on a regular basis, and cultivate relationships that build you up as a person. Surround yourself with people who love and support you.

Top 10 ways to sidestep a heart attack

Hum while you drive. Road rage can raise your blood pressure and trigger a heart attack.

Eat light. Digesting a very large meal can increase your heart rate and blood pressure.

Count your blessings. If you're optimistic, you're more likely to make healthy choices and feel less stress.

Broil some salmon. Cold-water fatty fish supplies heart-healthy oils, keeps veins open, and helps regulate your heartbeat. And season it with garlic. This flavorful herb keeps your arteries soft and flexible.

Walk the dog. The more you walk, the healthier your arteries and the lower your risk of blood clots. Spending time with a pet can also lower your blood pressure.

Get a flu shot. Respiratory infections and fever can sometimes trigger a heart attack.

Rent a comedy. Laughing helps reduce stress and less stress means a stronger immune system and a healthier heart.

Pop an aspirin. Ask your doctor about how aspirin reduces your risk of blood clots.

Put on some tunes. Enjoy your favorite music and you'll lower your blood pressure, too.

Give up a grudge. Anger, hostility, and anxiety are linked to rapid heart rate and high blood pressure.

Iron out your diet and help your heart

If you have heart disease, get tested for iron-deficiency anemia. Stunning new research suggests boosting low iron levels could lessen your need for diuretics and improve your heart and kidneys.

Iron is an essential mineral. This means your body needs it — but in the right amounts. Not enough, and your blood won't be able to carry enough oxygen. Too much and you risk a toxic buildup in your tissues and organs.

Know your risk. If you have low iron, you might feel weak and tired much of the time. You could feel too cold or too hot and have trouble fighting off sickness.

★ You're at risk for low iron if you haven't yet reached menopause and have heavy periods, or if you use an intrauterine device (IUD) for birth control.

★ Certain diseases, surgeries, or drugs can cause you to have a problem absorbing nutrients. This means your body won't get all the iron it should from the food you eat.

★ Iron deficiency frequently hits vegetarians since they don't eat meat — the best source of dietary iron.

★ Your kidneys are key to the right balance of iron in your body, so if you suffer from kidney problems, you're more at risk for anemia.

★ Postmenopausal women don't usually have trouble with low iron, but certain medical conditions can drain you of this important element.

If you think you might be at risk, talk to your doctor about a blood test to be sure.

Mind your milligrams. The recommended dietary allowance (RDA) for iron is 18 milligrams (mg) a day for premenopausal women and 8 mg a day for women past menopause and for men. Vegetarians should aim for about twice these amounts since iron from plant sources is harder for your body to absorb than iron from meat.

Balance the benefits. Don't forget to look at the big picture — some foods are better choices than others. While fortified cereals are usually a good source of iron, you still need to read nutrition labels. One cup of Kellogg's Rice Krispies contains less than 1 mg of iron while a cup of Total has more than 20 mg.

And although meat supplies you with easily absorbed iron, it contains heart-damaging fat and cholesterol. A 3-ounce serving of chicken livers contains 7 mg of iron, but it also serves up a whopping 536 mg of cholesterol. Choose instead a roasted chicken breast without skin. You'll get nearly 2 mg of iron but only 146 mg of cholesterol.

Round out your menu with other heart-friendly sources of iron, like beans and green leafy vegetables.

Sip the right beverage. If you wash down those iron-rich foods with green tea, coffee, or wine, your body won't see as much benefit. Compounds in those drinks — called phenols — interfere with iron absorption. So, drink green tea and coffee between meals instead. And, as always, drink wine sparingly.

If you want to boost your iron absorption, drink orange juice with your green leafies and legumes. Vitamin C helps your body digest iron from plant sources.

Consider supplements. If you follow a strict vegetarian diet, or suffer from a medical condition that makes you iron deficient, talk with your doctor about iron supplements.

Winterize your heart

Even with a snow blower, winter storms can mean big heart trouble. Experts say you're just as likely to have a heart attack using a snow blower as you are using a shovel. Apparently, moving the heavy machine around is as dangerous for people with heart disease as shoveling.

Here's how to avoid cold weather pitfalls — and look after your heart.

Pay for snow removal. Shoveling is a tough job even for people in great shape. Combine that with stress and a heart condition, and you have a recipe for disaster. If you can afford it, pay someone to clear your driveway and sidewalks during the winter.

Shovel smart. If you absolutely must shovel, make the tool do most of the work. Choose a lightweight one that suits your height. If the snow isn't too deep, use the shovel like a plow to push it to the edge of the walk.

And try to shovel early and often, since it's easier to keep clearing light snow. Take frequent breaks, and drink plenty of fluids. Above all, listen to your body. If something hurts or you feel winded, stop immediately.

Pace yourself. Many people wait until the weekend to catch up on chores, like shoveling. Others stay active between Monday and Friday, but turn into a couch potato on the weekends. Either way, these spurts of exercise are hard on your heart. Try to space your physical activity throughout the week.

Bundle up. Women who live where the temperature changes throughout the year have more heart attacks in mid-winter than any other season. But in parts of the world where the climate is mild all year — like Taiwan — there is never a spike in the number of heart attacks.

You can't blame this all on snow removal, though. Scientists say the temperature itself can be bad for you. Because cold weather narrows your arteries and therefore reduces blood flow to your legs, blood clots cause more heart attacks in winter.

Since you can't hibernate, outsmart the cold by wearing layers. If you get too warm, you can always take a scarf or jacket off. And skip the outdoor activities on very cold days. If you get restless, go to a mall to walk. Finally, keep your house well insulated and wear a sweater indoors whenever you feel chilled.

Ride out a storm. You know to stock up on groceries before a winter storm, but do you know to take a break? Changes in air pressure that occur during a winter storm can put a strain on your heart. Researchers say a reading of 1,016 millibars on the barometer — an instrument for measuring air pressure — is best for your heart. For every 10 points the barometer rises or falls, the number of heart attacks increases by 10 percent.

The moral of the story is to take it easy during storms since the barometer may move several points. You can catch up on your chores later.

Athlete's Foot

Bathe away pesky athlete's foot with herbs

You don't have to be an athlete to get athlete's foot. And you may not have to see a doctor to get rid of it. Most over-the-counter anti-fungal lotions will do the trick.

You know you have athlete's foot if your feet itch or burn, the skin between your toes is cracked and covered with tiny scales, or you have tiny blisters between your toes.

Though home remedies may not get rid of the fungi that cause the discomfort, they can soothe most of the symptoms.

Tea tree oil. The oil from the leaves of this Australian tree is widely used to disinfect skin and fight fungus. Rub the oil between your toes, and follow up with some baking soda to keep them dry. Continue to apply the oil three times a day for at least a week after the rash is gone. When you purchase tea tree oil at a local health food store, open the vial and make sure you can smell a strong, eucalyptus-like medicinal scent. This is a good indication the oil contains enough of the active ingredient.

Garlic. Garlic is a powerful anti-fungal agent. To take advantage of this smelly herb, crush a few cloves and steep them in hot water. When the water cools, soak your feet for several minutes and carefully dry them. You can also chop up a few cloves and slip them in your shoes, or sprinkle your feet with garlic powder. It may not make you popular with your friends, but it will definitely deter enemy fungi.

Calendula. The blossoms of this common garden marigold may fight irritation and encourage your cracked skin to heal. Steep two

teaspoons of the flower heads in boiling water. Wet a soft, cotton cloth
with the mixture and gently apply it to the irritated area.

Chamomile. A member of the aster family, the chamomile flower
can soothe irritated skin and speed its healing. Soak your feet in a bath
of cooled chamomile tea to reap the benefits of this garden herb.

Peppermint oil. Just like mint gum freshens your mouth, a peppermint bath can cool and refresh your feet. The menthol in peppermint oil numbs pain and relieves itching. Rub your feet with the oil,
but make sure you've diluted it with a carrier oil, like jojoba or sesame,
to prevent irritation. Or try massaging them with peppermint lotion.
If you notice any headaches, flushing, or a rash, you may have an allergy to menthol. Stop using peppermint and try tea tree oil instead.

Sage. To keep your feet dry, try a bath of sage and agrimony. Sage
is a natural antiperspirant. It may also have the power to soothe skin
irritation and kill fungi. Agrimony is an ancient herb from the British
Isles used for generations to heal minor skin irritations. Simmer both
herbs in water and let the mixture cool before bathing your feet.

You can mix and match many of these herbs to make aromatic foot-
baths. Soak your feet in sage tea with a few drops of tea tree oil and
peppermint oil. Or try a warm bath with a few drops of chamomile and
peppermint essential oils to soothe itching.

It's best not to self-treat foot fungus if you have diabetes or another circulatory problem. A minor foot irritation could lead to infection
or even amputation of your leg. Make sure you check your feet daily
for signs of injury and speak with your doctor immediately if you spot
any problem areas.

Stop infection from spreading to nails

Keep a sharp eye on your toenails if you have athlete's foot. The
fungi that infect your skin can spread to your nails. What's more,
toenail fungus is a lot harder to get rid of than athlete's foot and can
result in pain if you ignore it.

---

10 fungus-fighting footnotes

Foot fungi thrive in wet and warm conditions. Make these pests uncomfortable by trying these tips:

★ Wear flip-flops in wet public places, like swimming pools, locker rooms, and showers.

★ Spray antiperspirant on your feet to keep them from sweating.

★ Powder your feet with cornstarch, baking soda, or fungal powder to keep them dry.

★ Use a zinc oxide-based diaper rash ointment to seal any cracked skin between your toes.

★ Slide into sandals or prop your bare feet up in a sunny window. The fungi that cause athlete's foot hate sunshine.

★ Wear cotton socks with closed shoes to draw moisture away from your toes, and change your socks daily.

★ Put socks on before your underwear. You don't want to spread the infection to other areas.

★ Alternate between two pairs of shoes, and set your spare ones out in the sun on their day off.

★ Take off wet socks immediately and dry feet carefully, especially between your toes.

★ Buy shoes that breathe. Stay away from rubber or nylon shoes, and don't wear boots all day.

Nail disease, known as onychomycosis, begins when common, keratin-loving fungi move in under your nail. Your body immediately starts to produce more keratin — the protein in nails and hair — to replace what it lost, and your nails grow thick and yellow. Left untreated, they can become too thick to cut and will slowly separate from your nail bed.

You can detect nail fungus early by checking your feet regularly for symptoms of infection. Common warning signs include a foul smell or yellowish-brown stains or white lines across the nail. Your nail may also lose its shine and thicken.

Since nail fungus is hard to treat, your best bet is to prevent it in the first place.

★ Wash your feet daily with soap and water, especially between the toes and around the nails, and dry them carefully.

★ Change your socks often to keep your feet dry, so fungus can't breed.

★ Wear socks made of natural fibers, like cotton or wool, which can absorb moisture. Avoid nylon, polyester, or tight-fitting socks and hose that retain sweat.

★ Buy shoes with good ventilation and plenty of toe room.

★ Cut your nails short, straight across the top, and inspect them regularly.

★ Avoid any minor cuts to your toes. They can be an open door for fungi.

★ Give up nail polish and acrylic nails. Both will trap moisture under your nail and block oxygen passing through it.

If it's too late and you see signs of infection, don't hide them under a coat of nail polish. Instead, see your doctor. He can prescribe oral medication or a special nail lacquer to treat the fungus. Be patient — nails grow back very slowly. Most treatments take about three to six months to get rid of the problem.

There is only one known natural remedy for this pesky foot problem. Tea tree oil, available at health food stores, can be as effective as prescription medicine if you use it for six months. Apply the oil directly to your nail twice a day for best results.

If the condition gets worse, or you notice greenish spots under your nail, see your doctor. He can test your nails to make sure you don't have a staph infection or another condition that is more serious.

Sure-fire ways to wipe out fungi

One of the easiest ways to give athlete's foot the slip is to practice good hygiene.

★ Wash your feet every day with an antibacterial soap and dry them carefully, especially between your toes.

★ Bathe your feet twice a day in equal parts of vinegar and water. This foot wash increases the acidity of your feet, making them unfriendly to fungi.

★ Disinfect your shower and bath with a mixture of one part bleach to 10 parts water. Scrub down tiles and floors every two weeks to kill lurking organisms. Make sure you wear gloves to protect your hands from irritation.

★ Clean the insides of your shoes with alcohol or fungal spray and set them outside facing the sun. Fungi don't like ultraviolet light and will soon die.

★ If you just got rid of athlete's foot, wash your socks, towels, and sheets in very hot water before using them again.

Back Pain

Fold away back pain in 90 seconds

"'Fold and Hold' could help you relieve 75 percent of the common muscular aches and pains you experience," says Dr. Dale Anderson, a physician and pioneer in alternative healing. "It's simple, once you master some basic concepts and a few of the 'right moves'."

Anderson is speaking of his stretching method that can release tight, painful muscles without medication or surgery. It requires no supplements or machines. In fact, you can do it almost anywhere. It's surprisingly comfortable — and you won't spend a penny. Anderson explains Fold and Hold in his book *Muscle Pain Relief in 90 Seconds*.

"Muscle spasm is the chief culprit in most of the pain I see," he says. "And it is significantly improved by relaxing muscles that are in spasm. Relieving the spasm by relaxing and then gently stretching these muscles is the essence of Fold and Hold."

According to Anderson, a sudden movement can cause a muscle to spasm. To relieve the pain, you must re-create and exaggerate the original position. Here are the four basic steps:

Step 1: Find the tender spot — a sensitive area of intense pain.

Step 2: Fold gently around that spot.

Step 3: Hold this position for at least 90 seconds.

Step 4: Unfold carefully into your normal posture.

Here are a few exercises to release some of the more common muscle spasms in your back.

Hug your knee. Pull yourself up too quickly from a kneeling position and you may feel back discomfort when you stand, and sharp pain when you climb stairs. You probably strained the muscle that stretches from your back to the inside of your hip. Your tender spot might be near your groin.

To Fold and Hold over this spot, first lie down comfortably. Bend one knee and pull it gently up to your chest. Allow your hip to follow your knee so that it is also slightly off the ground. Adjust this position until it is comfortable. Hold for 90 seconds, then gradually unfold and rest for a few minutes.

Curl up tight. Straighten suddenly after you've been slouching over a table or sitting with your elbows propped on your knees, and you may feel a nagging ache along the center of your back. You've probably pulled one of the tiny muscles behind your stomach that hold your spine upright.

Anderson suggests you sit on a cushion on the floor with your knees pulled into your chest. Curl your whole body in until your forehead rests on your knees and your arms hug your legs. Shift gently to your left or right side until you find a comfortable, pain-free position. Hold this pose for 90 seconds and slowly uncurl. Rest for a few minutes. See photo on next page.

Let your leg hang down. If you twisted suddenly, you may now have intense pain in your tailbone when you sit or bend over. Your tender spot is probably at the base of your spine.

Lie down on your side, near the edge of your bed. Bend your bottom leg slightly so you won't roll over. Let your upper leg drop behind your body and gently hang off the side of the bed. Shift your position until the pain stops, and hold for 90 seconds. Bring your leg slowly back onto the bed and rest on your side for a few minutes.

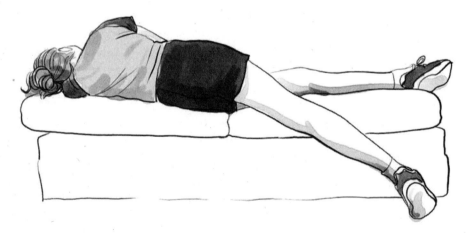

Reach for the sky. Slouching in front of the TV or reading in bed can cause upper back and shoulder pain. At least two different groups of muscles can spasm when you slump, making it hard to stand up straight. You can exaggerate the slouch for 90 seconds to relieve the pain, or try this simple stretch.

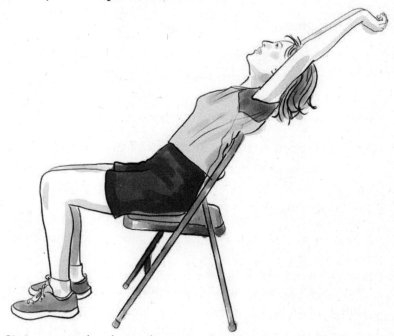

Sit in a straight chair, clasp your hands over your head, and gently pull your arms backwards, arching your back slowly. Hold this stretch for 90 seconds, then release. Periodically arch your back if you sit for a long time and you'll avoid this pain in the future.

Anderson cautions, "Fold and Hold is not painful or forceful. It does not involve 'cracking' or 'popping' vertebrae and joints into place. Nor does it painfully stretch or apply pressure to muscles that are already strained." So be careful not to push yourself beyond comfort and into pain.

"In short," says Anderson, "Fold and Hold treatment is always to go to the most comfortable position. Used correctly, Fold and Hold will ease or eliminate many pains."

Hobbies can build a healthy back

Don't let back pain cramp your creativity. Hobbies are really just a fun form of exercise — great news for your back, since exercise may help back pain more than rest. So, enjoy your hobbies. Just remember to think about the way you stand, sit, and bend, and you'll protect your back from strain.

Garden with gusto.

★ Don't lift and carry things that are too heavy for you. Fill that old play wagon with mulch and fertilizer. Stack small items on a skateboard, a sled, or even a shovel. Pulling and dragging these are easier on your back.

★ Use duct tape to attach a broomstick onto your trowel and you'll never have to bend over again. Make sure your fork and spade have handles long enough to reach your waist.

★ Kneepads aren't just for risky sports. Wear them in the garden and you won't have to bend to move a knee cushion every time you reposition.

★ Take frequent breaks to stop and stretch, especially if you spend a lot of time kneeling.

★ Don't feel like you must finish everything in one day. Set small goals — spend only 20 to 30 minutes weeding or pruning at a time.

Walk to win.

★ Warm up with gentle stretches before you start your day. Your vertebrae often swell while you sleep and you don't want to jolt your spine awake.

★ Walking isn't a fashion show, so wear shoes that match your activity. No street shoes allowed.

★ Walk around the block slowly at first, just to test your muscles. The next day, walk a little faster. Keep adding a block and speeding it up, until you can walk at a moderate pace for a total of 20 to 30 minutes, four times a week.

★ Teach your dog to heel. Having a companion is always fun, but a dog that drags you along on his leash is not fun for your back.

★ Dirt is much kinder to your feet and back than asphalt or concrete. Look for an earthen track without rocks or hidden holes.

★ Hills can put a different kind of strain on your back. When you walk uphill, don't lean forward, and keep your shoulders back. When going downhill make sure your knees are slightly bent when your feet hit the ground.

Tee off with ease.

★ Use your golf club as a stretching tool. Hold it horizontally in front of you, and, without arching your back, lift it to the sky. Then bring it back down to shoulder height and gently rotate your upper body to the right and then the left.

★ Start walking the course a couple of weeks before the golf season to get used to the terrain.

★ Start out with a shorter backswing, progressing to a full swing as you gain strength and range of motion in your back. However, you can significantly reduce your backswing without affecting your stroke.

★ Concentrate on turning your hips as you swing. This will relieve your back and improve your form.

Keep on crafting.

★ Set up your woodworking machines so you can stand comfortably.

★ Use a floor hoop for quilts. You'll be able to sit upright and still follow the powdered lines.

★ Stand up and stretch after every 10 minutes you spend crouching under the hood of your vintage car.

★ Sit in an armchair as you knit so your elbows can rest. Turn on a light over and behind your chair so you have to hold your shoulders back to see the needlework in your hands.

★ Install a high countertop in your kitchen so you don't have to hunch down to prepare meals. However, if you bake a lot, find a lower counter for kneading dough and rolling out pastry.

A lifetime of daily activity will keep your back fit and chronic pain at bay. So stay active, and enjoy the precious gift of a healthy spine.

New therapy beats back pain lying down

There's a hot, new back pain therapy sweeping the country. It's not surgery, it's FDA-approved, it offers astonishing results — and it's controversial.

Vertebral axial decompression (VAX-D) therapy uses a motorized table to gently stretch your lower back. In a typical half-hour session, you stretch and rest 15 times. A full course of therapy can consist of anywhere from 10 to 30 sessions. Most amazing, 70 percent of the people who tried it claimed they had significant pain relief even six months later.

By lightly pulling the vertebrae apart, VAX-D therapy eases pressure on the discs and nerves in your back. According to experts, this allows healing nutrients to circulate and speed recovery.

The controversy surrounds whether this therapy really cures herniated disks and nerve damage, or if it just offers temporary pain relief. Several studies have tried to prove that VAX-D physically changes the condition of your spine, but their results vary.

Another concern is the cost. VAX-D therapy can cost you several thousand dollars — much of it not covered by insurance. Before you make any decision, do your research.

Put the brakes on highway backaches

New cars have all kinds of improvements designed to support your spine and halt lower back pain — inflatable lumbar support pillows that fit the curve of your back, automatic seats that keep your knees lined up with your hips, and tilt steering wheels for the most comfortable grip.

Fortunately, you don't have to buy a new car to pamper your spine. Here are a few simple ways you can make the car you have a better deal for your back.

Set the standard. As soon as you settle into your car, sit up straight and adjust your mirrors. You want to see the road clearly without craning your neck. If you notice the mirrors need correcting while you are driving, you may have slumped in your seat. Straighten up and pull your shoulders back before changing your mirrors.

Cozy up to the wheel. Get close enough to the steering wheel that your shoulders don't have to stretch while you steer. To gauge this distance, move the seat up until your wrists rest on top of the wheel with your shoulders relaxed. Generally, you should be at least 10 inches away from the wheel.

Cushion your neck. Your headrest cannot protect your neck from strain if all it supports is a cushion of air behind your head. Adjust the headrest so your ears line up with the middle of the cushion.

Adjust the strap. In most cars, you can change the height of the safety belt anchor located over your shoulder. Line it up with your ears. It shouldn't rub the nape of your neck, or push your shoulder down. When the belt is set properly, it will hold your shoulders back, and you won't slump forward while you drive.

Get the right angle. Tilt the back of your seat so you are just slightly reclined. This will keep your spine upright without cutting off the circulation in your legs.

Add some support. Use a small, flat pillow to cushion your lower back. The best kind will fit comfortably in the curve of your spine — below the bottom of your ribcage. Attach it to the seat with ribbon or elastic and it won't shift out of place while you drive.

Steer it straight. There is a fine balance between controlling your car's steering and straining your arms while you hold the wheel. Though people disagree on the best hand position, the American Chiropractic Association recommends you alternate between two.

First, think of your steering wheel as a clock. Place your right hand on the wheel at a 3 o'clock position and your left at 7 o'clock. Every so often, switch your right hand to 5 o'clock and your left to a 10 o'clock position. Changing like this will keep one arm from getting too tired, while still giving you full control.

Don't go too low. Whether you have bucket seats or just ones so worn you sink into them, your back will eventually pay the price. Sitting with your knees higher than your hips can cut off your circulation and damage the sciatic nerve that runs down your leg. Add bulk to your seat with a loose pillow or a foam pad. Choose a wedge-shaped one that will prop your hips up to the line of your knees.

Exit with grace. Getting out of your car can be awkward and sometimes difficult. To save your back, don't twist, but turn. Keeping your legs together, turn your whole body towards the open door. Take both feet out at the same time and set them solidly on the pavement. Sit on the edge of the seat and pull yourself up with your leg muscles, not your back. A swivel cushion can make this process easier.

Finally, if you are taking long road trips, remember lower back pain is often a reaction to the constant vibration of the car. Take short rest stops every hour or so. Walk around your car a few times and stretch your muscles.

Massage your way to back pain relief

Massage is more than a treat. It's a powerful way to ease the aches and pains in your back — one you don't have to be rich to enjoy.

If you suffer from back pain, you may have tried a number of alternative treatments, like exercise, acupuncture, or simply relearning how to sit, stand, and lift. But research shows massage can increase your range of motion and ability to function, and reduce pain more than these other therapies.

At the Center for Health Studies in Seattle, massage patients used less pain medication and made fewer trips to the doctor outside of therapy.

Best of all, these back pain sufferers reported no side effects from massage and results that lasted at least one year. What's more, it's proven

---

12 top ways to baby your back

Try these tips from the American Chiropractic Association to help your back last a lifetime.

Rise and shine. Roll onto your side, sit up, and push off the bed with your hands.

Stand at attention. Keep your shoulders back, your knees bent, and shift your weight often.

Slow down. Schedule morning stretches, and think before you lift heavy objects.

Take a breather. To refresh your muscles and fight fatigue, breathe deeply.

Get up with grace. Use your arm and leg muscles when you stand up — not your back.

Don't play Twister. Align your toes with your nose when you lift things or watch television.

Chat sensibly. Don't cradle the phone between your shoulder and your ear. Hit the speaker button or use headphones.

Size up your purse. Leave extra stuff at home and switch shoulders often, or use a fanny pack.

Pad the floor. Place thick rubber mats in front of work areas like the sink.

Put up your feet. Use that ottoman next to your favorite chair.

Buy a dreamy mattress. Find one that supports and cushions your back.

Hit the sack. Get enough sleep to beat droopy shoulders.

---

that a positive attitude toward massage therapy can bring even better results. Researchers at Washington University treated more than 100 back-pain sufferers with either massage therapy or acupuncture. Those with the highest hopes for their treatment showed the most improvement.

So, keep your chin up. With a good attitude, you may already be on your way to recovery. Just remember to stick with the treatment to get the full benefits. People in these studies received a massage at least once a week for four to 10 weeks.

Although a licensed massage therapist will provide the best results, you can also give your back a hand at home.

Stretch out the kinks. Many massage therapists recommend gentle stretching to help keep muscles relaxed and flexible. So, banish stiffness and give your back a daily stretch. Here's an easy one to try. Lie down on your back with both legs out straight. Now, raise one knee, grab it with both hands, and slowly hug it to your chest. Try to point your toe toward your head to get the best stretch. Hold, count to five, and repeat with the other leg.

Roll with it. Fill a long sock with three or four tennis balls and lay it on the bed or floor. Lie down with your lower back resting on the sock. Roll gently from side to side, then up and down, letting the tennis balls massage your muscles. Your body weight should put just enough pressure on the tennis balls to give your back a mild work out.

Grab a partner. Massage really is a two-person tango. Ask someone you're comfortable with to be your back-rub buddy. Then begin learning and practicing together. Many books and videos teach easy-to-use massage techniques. The Internet is also a wealth of information. Start out slowly and carefully until the two of you develop a comfortable routine. The more you know, the better your back will feel.

Ice up and rub down. Cool the pain and ease the ache with an ice massage. Fill a paper cup with water and freeze solid. Tear the paper away from one end of the cup. Have someone massage your sore muscles with the ice for about 10 minutes. Repeat up to once an hour.

Massage can ease back pain for many people, but it can't melt away some back troubles. Here are four signs your back pain may mean a bigger problem.

★ Stiffness that is worse when you rest but fades with exercise may be a sign of arthritis.

★ Fever with back pain may be a symptom of infection.

★ Pain from a recent physical trauma like a fall could indicate a fracture.

★ If you're over 50 or have experienced sudden weight loss, your back pain could point to something more serious like a tumor.

If you have these symptoms or suffer from continual back pain that just won't go away, see a doctor. A variety of traditional and alternative treatments can have you back in the saddle in no time.

Cut caffeine and cancel out pain

Caffeine — friend or foe? While it helps many pain medicines work faster, experts believe too much caffeine can make muscle pain worse.

In a recent research project in Vermont, people who complained of back pain said they drank an average of three 8-ounce cups of coffee a day — that's a whopping 400 milligrams (mg) of caffeine. Those without back pain drank half that amount. Here's what caffeine does to your body.

Irritates muscles. Like little electric shocks, caffeine makes muscles twitch repeatedly. Too much of this and your back muscles become sore and weak.

Cuts down on oxygen. Caffeine narrows your blood vessels, one of the few physical symptoms doctors can find for chronic muscle pain.

Grates on sensitive nerves. Caffeine encourages the release of epinephrine, a hormone that stimulates your senses and intensifies every experience. Too much epinephrine and your nerves get so touchy they interpret every movement as a pain signal.

Cripples natural painkillers. Endorphins are painkillers your brain produces. Caffeine, however, reduces these natural "feel good" drugs. With nerves super-sensitive to pain, and no natural painkillers to soothe them, caffeine can amount to a big pain in the back.

Spikes stress levels. If you are under any kind of stress, caffeine will double it. Too much stress can lead to depression, which will weaken your immune system, making back pain worse.

Reduces calcium. When you drink coffee, you're flushing calcium out of your body. If you don't replace this calcium, you're more likely to get hairline fractures in your vertebrae.

Coffee isn't the only culprit in this caffeine conspiracy. Check out some of these other sources.

Hidden sources of caffeine		Amount (mg)
Excedrin, Extra Strength	2 tablets	130
Midol	2 tablets	120
Anacin, Regular Strength	2 tablets	64
Mountain Dew	12 ozs	54
Diet Coke	12 ozs	46
Starbuck's Coffee Italian Roast Ice Cream	1/2 cup	45
Sunkist Orange Soda	12 ozs	40
Diet lemon-flavored instant iced tea	8 ozs	36
Tea, brewed 3 minutes	6 ozs	36

Delete computer back pain

Scrooge wasn't grouchy just because he was a penny-pincher. Years of hunching over account books truly bent him all out of shape.

Times haven't changed all that much. You may sit for hours before your own computer, then wonder why your back hurts, your wrists are sore, your eyes are blurry, and your head is pounding. You might be grouchy, too.

Free yourself from all these aches and pains simply by correcting your posture. Sit up straight and take notice of the following tips to avoid computer burnout.

Align your monitor. While sitting at your computer, close your eyes and imagine you are looking straight ahead. Now open them and notice the first thing you see. This is your line of vision. The center of your screen should be 4 to 9 inches below this line. Generally, if you can see over your monitor, your screen is set too low. Prop it up with a wooden block or a heavy book.

Sit just so. Your best ally in the posture war is still your chair. Here's how to use it to your full advantage.

★ Make sure your chair is high enough. Your knees should line up with your hips while your feet stay planted on the floor.

★ Don't sit on the edge of your seat. Your back has no support and you'll start to slump.

★ When your hips are against the back of your chair, you should be able to fit three fingers between the back of your knee and the edge of your seat. If you can't, try another chair.

★ If your chair tilts, lean back slightly. If it doesn't, adjust your back support so you can sit at a slight backwards angle.

Straighten your wrists. The nerves running from your arm to your fingers pass through a tunnel of muscles in your wrists. When these muscles get inflamed from strain, they squeeze the nerves and cause pain signals to shoot up your arm. This is called carpal tunnel syndrome.

Keep your hands and elbows in a straight line and you can avoid this tunnel block. Position your keyboard even with your lap, propping your wrists up if necessary.

Key in to technology. Computer designers are busy developing ways to adapt their machines to your body. You can now buy a keyboard that looks like a fat boomerang. This "vertical split keyboard" (VK) divides the keys in half and angles the two sides so your wrists don't twist unnaturally while you type. The VK sits inside a padded frame that keeps your wrists higher than your fingertips, a good neutral position for your hand.

Another company is developing a more dramatic alternative, called a Keybowl, which can replace the keyboard entirely. Instead of keys, it uses a combination of ball positions to choose letters.

Look into these new keyboards and other computer accessories that can save your joints.

Look after your eyes. Everybody gets tired eyes at the end of the day. But the burning, itching, and blurred vision you experience after using your computer too long is serious enough to have its own medical term — computer vision syndrome.

The muscles behind your eyeballs stretch and relax as you focus near and far. If they stay fixed in one position for too long, however, you feel the strain. While the fatigue is only temporary, it can still be uncomfortable. In addition, when you stare at your screen, you forget to blink. This dries your eyes out, adding to your discomfort.

The simplest way to save your eyes while you work is to take mini-breaks. After every 20 minutes you spend in front of your computer, get up and walk around. Get a glass of water, talk on the phone, or focus on something far away. You get double benefit from these breaks — your eyes will relax and your back will stretch.

Ease the tension. Poor posture puts stress on the muscles of your neck and shoulders. When they cramp, you can get a major tension headache. So, don't twist your neck to look from a piece of paper on your desk to the screen. Instead, set up a vertical document holder parallel to your monitor. And remember to breathe in deeply every once in awhile. This will pull your shoulders back in line and relax the muscles in your neck.

Don't ignore your body while you work on the computer. Have a message pop up on your screen every 15 minutes with this friendly reminder: "Sit up, blink, and breathe."

Bites and Stings

Defend yourself from flying insects

It's hard to have fun in the sun when you're fighting off dive-bombing insects. Don't let these pests ruin your good time. An encounter with a bee, wasp, or yellow jacket can be very painful. And if you're allergic to their venom, it can turn deadly. Here's how you can avoid being stung.

★ Don't wear bright colors or floral prints.

★ Hold off on colognes and other cosmetics.

★ Leave real flowers at home, not on your shirt.

★ Wear long-sleeved shirts, pants, and shoes.

★ Rid your home and property of insect nests.

★ Clean up leftover soft drinks and food before they attract bugs.

★ Brush off insects gently. Swatting could provoke it to sting.

★ Run away when swarmed and find shelter.

If you do get stung, fast treatment is essential, especially if a honeybee was the culprit. A honeybee leaves its stinger in you. Use a credit card, knife, or your finger to scrape away the stinger before it pumps venom into you. Once you get it out, here's how to treat the wound:

★ Wash the area with warm water and soap to prevent infection.

★ Mix unseasoned meat tenderizer with water and apply the paste to the wound.

★ Ease the pain and swelling with an ice pack or ice cubes wrapped in a paper towel. Hold the ice on the sting for 20 minutes, and then leave it off for 10 minutes.

Top ways to handle a ferocious dog

Dog attacks are in the news more and more these days. And these reported bites are just a few of the millions that occur every year.

Stay out of the newspaper — and the hospital — by following these tips from the Centers for Disease Control and Prevention and the American Humane Society.

- Steer clear of strange dogs, especially if they're behind a fence or in a car.

- Allow familiar dogs to sniff you before petting them.

- Leave them alone when they're eating, sleeping, chewing on toys, or rearing pups.

- Avoid eye contact with aggressive dogs.

- Stand as still as a tree if one threatens you. Never scream or run away.

- Back away slowly only after the dog backs off.

- Fend off an attacking dog by "feeding" it your purse, jacket, or anything else handy.

- Curl up if knocked over. Stay still and cover your ears with your hands.

If you are bitten despite these precautions, here's what you should do.

- Wash the bite with soap and warm water.

- Report it to your doctor.

- Alert the local animal control agency.

Dealing with spider bites

Luckily, spiders like to stay away from people and only attack when bothered. The problem is — you won't know you're bothering one until it's too late. Be careful and wear gloves when you rummage through attics, garages, storage areas, and in piles of trash, wood, or leaves. And shake out stored shoes, towels, and bedding before you use them.

A spider bite will leave you with an itchy, swollen sore, which can lead to sweating, nausea, vomiting, and a severe headache. The bites of more harmful spiders — like the black widow and brown recluse — can even cause muscle spasms, fever, chills, breathing problems, and convulsions.

If you start having any of these symptoms, get medical help right away. Otherwise, just apply some simple first-aid to the bite.

★ Wash the bite with soap and warm water.

★ Tie a string around the area just above the bite to slow the spread of venom. Tighten it until it makes an indentation mark on your skin, but don't cut off your circulation.

★ Apply an ice pack to the area.

★ Avoid moving the bitten area.

How to steer clear of snakes

Nothing may be scarier than a slithering, hissing snake — especially if the snake is hissing at you. That's why nothing may be smarter than taking these precautions the next time you're enjoying the great outdoors.

★ Avoid alcohol and drugs so you'll be alert.

★ Cover up with boots, long pants, and long sleeves.

★ Travel with a buddy.

★ Watch where you put your feet and hands.

★ Leave snakes alone, even if they look asleep.

If you are bitten, proper care can save your life. Forget about those famous folk remedies for snakebites — sucking out the venom, applying ice, using a tourniquet, and drinking alcohol. They can do more harm than good. Instead, follow this advice.

★ Keep the bitten body part still. Use a splint if you have one.

★ Remove your watch, rings, and other pieces of jewelry. Otherwise, they could get stuck when swelling sets in.

★ Go to the hospital. It's the safest bet, even if you think the snake wasn't poisonous.

It's also important to remember what kind of snake bit you. Your doctor needs this information to give you the best treatment. You don't have to be a snake charmer to give an accurate description.

First, look at its head. Many poisonous snakes have triangular heads set off from their bodies. Their eyes are slit-shaped, not round. And they have pits, or indentations, between their nostrils and eyes. Take notice of their tails, too. Poisonous snakes usually have rings that go all the way around their tails.

Don't risk another bite to get a second look or capture the culprit. And don't waste too much time either. The most important thing for a snakebite is prompt medical attention.

'Bee' alert to allergies

An allergic reaction to a bee sting can kill you in less than an hour. No wonder bees, wasps, and yellow jackets cause more deaths than all other venomous animals.

That's why it's smart to carry an EpiPen at all times if you know you're allergic to insect stings. The EpiPen contains a dose of epi-nephrine that can treat severe allergic reactions, giving you time to make it to the emergency room. Use it as soon as you are stung.

Watch for a reaction to a sting even if you don't think you're aller-gic — especially if you've been stung several times. Common signs include swelling, nausea, dizziness, or a headache.

More serious reactions cause swelling in your mouth and throat, breathing problems, an irregular heartbeat, and fainting. Get to a doctor as quickly as possible if you notice any of these symptoms.

Breast Cancer

Soy sparks tumor growth

Women at high risk for breast cancer need to think twice about eating soy foods and taking soy supplements. One of soy's phytoestrogens — the isoflavone genistein — could make breast tumors grow faster.

Although earlier research suggested that soy could lower your risk of breast cancer, new studies sponsored by the National Institutes of Health paint a different picture.

When scientists at the University of Illinois added genistein to the diets of lab mice with breast cancer, their tumors grew larger. Some researchers think the same thing could happen to women who have a certain type of breast cancer. Other researchers think this data is not convincing.

Meanwhile, at the University of Texas, the results of a different study suggest that other components of soy might help lower breast cancer risk. The women in this small study consumed 36 ounces of soymilk a day with 99 percent of the isoflavones removed. This equaled less than 5 milligrams of isoflavones daily.

So if you enjoy eating soy foods, look for products with the lowest amount of isoflavones. Here are examples of typical servings along with the average amount of isoflavones they provide:

1/2 cup of soy flour = 50 milligrams (mg) isoflavones

1 cup of soy milk = 40 mg isoflavones

1/2 cup of tofu = 40 mg isoflavones

1/2 cup textured vegetable protein = 35 mg isoflavones

With the current popularity of soy products, you can be sure the studies will continue. Consider your risk factors to decide how much soy is safe for you.

Clobber breast cancer with chicken

Does the color of the meat you eat really matter when it comes to fighting breast cancer? At least one team of scientists thinks so.

Dr. Ralph J. Delfino and his fellow researchers at the University of California Irvine College of Medicine found that women who ate about 2 ounces of white meat a day had half the risk of breast cancer as those who ate less than an ounce. A normal-size serving is about 3 ounces.

"No matter how the food was prepared — blackened, barbecued, grilled, or pan-fried," Delfino says, "red meat didn't increase the risk, and white meat actually seemed to offer protection against breast cancer."

In earlier studies, women who ate the most red meat had a 78 percent higher risk of breast cancer than those who ate the least. And those who ate their grilled or fried meat heavily browned or charred had an increased risk as well — thanks to chemicals called heterocyclic amines (HCAs), formed on the surface of meat during high-temperature cooking.

Unfortunately, Delfino's study only looked at breast cancer, not other cancers linked to meats cooked by high-heat methods. To be on the safe side, consider baking, broiling, or stewing most of your meats.

If you want to cook on the grill occasionally, try making cherry burgers. Surprisingly, mixing chopped cherries with ground beef seems to reduce the HCA danger. And cherry burgers are moist and juicy, even though the fat content of the burgers is lower than regular burgers.

The amount of fat in your diet is another cancer concern. Although it's not yet clear what role fat plays in your chances of getting breast cancer, there's no doubt being overweight increases your risk. To keep your weight down, choose lean portions of meat and cut away any visible fat. Use fat-free milk and other dairy products.

In addition, replace bad fats, like lard and butter, with olive oil, which some studies show may even protect you against breast cancer.

3 powerful cancer-fighting beverages

Delight yourself with these delicious, refreshing drinks, and your taste buds will trick you into forgetting your nutritional goal is serious — to beat the odds of getting breast cancer.

Grape juice spritzer. Blend a cup of Concord grape juice, half a cup of club soda, and a dash of lemon juice. Pour over ice and — bottoms up. Makes a great stand-in for alcohol-spiked punch.

Banana-carrot smoothie. Toss a medium banana and half a cup of plain or vanilla yogurt into your blender. Add two cups of fresh carrot juice — or substitute a cup of apple juice for one of carrot— and a few fresh mint leaves. This drink is great as a light meal, too.

Spicy apple iced tea. Place a few slices of a sweet apple in the bottom of your teapot. Sprinkle with sugar and cinnamon to taste. Add two tea bags, pour in two cups of boiling water, and steep. Let cool and pour over ice. Add lemon or mint if you wish.

These juicy blends are rich in vitamin C, beta carotene, quercetin, and other flavonoids — all powerful antioxidants. That's what makes them so beneficial to your breasts.

Soak up sunshine to lower your risk

A sunny day can lift your spirits and lower your risk of breast cancer. Women who live in the sunnier southern parts of Europe and North America, according to a recent study, get breast cancer less often than their northern sisters.

Sunshine's gift of vitamin D is probably responsible. To reap the benefits of the "sunshine vitamin," spend at least 30 minutes a day in the sun, but avoid the hours between 10 a.m. and 4 p.m. when the sun's rays are strongest. You can also get this important nutrient by eating fish and drinking fortified milk.

Try these other nutritional tips to help in your fight against the menace of breast cancer.

Pour yourself a colorful drink. Tomatoes, carrots, and dark-leafy greens do more than brighten your plate. They provide vitamins and minerals that help you combat breast cancer.

But did you know drinking your veggies might be even more protective? Research suggests that two important cancer-fighting nutrients — alpha-carotene and lutein — are more available in juice than in whole vegetables, raw or cooked.

Make flax a breakfast habit. A heaping tablespoon of ground flaxseed a day could lower your breast cancer risk. A simple way to get flaxseed into your diet is to sprinkle it on your cereal each morning.

Bulk up your resistance. Eating whole grains, according to some studies, will help guard you against breast cancer. Whole grains are a good source of fiber, which can lower the estrogen circulating in your body. This is particularly important if you are premenopausal. Fruits and vegetables are also good sources of fiber.

Drink green tea. Women in China and Japan are six to 10 times less likely to get breast cancer than North American and Western European women. And green tea could be one of the reasons.

"There are, of course, many dietary and other differences to be examined," says Dr. Gail Sonenshein, a professor of biochemistry at Boston University School of Medicine. "Although we don't believe green tea by itself will prevent breast cancer," she says, "it may prove beneficial when used in combination with other dietary factors."

Don't drink alcohol. According to USDA guidelines, even one drink a day can raise your risk of breast cancer. If you drink occasionally, stick to a one-drink limit.

By choosing more healthy foods and fewer sugary treats and empty calories, you'll boost your immune system. The reward will be resistance to breast cancer as well as many other diseases.

Sidestep breast cancer — at any age

Being physically active after menopause can almost make up for a lifetime of taking it easy, at least as far as breast cancer is concerned. A new study says you can slash your risk of breast cancer by 40 percent — and you don't even have to go to a gym to do it.

"This study is great news for women who, so far in their lives, have not been physically active," says Dr. Christine Friedenreich, research scientist with the Alberta Cancer Board and the University of Calgary. "Our data show it's never too late to start — and once you do, your risk of breast cancer plummets by 40 percent."

The news is even better if you have been on the go all along. "For those who have been active throughout their lives," says Friedenreich, "their risk of breast cancer is reduced by 42 percent."

It's not exactly clear why lifelong activity brings such good results, but strengthening your immune system and helping you maintain a healthy weight are two good reasons. Controlling your weight is a big plus because obesity, especially abdominal fat, is a major risk factor for breast cancer.

The best activities aren't necessarily lifting weights, doing aerobics, or taking brisk walks. Based on this study, these activities don't seem to offer the best protection.

"It is not simply recreational activity that counts," says Friedenreich. "In fact, we found the greatest risk decreases with occupational and household activity. My advice to women is to be as active as possible in all aspects of their daily lives."

So don't skip your chores before you rush off to exercise class. Scrubbing pots and pans and unloading the dishwasher may do you just as much good. And adding some of the following activities to your daily routine will help keep your breasts healthy, too.

★ Use stairs as often as possible. Carry smaller loads when putting things away upstairs so you'll have to make several trips.

★ Park a block or two from your destination and walk instead of driving around looking for the closest parking space.

★ Load your own groceries into your car. If you have just a few bags, carry them out. Don't use a cart.

★ Take the longest route, or the one with the most steps, when carrying out the garbage or bringing in the groceries.

★ Put canned goods and other heavier items on higher shelves in the pantry to give your arms a workout.

★ Pick up and carry flowerpots and gardening supplies rather than rolling them in a wheelbarrow.

★ Water outside flowers and shrubs with a watering can instead of using the garden hose.

★ Pack two smaller bags when traveling and carry them. Leave the rolling bag at home.

★ Sweep, rake, or blow leaves off your driveway.

★ Walk your pets and give them baths.

★ Go to the park with your grandchildren. Push them in swings and catch them at the bottom of the slide.

Getting more action into your life will also do wonders for your bones and your heart. Think about other activities you can do and put them on your daily to-do list.

Burns

Extinguish household burns

Your home is your castle. Unfortunately, it can also be a royal source of danger.

Burns often occur in the home. Cooking equipment, heaters, flammable clothing, scalding water, and smoking materials like cigarettes, matches, or lighters all represent potential hazards. Older people and children are especially at risk for burns, which are classified into one of three degrees.

- ★ First degree. Only the top layer of skin is burned. The skin is red and painful to the touch.

- ★ Second degree. These deeper burns are more painful. The skin may blister and swell.

- ★ Third degree. The burn leaves the skin blackened or sheet-white, and it can break open. You must get emergency help quickly.

Prevent burns in your home by taking the following precautions.

Turn down the temperature. To avoid scalding from hot water, lower the temperature setting on your water heater. Make sure it does not go above 120 degrees.

Watch hot pots. Turn pot handles away from the front of the stove, and use mitten potholders when handling them.

Top tips for treating burns

Ouch! Maybe you should have used an oven mitt. Here's what to do in case you get burned.

Cool down. Run cold water over the burn for about 10-15 minutes. You can also soak the burned area in cold water or cover it with wet towels. Don't use ice.

Cover it. If your clothing irritates your skin, cover the burn with a gauze bandage.

Nix ointments. Don't apply butter, mayonnaise, or commercial burn ointments to the burn. They slow healing and increase your risk of infection.

Ignore blisters. Don't pop a blister. It's your body's way of protecting the burned tissue. If one breaks, apply a light layer of antibiotic cream.

Get help. Seek medical help for bad burns. If your burn is larger than your palm, it could be serious. Also see a doctor if you spot signs of infection, such as worsening redness, pus, offensive odor, and fever.

Test your food. Be especially careful of food cooked in a microwave. The outside might feel cool, but the middle can be scalding hot. Food can also be much hotter than its container.

Clear counters. Avoid spills and other accidents. Keep cups or dishes of hot food or drink away from the edges of counters or tablecloths. Don't let cords of appliances dangle over the counter.

Snuff out smoking. Quit smoking. Not only will you lessen your risk of burns, you'll slash your risk for all sorts of health problems. If you can't quit, make sure not to smoke in bed, when you're sleepy, or after you've been drinking alcohol.

Wear safe clothing. Sturdy fabrics like denim, wool, polyester, nylon, and silk are your best bet. Don't wear loose clothing when using the stove. Bathrobes with long, floppy sleeves are especially dangerous.

Gear up. To avoid painful chemical burns, wear rubber gloves and protective eye goggles when using household chemicals like oven cleaner.

Heat sensibly. Don't overfill your kerosene heater or fill it with gasoline. Never use cooking equipment to heat your home.

Child-proof your home. If you have children or young visitors, take steps to keep them safe. Store chemicals in a high place out of their reach. Don't keep candy or other tempting goodies above the stove. Cover your electrical outlets, and store matches and lighters in a locked cabinet.

Use caution and common sense to sidestep burns — and your "castle" will be truly fit for a king.

Cataracts

Easy ways to steer clear of cataracts

You may be a good driver, but a cataract in one or both eyes means you're more likely to have an accident. As cataracts gradually cloud your vision, it gets harder to distinguish between light and dark and to see what's in the shadows. In one study of older drivers, those who had wrecks were eight times more likely to have this vision problem than those who had no accidents.

Get in the drivers seat when it comes to cataract prevention.

Grab some shades. Avoid sunlight altogether during the brightest part of the day, and wear sunglasses any time you go out in the sun. Researchers say your rate of cataracts is about 60 percent higher if you don't wear sunglasses on a regular basis. Keep those dark glasses on in the car, too. Most people don't realize how much light can bounce off the hood and stream in through the windows.

If you use the herb St. John's wort, be especially careful. It makes your eyes even more sensitive to light.

Don't smoke. The more you smoke, the greater your chances of cataracts. If you need another reason to give up this dangerous habit, just think about protecting your peepers.

Avoid alcohol. Over 17,000 doctors took part in a study that, in the end, proved a connection between alcohol and cataracts. Those who drank every day had a 31 percent greater risk of cataracts than those who had alcohol less than once a month.

Choose an "eye-deal" diet. What you see on your dinner plate can influence how well you see everything else.

★ Eat lots of apricots, carrots, spinach, strawberries, tomatoes, and other brightly colored fruits and veggies. They are full of antioxidant vitamins A and C, which keep your eyes healthy by fighting free radicals.

★ Make a peanut butter sandwich using whole grain bread. Toss wheat germ in your cereal and sunflower seeds on your salad. Serve up a steaming bowl of brown rice. You'll cut your cataract risk in half by getting enough vitamin E every day from seeds, nuts, and grains like these. Cooking with canola oil is another way to add this antioxidant vitamin to your diet.

★ Start your day with a fortified cereal, have a tuna salad sandwich on whole wheat bread for lunch, and include a baked potato with mushrooms at dinnertime. These are foods that give you a healthy dose of three protective B vitamins — niacin, thiamin, and riboflavin.

★ A protein deficiency can put you at greater risk of cataracts. So, include fish, turkey breast, other lean meats, and low-fat dairy foods. Or get the same benefit by eating different plant proteins together. Beans and rice or black-eyed peas and corn bread are good choices.

★ Treat yourself to a spicy Indian curry dish with turmeric. It contains curcumin, an antioxidant that just might help you keep clear of cataracts.

Notice what you need to avoid, as well. Saturated fats like butter, lard, and coconut oil can increase your chances of developing cataracts. Use canola and olive oil instead. Salt is another threat to good vision. Keep it to a minimum by spicing up your meals with herbs. Curcumin, an ingredient in turmeric — used in many Indian dishes — is an antioxidant that's particularly good at fighting cataracts.

Beware of sight-stealing meds

Blurred faces, dull colors, light sensitivity — you suspect a cataract. But a medication you're taking for another condition could just as easily cause symptoms like these.

If, for example, your eyesight seems to be getting dimmer, the high cholesterol drug Lipitor could be the culprit. Switching to another medication may seem like the obvious thing to do, but talk it over with your doctor. Two other drugs prescribed for high cholesterol, Zocor and Pravachol, can actually make cataracts worse if you already have them.

According to the American Optometric Association, if you have certain vision problems, a medication could be the cause.

Vision problem	Check the medication you are taking for...
Blurred vision	acne, angina, anxiety, arthritis, congestive heart failure, depression, diabetes, high blood pressure, leg cramps, nausea or vomiting, pain, thyroid problems, tuberculosis, ulcers
Difficulty telling apart colors	acne, arthritis, breast cancer, congestive heart failure, heartbeat irregularities, impotence, tuberculosis
Sensitivity to light	acne, allergies, anxiety, arthritis, diabetes, ear infections, heartbeat irregularities, high blood pressure, leg cramps, psoriasis, respiratory infection, seizures, sinus infection, skin infection, thyroid problems, ulcers, urinary tract infection

This list is not complete. If you're not sure how a medication could affect your vision, call your doctor.

Better vision: a clear benefit of HRT

Think about your eyes if you're thinking about hormone replacement therapy (HRT).

While everyone faces the threat of cataracts as they age, after 50, women are at greater risk than men. This is probably due to hormonal changes that come with menopause. In addition, if surgery brought on your menopause rather than it occurring naturally, your chances of developing cataracts are even greater.

Estrogen, however, protects against cataracts — and the longer you take it the greater the benefits. Women on estrogen for more than 10 years cut their risk of cataracts by 60 percent, compared to non-users. Even if you've only been on HRT for one to two years, your risk is 20 percent lower.

Unfortunately, new information about estrogen therapy indicates greater health risks — breast cancer, heart disease, heart attacks, strokes, and blood clots — than previously believed. The Food and Drug Administration advises doctors to prescribe estrogen only when benefits clearly outweigh the risks, just long enough for successful treatment, and at the lowest effective dose. If you are considering taking estrogen, be sure you discuss all the risks and benefits with your doctor first.

Cold Sores

Kiss off cold sores with amazing treatments

The burning, itchy, tingling of cold sores may make it hard to pucker up for a little smooch. But relief — and romance — may be closer than you think. The FDA recently approved a nonprescription medication for cold sores. The new cream, called Abreva, works best if you apply it at the first sign of a flare-up.

Unlike the prescription medication, the active ingredient in Abreva, docosanol, doesn't work by destroying the herpes simplex virus that causes cold sores. Instead, scientists believe, it changes the skin cells so they create a barrier against the virus.

You may find it well worth the cost at $15 a tube, but if you prefer a different approach to healing, look for these remedies in herb shops or drugstores.

Lemon balm. When you use a cream made from this minty herb, you are likely to feel much better by the second day, the time when people say cold sores usually hurt the most. According to research, healing time is much shorter for people who use it four or five times a day. On top of that, the period between outbreaks might be longer.

Zinc. Getting zinc in your diet — from meat, shellfish, beans, and grains — will help prevent cold sores. But if you get one anyway, dab on some zinc oxide and glycine cream as soon as you notice it. Sores heal faster in people who use this preparation within 24 hours of the first symptoms. They also had less blistering, soreness, itching, and tingling. Or place a zinc lozenge directly on your sore and let it dissolve slowly.

Aloe vera. If you have an aloe vera plant growing in your window, break off a tip of the cactus-like leaf and squeeze on the soothing, healing gel the next time you get a cold sore. Aloe vera lip balm works great, too. Apply it three times a day until the sore dries up.

Aloe vera not only reduces inflammation and attacks the virus that causes cold sores, it also fortifies your skin with B vitamins, vitamin C, and amino acids.

Ice. As soon as a sore appears, apply ice for 15 minutes a day to hasten healing and numb the pain. Drinking a cold liquid or sucking on a frozen treat might also work.

Milk. To stop a cold sore early, or heal a fully formed one faster, dip a soft, clean cloth in milk and apply it directly to the cold sore. Press for five seconds and remove for five seconds. Continue this process for five minutes. Repeat every few hours. Some experts think the protein in the milk speeds healing.

Pepto Bismol. At least one person reports getting relief from applying Pepto Bismol when a cold sore appears. Strange as it sounds, it might really work. That's because research shows a key ingredient in this diarrhea medicine is effective against cold sores.

Discover the healing power of tea

The simple pleasure of sipping a cup of tea not only soothes your spirit, it can settle an upset stomach and protect you from cataracts, cancer, and heart disease. Now, researchers say, you may have tea to thank for fewer cold sores, too.

"Tea has long been believed to have medicinal properties, and our results justify this belief," says Dr. Milton Schiffenbauer. He and his fellow researchers at Pace University in New York are discovering the power of tea to fight viruses, including herpes simplex, the one that causes cold sores.

Whether you prefer hot tea or cold tea, black tea or green tea, when it comes to cold sores, it may not matter. "My results were with cold tea, but I do not think that temperature makes a difference," says Schiffenbauer. "In addition, I am now doing work with green teas, and I find my results to be very promising."

Although the work isn't complete and additional studies might be needed to support these findings, it looks like all kinds of tea — blended or unblended, filtered or unfiltered, even bottled tea drinks — like Snapple, Bigelow, and Arizona — may destroy the cold sore virus.

In addition to drinking tea, you'll be glad to know there are several more ways to keep cold sores at bay.

Take an aspirin. A 45-year-old man, recovering from a heart attack, was also troubled with severe cold sores. Under his doctor's care, he started taking small, daily doses (125 milligrams) of aspirin for his heart. Amazingly, after three months, his cold sores disappeared.

This sparked a study to see if aspirin had the same effect on other people. The results showed that the people who took aspirin had milder cases, and those who used aspirin long-term had longer periods without sores.

If you want to use aspirin, but not on a regular basis, experts say your best bet is to take one as soon as you notice the tingling that precedes a cold sore. Then take one every day until the symptoms disappear.

Load up on lysine. If cold sores are causing you pain and embarrassment, an amino acid called lysine might be your best bet for protection. According to doctors at Indiana University Medical School, lysine can prevent cold sores from reappearing in chronic sufferers. And even though some people developed cold sores again, they had fewer outbreaks, and the sores went away faster.

Good sources of lysine include wheat germ, poultry, pork, ricotta cheese, and cottage cheese. It's also available as a supplement at many health food stores. If you have frequent flare-ups, researchers recommend taking a small dose of about 500 milligrams (mg) a day, then up to 3,000 mg a day during an outbreak.

People who want to try lysine supplements should have their cholesterol levels checked first. Some studies suggest that lysine can cause the liver to produce too much cholesterol.

Lysine comes with another warning, too. To get the protective benefits, avoid foods containing arginine, a substance that prevents lysine from working. Lay off such favorites as peanuts, seeds, whole grains, rice, and gelatin.

Say yes to yogurt. Just be sure to eat yogurt with the live *Lactobacillus acidophilus* culture if you want to fend off cold sores. If you aren't fond of yogurt, you can get the culture in capsules at a health food store. But remember, the culture has to be live and must be kept refrigerated.

Eat a nutritious diet. A healthy immune system is necessary for fighting any virus, and herpes simplex is no exception. A well-balanced diet, with plenty of vitamin C, vitamin E, folic acid, and zinc, will help you fend off the cause of cold sores.

Colds and Flu

Simple secrets soothe your sore throat

Being sick is tough to swallow. Especially when you have a sore throat. Whether it's scratchy, tickling, raw, or just plain painful, your throat demands relief. Here are a few easy ways you can lend a hand.

Grab a gargle. Mix up one of these comforting brews for your throat and give it a good gargle about twice a day — just don't swallow.

- ★ Stir a half-teaspoon of salt into a cup of warm water.

- ★ Add a teaspoon each of salt, baking soda, and sugar to half a glass of warm water.

- ★ Dissolve two aspirin tablets in a glass of warm water — just make sure they're not coated or buffered aspirin. And don't substitute acetaminophen. It won't work.

- ★ Brew some strong tea and gargle with it either warm or cold.

Slurp some soup. Chances are your mother served chicken soup when you were sick. And chances are you felt better. The warm liquid provides relief for your aching throat and other cold symptoms.

Sip some tea. Warm beverages like ginger and hyssop tea also calm your throat. Make a pot of ginger tea by putting three or four slices of the fresh root in a pint of hot water and simmering for 10 to 30 minutes. You can find hyssop tea bags at most health or nutrition stores. Follow the manufacturer's brewing instructions. For added relief, stir a spoonful of honey or squeeze a lemon into your cup.

Is it the flu or anthrax?

It's only natural to worry. After all, anthrax has gotten its share of publicity. And inhalational anthrax, the deadliest form of the disease, shares many symptoms with the flu. But the next time you start feeling sick don't panic. According to the Centers for Disease Control (CDC), under normal circumstances, your odds of developing anthrax are only about 1 in 300 million.

See your doctor if you develop these symptoms:

★ Fever (temperature over 100), sometimes accompanied by chills or night sweats

★ Cough, usually a dry cough, along with chest pain, shortness of breath, fatigue, and muscle aches

★ Sore throat, followed by difficulty swallowing, headache, nausea, loss of appetite, abdominal pain, vomiting, or diarrhea

★ A sore, especially on your face, arms, or hands, that starts as a raised bump and develops into a painless ulcer with a black area in the center.

If you have a stuffy or runny nose, you almost certainly have the flu and not anthrax.

Contact your state health department if you have more questions or visit the CDC's Internet site at <www.cdc.gov>.

Chomp into a chili pepper. These spicy little peppers, also known as cayenne peppers, numb your sore throat so you can swallow without pain. You don't have to eat them straight — chop them into your favorite recipe or sprinkle cayenne powder on almost any dish. Just be sure you start off with a light hand to test your tolerance.

Pass the pomegranates. The bright red juice of the pomegranate, a fruit common in the Middle East, is not only a delicious way to get your fluids, it's also loaded with vitamin C.

Choose and use drugs wisely. It would be nice to knock out your sore throat with an antibiotic. But that only works for bacterial infections, like strep throat. Even the world's strongest antibiotic is powerless against viral infections, like common colds and flu. Worse, taking an antibiotic for a viral infection can cause bacteria to become immune to antibiotics.

If you do have strep throat, make sure you don't stop taking your antibiotics just because you feel better. Finish the prescription to finish off the bacteria.

If you use an over-the-counter product, choose one specifically for sore throats. There's no use treating symptoms you don't have. And there's no use trying to treat yourself if your sore throat is the sign of something more serious. If you have a severe sore throat that lasts more than a week, see your doctor.

---

6 top tips to survive the flu

In spite of everything you did right, you still got a cold or the flu. And the only place you want to be is in bed. Get plenty of sleep, and keep these helpful items nearby.

Stock up on tissues. Handkerchiefs only hold and spread your germs. Instead, use tissues with lotion that will soothe your nose.

Fill a jug of water. Drink, drink, drink to flush out the toxins and hydrate your body. To tickle your taste buds, add a little lime or lemon juice.

Make a cooling compress. Soothe your aching head with a home-made ice pack. Wet a clean sock, stick it in a zip-lock bag, and place it in the freezer. When it's nice and cold, lay it over your forehead.

Plump up plenty of pillows. Pamper yourself with soft, fluffy pillows. By elevating your head, you'll breathe and rest better.

Mask the light. Buy an herbal sleep mask to ease your headache and shut out the world.

Treat yourself to tangerines. Fruit juice is great, but tangerines are a delicious, fun way to get your vitamin C.

Wash your hands to wipe out germs

When it comes to spreading germs, you have to hand it to hands. Although colds can be spread through sneezing and coughing, you're actually about 60 percent more likely to catch one from a simple handshake.

That's because once the germs are on your hand, it's easy to transfer them into your body by touching your eyes, nose, or mouth.

But don't despair. With a little soap and water, you can take a hands-on approach to colds and flu prevention.

Salute cleanliness. Leave it to the United States Navy to sink the common cold. Navy recruits who were ordered to wash their hands at least five times a day slashed their rate of respiratory illness by 45 percent.

Of course, you don't have to be in the armed services to be at risk for colds and flu. Everyday objects such as telephone receivers, kitchen faucets, and sponges hide all sorts of germs. And everyday activities like cleaning your house or doing your laundry can expose you to germs.

With so many enemy germs out there, it might be a good idea to take a tip from the Navy. Try to wash your hands at least five times a day. It can't hurt, and you just might cut your risk of colds and flu in half.

Scrub smarter. Here's a scary statistic. While about 95 percent of Americans claim to wash their hands after using a public restroom, only two out of every three people actually do.

That's a shame because there's really no excuse not to wash up. It's not only one of the best ways to fight germs — it's also one of the easiest. Just wet your hands, use bar soap or apply a dollop of liquid soap, about the size of a quarter. Scrub your hands vigorously for at least 15 seconds, says the Centers for Disease Control. That's about as long as it would take you to recite the alphabet. Then rinse well and dry.

It doesn't even matter how you dry off. Whether you use cloth towels, paper towels, a mechanical dryer, or just let your hands air-dry. They still remain clean.

Always wash your hands before and after you cook a meal, before you eat, and after you use the bathroom. Make an effort to wash more often when someone in your house is sick.

Sidestep special soaps. If you're looking for extra protection from colds and flu, don't reach for antibacterial soap. Viruses, not bacteria, cause colds and flu. So an antibacterial soap won't work any better than regular soap.

Plus, using antibacterial soaps too often might actually help certain bacteria develop a resistance to antibiotics and become stronger. In other words, you might be doing more harm than good.

The important thing is to wash your hands properly and frequently. Put away those fancy antiseptics and stick to good, old-fashioned soap and water.

Pay less for cold protection

Take vitamins and other nutritional supplements and you can give your immune system a healthy boost. You probably won't get sick as often, and your colds may not last as long.

But why pay full price for better health? You can find plenty of deals if you look hard enough.

Here's just one example. Save up to 50 percent on vitamins and other nutritional supplements at Total Health. Check prices or place an order at their Web site <www.totaldiscountvitamins.com>, or reach them at:

Total Health
170 Fulton Street
Farmingdale, NY 11735
800-283-2833

It's easy to find discounts on your own. Start by browsing through newspapers and magazines for deals. Comparison shop. Seek the best bargains at drugstores, supermarkets, specialty shops, and discount stores. If you have access to the Internet, you'll discover even more savings.

Amazing ways to boost your immune system

Without a strong immune system, your body is like a castle without a drawbridge or a hockey team without a goalie. You have no defense against intruders.

On the other hand, a healthy immune system fights off germs so you don't get sick. It's like stopping a cold before it starts.

Fortunately, it's not difficult to bolster your defense against colds and flu. Check out these surprising ways to strengthen your immune system.

Deal with it. Sit down for a game of contract bridge and score a Grand Slam against sickness. When you play this complicated card game, you stimulate your dorsolateral cortex, the part of your brain involved in memory and planning ahead. This region spurs your thymus gland to produce more T-cells, which fight off viruses and other germs — whether they attack from the North, South, East, or West. A recent study found that a group of older women raised their T-cell levels after playing contract bridge for an hour and a half.

Take a walk. Avoiding a cold might be as simple as putting one foot in front of the other. Regular, gentle exercise, like walking, helps fortify your immune system by stimulating natural killer cells that stop viruses and bacteria. Exercise is especially helpful for seniors. Women over 67 who walk or exercise regularly have fewer respiratory infections than others.

Just don't overdo it. Activities that are more strenuous like rowing or distance running can temporarily weaken your immune system and leave you more susceptible to colds and flu.

Relax. Stress can hamper your immune system and open the door to colds and flu. Learning how to handle stress, on the other hand, can protect you. An Ohio State University study of 33 medical and dental students demonstrated the power of self-relaxation. During a high-stress period right before exams, the students practicing relaxation techniques had stronger immune responses than their peers. The more often you practice these techniques, the stronger your immune system becomes.

Laugh out loud. Another great way to counter stress is through humor. It's no joke — good, hearty laughter offsets the effects of stress hormones and gives your immune system a major boost. Watch a funny movie or TV show or swap jokes with a friend. Fighting illness has never been so much fun.

Look on the bright side. The old song "Accentuate the Positive" isn't just catchy — it can also keep you from catching a cold. People with a negative outlook on life are almost four times more likely to come down with a cold than optimistic people. On the other hand, if you have a positive outlook and an outgoing personality, you'll have one more thing to be happy about.

Hang up on your stuffy nose

You might not be coming down with a cold after all. Maybe you're just talking too much or working too hard.

If you spend a lot of time on your cellular phone, your nose might feel stuffed up. That's because the electromagnetic field of the cell phone increases your skin temperature and causes the blood vessels in your nose to dilate.

Researchers in London found that even a short conversation significantly raises your skin temperature. You can avoid the stuffy nose feeling by using an earpiece instead of holding the phone against your face.

Another study, this one in Finland, found that common office supplies might also supply you with cold symptoms.

If you handle self-copying, or carbonless, paper, you might be increasing your risk for a sore throat by a whopping 80 percent. You might also get headaches, wheeze, and cough more often.

Spending a lot of time near the photocopier can irritate your nose, and sitting in front of a computer all day can leave you with headaches and fatigue.

So, don't rush to the drugstore to fix your cold symptoms, try fixing the technology in your life, first.

Check your kitchen for cold and flu cures

Don't spend a fortune on remedies for cold and flu symptoms. Sometimes, help is right in your own kitchen.

Feel fine faster. Take echinacea at the first sign of a cold or the flu and your symptoms may be gone within 24 hours. This popular herb comes in several forms, including liquid extract, tablets, and capsules.

Another natural remedy, elderberry, has people claiming to recover from the flu 200 percent faster. The extract, called Sambucol, even helps reduce fever. Look for elderberry as an ingredient in commercial syrups and lozenges.

Calm that cough. Prescription cough remedies can be costly in more ways than one. One, benzonatate (Tessalon), temporarily deadens the nerves in your airway and reduces your cough reflex. However, if you chew or suck on the soft capsules, you could completely deaden the nerves in your mouth and throat. You could choke, suffer a cardiovascular collapse — or even die.

For a safer alternative, mix 8 ounces of warm pineapple juice and two teaspoons of honey. It will provide natural, tasty relief.

Breathe a bit better. A cup of warm tea can soothe a sore throat, but it also contains a natural antihistamine that can open your stuffy nose. Quercetin, a phytochemical in tea, controls the membranes in your body that release histamine — a substance that dilates your capillaries and makes your nose feel clogged.

Other good sources of quercetin are buckwheat, citrus fruits, and red onions.

Boost your immunity. Garlic has as much anti-infection power as penicillin. It not only kills bacteria, but viruses and infectious fungi, too. It will give your immune system a boost and make you sweat, a natural way to get rid of waste. If that's not enough, garlic adds great flavor to your meals.

So next time you get a sniffle, don't rush to the pharmacy. With all these healing foods and herbs at your disposal, staying home might be the best medicine.

Exercise in spite of illness

You're not feeling on top of your game — but that doesn't mean you have to stay on the sidelines. Even when you're sick, you can still exercise your right to exercise. Just go about it sensibly.

Draw the neckline. To determine whether you should exercise or not, take the neck test. If your symptoms are above your neck — such as a runny nose, a sore throat, or sneezing — go ahead and do some moderate exercise. If you feel good after 10 minutes, pick up the pace. If you feel awful, stop and try again later.

However, if your symptoms are below your neck — such as a hacking cough, fever, chills, sore muscles and joints, diarrhea, or vomiting — you should stay in bed. Exercising with "below-the-neck" symptoms can lead to dehydration, heatstroke, and even heart failure.

Ease into it. If you skipped a few days of exercise because you weren't feeling well, don't jump right back into your routine as soon as you feel better. For every day you were sick, spend two days working out at a lower than normal intensity. For example, if you were sick for three days, work out at a less intense pace for six days.

Combat the cold. Because most colds occur during winter months, take extra care when exercising. Here are some helpful tips for working out in cold weather.

★ Dress in layers with something wind and waterproof on top.

★ Wear a scarf over your mouth and nose. This helps warm the air you breathe.

★ Stretch to warm up your muscles before you begin. Cool down after your workout, too.

★ Drink plenty of fluids. Even though you might not feel as thirsty in cold weather as in hot weather, your body still needs fluids just as much, if not more. Bring a water bottle with you.

Choose wisely. If it's too cold or icy, don't risk exercising outside. Go to a gym or walk around the mall instead. You could also try exercise videotapes for a stay-at-home alternative. Just make sure you choose tapes that match your level of fitness. For example, if you're a beginner, don't buy or rent a tape for experts. Switch things up by using a few different tapes. That way, you won't get bored with the same old routine.

Colon Cancer

Make the right diet decisions

You can count on a healthy diet to help you resist many illnesses. But when it comes to colon cancer, it may not be that simple.

Researchers recently compared three diets to see what effect they had on colon cancer risk in older women. Surprisingly, a healthy diet of fruits and vegetables, fish and poultry, whole grain breads, fruit juice, and low-fat dairy products was not protective.

Equally unexpected, a typical western diet of processed and red meats, soda and sweets, refined breads and potatoes, and high-fat dairy products did not increase the risk. Nor did a diet with lots of calories coming from alcohol.

But the experts say not to give up on a healthy diet. Their study suggested it could shield women under 50 from colon cancer. And a healthy diet affects you indirectly no matter what your age. For example, obesity raises your chances of getting colon cancer, and a nutritious diet can help you keep your weight down.

While you may not find the perfect overall diet, previous studies have suggested certain foods might help you dodge colon cancer.

Care for your colon with curcumin. A love of Indian and Thai food may put you a step ahead in preventing colon cancer. Turmeric, the spice that gives these dishes their yellow color, contains curcumin. This antioxidant phytochemical not only fights colon cancer, it battles breast, skin, stomach, mouth, liver, blood, and lung cancers, too.

Reduce risk with rye. Have high-fiber veggies on whole-meal rye bread for a sandwich your colon can appreciate. It's not clear exactly what role fiber plays in fighting cancer. Recent studies have questioned whether it helps prevent colon cancer. But research shows rye bread can improve your bowel movements and may lower the concentration of some cancer-causing compounds in your colon.

Protect yourself with legumes. A dish of black beans can be an outstanding addition to your cancer-prevention diet. They are high in resistant starch, which passes undigested through your stomach and small intestine. It then settles in your colon where bacteria tackle it, producing butyrate, a fatty acid that helps prevent cancer.

Researchers at the University of Illinois found seven kinds of beans were tops in resistant starch content. Black beans were highest at 27 percent, with 63 percent of the resistant starch making it to the colon before being digested. Corn and barley were the top whole grains, while heavily processed flour was on the low end with less than 2 percent resistant starch.

Trim the threat with milk. If you are among those who drink the most milk, you may be one of the least likely to get colon cancer. Researchers from Finland found this protective effect in a 24-year study of more than 10,000 people. They think lactose, the type of sugar found in milk, may encourage the growth of healthy bacteria that block the development of cancer.

Other dairy products may not be as helpful, though. In this study, cheese and buttermilk seemed to raise the risk of colon cancer although scientists aren't quite sure why. And eating butter raised the risk of rectal cancer slightly.

Crush cancer with cabbage. This inexpensive, low-calorie vegetable — eaten steamed, stuffed, or shredded raw in a salad — goes right to work producing anti-cancer enzymes to protect your colon. Studies from around the world find plain cabbage and its fancier cousins, Chinese cabbage and brussels sprouts, guard you from not only colon cancer, but breast, bladder, brain, lung, and stomach cancers as well.

Broccoli, spinach, kale, and other green vegetables are also powerful players in your battle against colon cancer. Their key weapon is an antioxidant called lutein.

Focus on the right fats. Joanne R. Lupton, Texas A&M University professor and research scientist, has spent the last 20 years studying the effects of diet on the colon. She now believes the kind of fat you eat helps determine whether cells in your colon will become cancerous.

"Fish oil seems to protect against colon cancer while corn oil not only does not protect against it but appears to promote it," says Lupton.

Other studies find olive oil, popular in southern European countries where people tend to have a lower rate of colon cancer, a protector. Still others find safflower oil a risk.

Research continues on these and other foods that may help you fight colon cancer. Meanwhile, stick to your healthy diet for a better chance of defeating any disease, including cancer.

Keys to locking out colon cancer

Being overweight raises your risk for colon cancer, but exercising regularly will cut your risk. So say researchers at the University of Arizona, who have uncovered a specific compound in your colon that boosts cancer risk — but is lowered by exercise.

Their study shows if you are overweight and inactive you are more likely to have high levels of a compound called prostaglandin E2 (PGE2). But exercise lowers the amount of this substance in your system. In the study, previously inactive participants who took a 30-minute jog or a 60-minute walk each day lowered their PGE2 by 28 percent.

Researchers think the PGE2 level may indirectly play a role in colon cancer by stimulating your body to make insulin. Lab studies have shown that insulin affects the growth of colon cancer cells. So by keeping your weight down, you may avoid colon cancer along with many other obesity-related diseases.

One more benefit from exercise is that it makes you thirsty. Men in a different study who drank the most water had a 92 percent lower risk of colon cancer than those who drank the least. Plus water helps keep your weight down. So try to get at least eight glasses of this refreshing beverage each day.

Fresh herbs: #1 disease fighters

While you are busy gobbling up healthy fruits and vegetables, don't miss out on one of the best sources of antioxidants — fresh herbs. Oregano, in particular, is a powerhouse.

A recent study found one tablespoon of fresh oregano packs an antioxidant punch equal to that of an apple. Gram for gram, it is 42 times more powerful than the apple, 30 times more than a potato, and 12 times more than an orange.

The antioxidants you get in oregano — and other leading herbs like dill, thyme, rosemary, and peppermint — help you fight a number of diseases, including many cancers, heart disease, and stroke. So toss them into salads, add them to dressings, sprinkle them on pizzas, and stir them into soups and pasta dishes.

Just be sure you use fresh ones. Dried herbs may still have flavor, but they don't measure up to the fresh ones in antioxidant strength.

Double your defense with aspirin and screening

Aspirin seems to be the answer to everything these days — even colon cancer. A new study has found taking one baby aspirin a day (80 milligrams) may cut cancer risk by 19 percent. Surprisingly, the smaller dose in the study was more effective than the regular dose of 325 milligrams.

Earlier studies have gone back and forth on the protective effects of aspirin for colon cancer. But this latest study gives scientists hope that aspirin will be another piece of ammunition to battle a disease that takes about 56,000 lives each year.

But it shouldn't be the only weapon in your arsenal. If you want to bring out the big guns, you should consider screening tests. They are, by far, the most effective way to protect you from colorectal cancer.

Your doctor may recommend a colonoscopy if you are at high risk for colon cancer — meaning you have a family history of the disease or suffer from inflammatory bowel disease — or if another test requires a follow up. But if you are over 50, you should schedule a screening even if you have no risk factors, says the American Cancer Society.

By taking aspirin and getting tested at the appropriate time, you'll double your defense against the third leading cause of cancer deaths in the U.S. But aspirin may cause side effects, like stomach problems, so talk to your doctor first to see if aspirin therapy is a good choice for you.

Magic bullet shoots down cancer risk

You'll be happy to hear the latest news if colon cancer runs in your family. A simple vitamin may lower your risk.

Previous research has shown you're twice as likely to get colon cancer if you have a parent or sibling with the disease, says Charles Fuchs, M.D., of the Dana-Farber Cancer Institute. But Fuchs and his fellow researchers offer a solution to that problem, and it's an easy one to swallow. They found that a diet high in folic acid — a common B vitamin — might help defend you against the added family-related risk.

Getting more of the essential amino acid methionine, and limiting alcohol, also helped lower risk, Fuchs found. All three are known to affect a process called methylation, which plays an important role in building a cell's DNA. He thinks it's possible that families with a pattern of colon cancer have a defect in this process, making them more susceptible to disease.

To help ward off colon cancer, try eating more folic acid, which you'll find in fruits, vegetables, and foods made with enriched flour. A cup of pinto beans, kidney beans, or spinach will give you between 200 and 300 micrograms (mcg) each. Green peas contain about 100 mcg; and orange juice, cauliflower, and broccoli provide a little less.

If you find it hard to get 400 mcg per day — the amount used in the study — from diet alone, try a multivitamin containing folic acid. It just may be the magic bullet you need to help you steer clear of colon cancer.

Top 3 tests for colon cancer

Screening is the best way to avoid colon cancer. You have the power to defeat this disease just by saying "yes" to these three easy tests.

Fecal occult blood test. This is your first line of defense. It checks for blood in your stool. It's the simplest and cheapest, but unfortunately, the least accurate of the tests. Have it done every year. If it turns out positive, you'll need additional tests.

Flexible sigmoidoscopy. Experts recommend you have this test done every 3 to 5 years. During this procedure, the doctor can find and remove polyps to test for cancer. It is accurate but only reaches about a third of the colon.

Colonoscopy. This highly accurate test checks your entire colon. Having it done just once reduces your risk — by a whopping 60 percent — of getting and dying from colon cancer over the next 10 years. It is recommended annually for those at high risk.

Constipation

Smart advice for kicking constipation

Constipation has long been blamed for causing every disease known to man. Today we know that's not true, but it can lead to certain conditions such as hemorrhoids, diverticulosis, and possibly some forms of cancer. Surprising new research has even linked it to Parkinson's disease.

Constipation bothers eight out of 10 people with Parkinson's, but doctors always thought it was an uncomfortable side effect. Now, new research suggests it could be an early symptom of Parkinson's or a warning signal that you may be at risk for the condition. In a long-term study of 7,000 men, those who had fewer than one bowel movement a day had almost three times the risk of Parkinson's disease compared with men who had one movement a day.

Although the connection is not yet clear, research suggests that whatever affects motor function in Parkinson's disease may also affect activity in the colon.

Don't panic if you suffer from constipation, though. Most constipated people won't ever come down with Parkinson's disease. Alert your doctor only if you have frequent constipation that doesn't respond to laxatives along with a family history of Parkinson's. In the meantime, treat your problem with one of these tried-and-true remedies.

Feast on fiber. Include at least 20 to 35 grams of fiber in your diet each day. That means eating more whole grains, legumes, and produce. If you don't normally eat this roughage, add it to your diet gradually. Otherwise, you could actually worsen your constipation.

Experts suggest upping your intake by 10 grams a day until you reach the recommended amount. That's about three servings of fruits and vegetables, one bowl of raisin bran, or one serving of beans. The fiber in these foods will make your bowel movements bulkier, softer, and easier to pass.

Drink plenty of water. Water keeps your insides lubricated and working like clockwork. It's especially important with a high-fiber diet, since the water helps fiber-filled food flow through your digestive system. Drink at least eight glasses of water each day to reap all its health benefits.

Get moving with exercise. Dance, jog, garden, play with your grandkids — exercise any way you want, as often as possible. Besides all the other ways it makes you healthy, breaking a sweat also helps you get regular.

Set your body like a Swiss clock. Never ignore an urge to go. That's your body trying to do its job, so let it. After a short while, you'll train your bowels to chime in at the same time every day.

Look for other constipation causes. Calcium and iron supplements, along with some medications, can sometimes wreak havoc with your system. If calcium is the culprit, try taking your supplements in two small doses instead of one big one. Taking them at mealtime could help, too.

To iron out constipation from iron supplements, stop taking them altogether. Postmenopausal women and older men don't need the extra iron. If you suspect your pain relievers, diuretics, antacids, or other medications are causing your problem, talk to your doctor. She can recommend a similar medication without the side effects.

Cheer up to clear up constipation

You may feel sad and anxious all the time and blame it on your chronic constipation. But you could have it backwards. Those feelings of depression may actually cause your constipation. By dealing with your emotional problems, you may clear up your physical ones as well. Try these solutions to help loosen up both your mind and body.

Get regular with biofeedback. Feelings of sadness, anxiety, and low self-esteem seem to upset your bowels, European researchers have found.

Top 12 high-fiber treats

Treat yourself to a quick pick-me-up and fast constipation relief —
all with one snack. Just choose any food on this list of all-natural,
high-fiber all-stars.

- Raisins
- Apples
- Whole grain toast
- Popcorn
- Dried plums (prunes)
- Celery sticks
- Dried apricots
- Bowl of cheerios
- Orange
- Bran muffin
- Baby carrots
- Strawberries

These emotions cause the blood flow and nerve signals in your large
intestine to actually slow down, causing your uncomfortable symptoms.

An encouraging study from England suggests biofeedback may give
you relief. After an average of five biofeedback sessions, only nine people in the study still needed laxatives, compared to 34 before. And only
nine had to strain afterward, while 26 did before.

During biofeedback, you monitor your bodily functions with a
machine. For instance, you can see and hear your heart beat or your
breathing rate, and you can then change it for the better. Many local and
national organizations offer biofeedback devices that hook up to your
personal computer. Check with your doctor for more information.

Practice relaxing every day. You don't need a scientist to tell you stress
can make life miserable. And you don't need a scientist to do this easy,
stress-busting breathing exercise. For 15 to 20 minutes each day, sit in a
quiet, comfortable room, and focus only on your breathing. Repeat one
word of your choice, "peace" for example, every time you breathe. By the
time you're finished, you'll have flushed out all the day's stress and worries.

Seek professional advice. If you feel overwhelmed by depression or anxiety, tell your doctor. It's not a shame to seek help from a therapist or from a loved one or friend. Facing your problems and working through them could be painful at first, but it's the first step on the path to feeling better — both mentally and physically.

Corns and Calluses

Natural cures for a 'corny' problem

You wouldn't walk around with a kernel of corn wedged into your shoe. So why endure the pain of a natural corn? Here are some simple garden-variety cures that will help you solve this uncomfortable problem.

Squeeze a zesty lemon. The citric acid in lemon juice can soften your skin, so apply it to a corn when it is still tender. Gently swab the affected area with fresh lemon juice and let it dry. You can also tape a piece of lemon peel to your corn before going to bed and let it heal your skin throughout the night.

Apply some pampering papaya. This tropical fruit has exotic compounds that can smooth your skin. Pour some fresh papaya juice on your foot, or cut a slice of papaya and secure it in place with a bandage. Leave it on overnight.

Peel a pineapple. The juice from a pineapple can dissolve the keratin buildup that results in a corn. Apply a small piece of the peel to your foot and let it sit for a while. But don't leave it on healthy skin for too long. The bromelain in this exotic fruit is so strong it can wipe out the fingerprints of pineapple harvesters.

Coat with creamy calendula. This common garden marigold heals skin and fights inflammation. Smear on some calendula salve from a nearby health store two or three times a day to banish pesky corns.

Dab on dandelion juice. The sap from this field flower may kill corns. Break a dandelion stem in two, and apply the white sap to the bump. Australian shepherds say it will turn the corn black before it drops off in a few days.

Cool it with cactus juice. Smooth on some aloe-based gel to moisturize and help smooth irritated skin.

Chop up an onion. Tape a slice of onion to your corn every night. Your bumpy skin should even out in a couple of weeks.

Wrap it up with vinegar. The Amish claim that a simple poultice of vinegar, bound to the corn, will root it out in no time.

Soak in seltzy baths. Twiddle your toes in a warm bath of water with either baking soda or Epsom salts to soften your skin.

Even though these remedies can soothe, and possibly remove, an existing corn, it is best to prevent them in the first place. Wear only well-fitting shoes with plenty of wiggle room, and pad any skin that rubs against your shoes.

You can also cover an existing corn with a moleskin cushion, corn pad, lamb's wool, or toe sleeve to relieve pressure on the skin and give it time to heal.

Diabetics: Don't cut corners on foot care

Diabetic foot care is not for amateurs. For the sake of your health, have a podiatrist care for your feet. An innocent-looking callus can lead to a dangerous ulcer. If you try to cut the skin away, you could cause a massive infection. As a diabetic, you know an infection can quickly turn to gangrene — a major cause of amputations.

So keep an eagle eye on your feet, but leave the cutting to an expert.

★ Check your feet daily for corns; calluses; blisters; warm spots; dry, cracked, or thickening skin; ingrown toenails; or swelling.

★ Don't use over-the-counter corn removers. These can be too harsh on your skin and cause more problems.

★ Let a podiatrist cut your toenails and care for corns, calluses, and any other foot problems you have.

Top 5 solutions for calloused soles

Thick-skinned soles that crack and peel need some tender loving care. Try these callus-control cures to rid yourself of skin buildup.

Soak your feet. Use warm water and baking soda to soften the callus. Or soak in cooled chamomile tea, then wash with soap and water to remove any stains. Gently buff away rough skin with a pumice stone.

Coat with aspirin. Make a paste of five or six crushed aspirin tablets and one tablespoon each of water and lemon juice. Coat your callus with the mixture, and cover with a plastic bag. Wrap your foot in a warm towel, and stay off it for about 10 minutes. Rub away rough, dead skin with a pumice stone.

Slather on lotion. Generous applications will keep your skin soft and smooth.

Take the pressure off. Buy heel pads to cushion the sole of your foot.

Pad your floor. Set down thick carpet scraps or a rubber mat in areas you use frequently, like around the sink or bathroom mirror.

Salon safety tips worth knowing

A group of women mysteriously came down with leg sores after going to the pedicurist. It turns out the unsterilized whirlpool footbath was infected with bacteria. Make sure you protect yourself at the salon by taking these precautions.

★ Take your own manicure set with you. You will know that your tools are clean and have only been exposed to your own germs.

★ Ask your manicurist to keep your toenails cut straight across — not too short and not too long. You don't want to tempt ingrown toenails or risk a hangnail.

★ Have your nail technician gently push your cuticles back before she applies nail polish. Never trim your cuticles because the tiny cuts could become infected.

★ Avoid acrylic nails. They can trap moisture under your nail where fungus can grow. You may also have an allergic reaction to the chemicals used to build acrylic nails.

★ Ask your manicurist if she uses tuberculocide to disinfect her instruments. Most salons use a simple germicide that doesn't kill bacteria and viruses.

★ Don't let your technician remove your calluses with a motorized buffer. Unsterilized buffing sanders can transfer fungi from foot to foot.

Re-lace your shoes for top foot comfort

Not all feet are made alike but, unfortunately, most shoes are. And a badly fitting shoe can rub in all the wrong places. Relieve the pressure and prevent calluses — or worse — by simply lacing your shoes in a different way.

Set your instep free. If you are blessed with a high instep, the top of your foot may rub against the inside of your shoe. Begin threading your shoelace through the bottom set of eyelets as usual — those nearest your toes. At midfoot, stop crisscrossing the laces and thread each end through the holes on the same side of the shoe, instead. This leaves the space over your instep free of laces. Once you have passed the high point of your foot, start to crisscross the laces again up to the last eyelets. This should give your instep some breathing room.

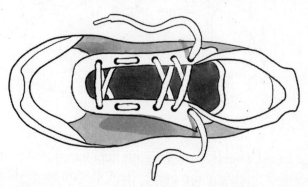

Leave room to spread out. If your foot is wide, begin your laces at the bottom set of eyelets as usual, but don't crisscross them. Instead run the laces through the eyelets up each side without crossing over the foot. Once past the widest part of your foot, start lacing as usual.

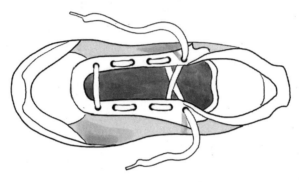

Tighten up on narrow feet. If your feet slip inside your shoe, double lacing will pull the sides tighter around the narrowest part. Go ahead and lace as usual across the first pair of eyelets. Then you will begin lacing through each hole twice.

Crisscross to the next set of eyelets then feed each lace back into the same eyelet on the opposite side. Your laces should cross both diagonally and horizontally between each pair of eyelets.

Pull the laces snuggly against your foot before moving on to the next set of eyelets. Once past the narrow part of your foot, crisscross the rest of the eyelets as usual.

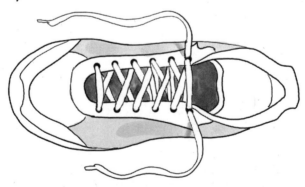

Hedge in thin heels. To keep your heel secure, lace your shoes normally until you reach the top two eyelets. Go through them once, then cross the laces over horizontally and go through the opposite eyelet again. This double lacing should really support your heel.

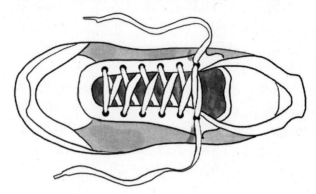

To keep your laces even tighter, you can knot the end of each lace right up against the eyelet.

Feed your lace back into the hole it just came out of, leaving a small loop. Bring the end back around and run it through the loop. Now pull it tight and tie your shoes as usual.

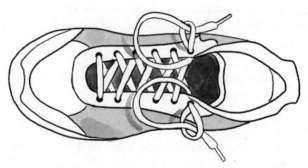

Let your toes wiggle. Pressure on your toes is sure to give you corns. Give your toes plenty of room by starting your laces at the top eyelet — nearest your ankle.

Feed a lace almost all the way through the upper right eyelet. Leave enough dangling to tie one side of a regular bowtie knot. Run the long end of the lace along the tongue of your shoe to the bottom left eyelet and come up through it from below. Thread over to the bottom right eyelet. Lace under to the next left eyelet, then over and across to the right eyelet. Continue lacing until you reach the upper left eyelet. Tie off as usual.

With this low-cost lacing method, all your shoes should custom-fit in no time. And you can say goodbye to unsightly corns and calluses.

Wave goodbye to warts

If you think the bumps on your feet are corns, don't even think about operating on yourself. Besides the obvious dangers of do-it-yourself surgery, you could have warts, a very different skin condition. Warts are small, hard growths caused by a virus. Cutting into them could cause bleeding and infection.

Your doctor can remove warts by freezing them, treating them with chemicals, or burning them with a laser. If that's a little unsettling to you, try these gentler home remedies. They might take a month or more to work, but at least they're painless.

- ★ **Castor oil.** Apply castor oil to the wart and cover it with a bandage. Do this twice a day until the wart disappears.

- ★ **Banana peel.** Tape a piece of the inside of a ripe banana peel to your wart, changing it daily after bathing.

- ★ **Vitamins A and E.** Break open a soft capsule of either supplement and rub on the wart once a day.

- ★ **Vitamin C or aspirin paste.** Crush a few vitamin C or aspirin tablets, and then add a bit of water to make a paste. Smooth it on the wart and cover with a bandage. Both vitamin C and aspirin contain helpful acids.

- ★ **Pineapple juice.** This juice boasts a powerful enzyme that warts don't like. Soak a cotton ball in fresh pineapple juice and wash the wart with it regularly.

- ★ **Beta carotene.** High doses of beta carotene have cured some people of warts, but it can turn your skin yellow. A dentist in Ohio took eight 15-milligram capsules of beta carotene daily. By the end of the fourth month, his warts were gone.

★ **Potato slice.** Certain chemicals in raw potatoes can mash warts. Rub a raw potato on your trouble spots several times a day.

★ **Lemon juice.** A folk remedy suggests holding a cut lemon on the wart several times a day.

★ **Onions.** This age-old cure requires you to rub a sliced onion on your wart frequently. But since onions have an unpleasant smell, you might want to try the other remedies first.

Cuts and Scrapes

Try a no-nonsense approach to wounds

Sharp knives, razor blades, broken glass, rough pavement, nails, pins, and other objects make life one big obstacle course. No matter how careful you are, you're bound to get hurt sometime.

Here's a step-by-step guide for dealing with minor cuts and scrapes.

Banish blood. Using a clean cloth or tissue, apply direct pressure to the wound until the bleeding stops. This can take up to 10 minutes.

However, if you step on a nail or have a similar puncture wound, you want to make sure it bleeds enough to flush out bacteria. In that case, squeeze around the wound to help it bleed.

Clean the cut. Rinse the cut with running water or wipe it with a wet cloth. Wash the area with a mild soap. Dip tweezers in rubbing alcohol and use them to pluck out dirt particles stuck in the wound.

Other options include swabbing the cut with antiseptic wipes or even licking the wound. Saliva helps kill bacteria and promote healing.

Rub it on. You might want to rub on some antibiotic cream. This works better than alcohol or hydrogen peroxide. But some experts claim it's unnecessary. Consider it an optional step.

Top home remedies for cuts and scrapes

Don't worry if you don't have a state-of-the art first-aid kit. You can treat minor wounds with these everyday items.

Peel a bandage. If you don't have an ordinary bandage, a banana peel will do. So will a slice of raw potato. Just tape it over your scratch.

Think small. Save those little packets of ketchup and mustard you get in fast-food restaurants. Keep them in the freezer and use them as miniature ice packs for tiny injuries.

Tea off. Wet tea bags soothe shaving nicks and other small cuts. They also work great for sunburn.

'Bee' resourceful. Honey keeps wounds clean, kills bacteria, and prevents scarring. Spread honey on a bandage rather than directly on your skin.

Sprinkle on relief. Cinnamon kills bacteria, numbs pain, and stops bleeding. After you wash and dry your cut, shake on some cinnamon powder and cover with a bandage.

Stick to it. To remove a splinter, dab on some white glue, let it dry, then peel off the glue and the splinter. A piece of tape works for tiny splinters.

Wrap it up. Believe it or not, a small cut will heal quicker without a bandage. But if the wound is likely to get dirty or if your clothes rub against it, it's probably a good idea to apply one.

Make sure to change the bandage every day to keep the wound clean. Petroleum jelly will keep the bandage from sticking to your wound.

Leave it alone. Don't pick at scabs. They're one way your body protects small wounds from infection. Instead, let scabs fall off after the skin has healed.

Get emergency help. If your injury is serious, don't rely on self-help. Here's how you can tell if you need to visit the emergency room.

★ heavy bleeding, especially after more than 15 minutes of direct pressure

★ gaping, jagged slash more than one-quarter inch deep

★ muscle or bone showing

★ cut on face, knee, elbow, or knuckle that doesn't close on its own

★ deep puncture wound made with a dirty object, especially if you haven't had a tetanus booster in the past 10 years

★ signs of infection, including redness, swelling, discharge, fever, and red streaks spreading from the wound site

Know what to do in case of an injury, and you'll be able to move through life's obstacle course with confidence.

Depression

Perk up with at-home pain relief

Many people suffering from chronic pain believe they have no control over it. They are wrong.

Pain — and the depression that comes with it — are not just part of growing older. You can learn to take back your life with these mind and body exercises.

Soak in some music. If taking pain medication has you down, let a little music therapy help tune out the ache. To experience a "sound bath," put your favorite relaxing music on and strap on your headphones. Then lie back, close your eyes, and let the music wash over you for about 20 minutes.

If you don't have headphones, aim your feet at your stereo speakers. The vibrations will travel from your soles through the rest of your body. These vibrations, experts say, may slow the tempo of your heartbeat and breathing, and reverse the effects of pulse-pounding pain and stress.

Try a "toning" trick. Some experts believe making your own music has even more pain-fighting benefit. Find out for yourself by creating a sound, or tone, in this special way.

★ Sit in a comfortable chair, close your eyes, and take a deep but regular breath.

★ Hum a sound — a vowel, for instance.

★ Start in a low pitch, gradually bring it higher, and then drop it back down again.

★ Press your palms to your cheeks while you hum and feel the vibrations.

★ Stop after five minutes, rest your hands in your lap, and concentrate on how your body feels.

★ Repeat for another five minutes.

You'll find that toning gives your whole body a massage from the inside out. To get the benefits of music all day long, try humming in the shower, or singing with your car radio. You'll increase your energy and produce endorphins, your body's natural feel-good chemicals.

Exercise past pain. Working out shouldn't make your chronic pain worse. It can actually do the opposite — free you from pain. In fact, *not* exercising may be what is making you feel bad.

Simply take a walk or practice pool aerobics, yoga, or "jarming." This last exercise involves swinging your arms as if you were running or conducting an orchestra.

Experts aren't sure why, but even an isolated workout, like jarming, eases pain throughout your body long after you've cooled down. It could be those endorphins again.

Plan your day. Like most chronic pain, yours probably comes and goes like the ocean's tide. Your aches run on an internal clock similar to the one that times your sleep schedule.

Get to know your pain clock, and take advantage of the "low tide" of your pain. That's the best time to accomplish all your important daily tasks — like grocery shopping, doctor appointments, and visits with the grandkids. Then handle less important tasks if you can.

Breathe back to health. According to a Gallup poll, more than half of all American senior citizens suffer from daily pain. If they only knew relief is just a breath away.

★ Relax in a quiet room and close your eyes.

★ Concentrate on your breathing, without changing the way you breathe.

★ Be conscious of the start, middle, and finish of every breath.

★ Feel your chest expand and contract.

★ Calm your mind and think only positive thoughts.

★ Continue to breathe like this for 15 to 20 minutes.

Time spent this way reduced feelings of depression, sleeplessness, and pain in women with fibromyalgia, a chronic pain condition. Researchers believe deep breathing and calm thinking reduce your levels of cortisol, a hormone your body releases during stress. While the effects are long lasting, you must practice it often. Women in the study meditated for about an hour, six days a week.

In that Gallup poll, two out of three people said they wait until their pain is unbearable before they visit their doctor. Don't be part of that statistic. No matter how you treat your chronic pain at home, see your doctor for a proper diagnosis.

Fight depression with feel-good foods

A better diet means a better mood. With a balance of just the right nutrients, your brain stays on an even keel. Here's an example of what one mood-boosting day could look like.

Take a break from stress with breakfast. Start your day this way if you have a big meeting or stressful appointment.

★ grape juice

★ toast with low-fat margarine or jam

★ black coffee with sweetener

In a recent study, this exact meal seemed to help tense people cope better with stress. It works because it's stocked with carbohydrates but is short on protein.

Carbs boost your levels of tryptophan, an amino acid that helps build the chemical serotonin. And serotonin is in charge of keeping you calm and assertive. Protein, on the other hand, keeps tryptophan — and serotonin — brain levels low.

Just remember, not all high-carbohydrate foods are good choices, since some contain enough protein to counteract their benefits.

Grab lunch on the go-get-em. If you're down in the dumps, get energized with this B vitamin-packed meal.

* ★ turkey sandwich on whole wheat

* ★ sweet potato fries

* ★ fresh fruit salad

Often, your feelings of depression point to just one problem — a shortage of thiamin, B6, B12, and folate. And as a senior, you're even more likely to run low on these nutrients. It may also cheer you up to know that turkey contains that all-important amino acid, tryptophan.

Ditch the dinner doldrums. If you want your brain to run at peak performance, you need omega-3 fatty acids. They'll balance out your store of omega-6 fatty acids, a process that's crucial for mental health.

* ★ salmon filet with lemon and dill

* ★ black beans and rice

* ★ fresh salad with tomato, mushrooms, and broccoli

Salmon is a great source of omega-3, plus, you'll sidestep sluggishness and the grumps with iron from the beans. To help your body use all that iron, the lemon and salad will provide vitamin C. Last but not least, the mushrooms and the fish will punch up your selenium levels, another brain-boosting mineral.

Stimulate your mood with a snack. Eat something chocolate-y and delicious, and your mind will pay you back by being happy and attentive.

★ low-fat chocolate frozen yogurt banana split

Finger-licking foods cause your body to release endorphins, chemicals that give you a natural high. And for good measure, the bananas will give you some extra B vitamins.

Hidden cause of depression symptoms

Your tiredness and lack of appetite may not come from depression. They may be signs of a magnesium deficiency.

Besides depression-type symptoms, a lack of magnesium also causes muscle cramps and foggy thinking. So it's important to eat foods rich in this essential mineral.

Lean on low-fat yogurt. One cup of this dairy delicacy can put you well on your way to magnesium's dietary reference intake (DRI).

Cook up a side of spinach. Green leafy vegetables are magnesium-rich marvels.

Wake up with bran. Find your magnesium in unprocessed foods like whole grain breads and cereals.

Net some oysters. Fish in the sea for some of the most potent magnesium sources.

Beat fatigue with black beans. Open your menu to other all-natural foods like legumes and nuts.

Ease your muscles with avocados. This exotic fruit is good in guacamole or sliced on a sandwich.

These magnesium powerhouses all will help you reach your DRI, which is 320 milligrams for women and 420 milligrams for men.

Make your good mood blossom

Gardeners and scientists agree — gardening sprouts happiness. Maybe it's the basic connection with the earth or maybe the pleasure you get from nurturing a living thing. Perhaps it's just breathing in all that fresh air. Whatever the reason, many people feel relaxed and content the moment they pick up a spade.

Find peace among the plants. It's called horticultural therapy and it's sweeping health and rehabilitation facilities worldwide.

People just seem to heal faster and feel better when they're around growing things. Several studies show simply looking at plants and trees can help you cope with pain. Whether it's a hospital room with a "greener" view, a bedside basket of flowers, or access to a full-blown garden, patients that are somehow closer to nature are able to tolerate pain longer and need less pain medication.

So, prune, water, pick, and weed. You'll get stronger, happier, and healthier.

Battle the winter blahs. The wintertime blues are not just in your head. Your body is actually starving for sunshine. You feel depressed and sluggish when there's less natural light because your body produces less melatonin, a hormone that helps regulate your sleep cycle.

A smart solution — feed it some daylight. Right after you wake up is the best time to get outside, since morning sunshine increases your melatonin level the most.

That means don't give up gardening just because the weather's bad. There will be good days when you can putter around outside. Otherwise:

★ Grow an indoor herb garden.

★ Fuss with your houseplants.

★ Discover the art of bonsai.

★ Build a greenhouse.

★ Force some bulbs.

If all else fails, sit by a window and start planning for spring. Draw up a landscape design, order seeds and bulbs, or plot out a vegetable garden. Besides pumping up your daily dose of sunshine, it will give you something to look forward to.

However, if you still find yourself overeating, oversleeping, and lagging about, you could be suffering from a severe form of depression called Seasonal Affective Disorder (SAD). In that case, talk with your doctor.

Value your success. Gardening takes planning and hard work. No wonder there's nothing more satisfying than harvesting a bumper crop of tomatoes and peppers, or watching cars brake in front of your home to admire your flowerbeds. That feeling of accomplishment can really lift your spirits.

Feel "scent"-sational. The scents in your garden may be as important as the look. Plant lavender and you may feel more cheerful. Plant rosemary and you could feel more alert and ready to take on the world.

Aromatherapy is nothing new. Scents have been used in healing for hundreds of years. But now, treating depression and anxiety with aromatherapy has scientific backing. Although essential oils are the most potent way to get proven benefits, try planting your own crop of aromatic therapy.

Let happiness bloom. Flowers produce happy emotions — almost immediately. You get a bouquet and you can't help but smile. Even better, that happy feeling lasts longer than you would think — according to research, for days.

Transform your garden into a flowering oasis by planting annuals, perennials, and bulbs. Then bring them indoors by the vase-full and improve your mood in every room.

Don't stop there. Clip some of your prized pansies or treasured tulips and pass on your happiness to family and friends. You'll feel more connected by sharing.

Exercise your right to happiness. Exercising could dig you out of the dumps just as well as antidepressant medications. To get this benefit, you don't need to follow a hectic workout routine or join a gym. You just need to stay active in your everyday life. Believe it or not, caring for your cabbage and carrots and battling weeds and bugs is a great form of exercise.

Top ways exercise blasts the blues

Fame and fortune won't make you happy. Be good at what you do, feel pride in your accomplishments, and share with loved ones — that's the trick. All this is easier than you think.

A yoga class, a walking club, or gentle martial arts, like tai chi, are great for strengthening your body and increasing your ability to relax and handle stress. At the same time, you'll ease depression — without medication. Here's how you can find true happiness through an exercise class.

- ✪   Build pride learning something new, and pump up your self-confidence as you shape up.

- ✪   Meet new people who share your interests and your concerns.

- ✪   Have fun.

- ✪   Get out of the house.

- ✪   Fight the fear of losing your function and freedom.

- ✪   Improve your posture and lose that depressed, slumped look.

- ✪   Sleep better.

- ✪   Defeat that fear of falling while improving your balance and coordination.

- ✪   Increase your appetite and crave more blues-busting foods.

- ✪   Breathe deeply for even more relaxation.

- ✪   Stay happy by committing to an ongoing class.

Diabetes

New guidelines mean better future for diabetics

You no longer have to nibble on carrot sticks instead of a cookie just because you have diabetes. The American Association of Clinical Endocrinologists (AACE) now says up to 10 percent of your daily calories can come from sugar — if you adjust for the extra calories.

A task force from the AACE and the American College of Endocrinology revised the original 1994 guidelines for diabetics. Their aim is to help keep blood glucose as close to normal as possible and to avoid long-term complications of the disease.

Diagnose it earlier. The old guidelines recommended screening high-risk people at age 45. But too many were already suffering from complications of diabetes by the time they were screened. The AACE now says doctors should screen high-risk people at 30 instead. You're at high risk if you:

- ★ have a family history of diabetes.

- ★ are likely to develop heart disease.

- ★ are overweight or don't exercise regularly.

- ★ delivered a baby weighing more than 9 pounds or had diabetes during pregnancy.

- ★ have high levels of blood fats (triglycerides).

- ★ have low HDL cholesterol.

★ are a member of an ethnic group more likely to get diabetes, such as Hispanics, African Americans, Asian Americans, or Native Americans.

Lower your target blood sugar. Experts now say diabetics should strive for blood sugar of less than 110 mg/dl before a meal and less than 140 after. If these numbers seem lower than you remember, it's because they are. Keeping tighter control over your blood sugar will pay off with fewer complications later in life. Stick with these new guidelines if you hope to avoid kidney disease, blindness, amputations, and heart disease.

Get your ratios right. The AACE recommends your diet include 10 to 20 percent protein, 55 to 60 percent carbohydrates, and less than 30 percent fat. Keep salt in your diet to less than 3 grams a day.

Don't sweat the glycemic index. The glycemic index is an exhausting list of foods with how much glucose each one generates in your body compared to a slice of bread. Confused? So were many diabetics who tried to use it. The American Diabetes Association now says your total carbohydrate intake is more important than the glycemic index. If the index works for you, continue using it. But if you can't get the hang of it, don't fret. Just track your carbohydrates carefully.

Control your calories. Just losing 10 to 20 pounds can make a big difference in your blood sugar, blood pressure, and blood fats. You don't even have to reach your ideal weight — simply start by keeping this much weight off. Although this information isn't new, the AACE thought it was important enough to repeat.

Be careful with alcohol. The guidelines still say you should be cautious about drinking. If you have neuropathy, a pancreas disease, or high levels of triglycerides, avoid alcohol. If you don't have these problems and your blood sugar is under good control, you can choose to have a drink now and then. Just remember to count the calories. Avoid sweet liqueurs, and have your drink with food, not on an empty stomach.

The AACE guidelines represent the most up-to-date medical advice for diabetics. If you want to fight diabetes, these are your rules to live by.

Can aspirin cure diabetes?

It may be the latest medical miracle. Researchers at Harvard Medical School and the University of California San Diego reversed insulin resistance in overweight mice by using extremely high doses of aspirin. Trials of aspirin therapy are now underway on diabetics and obese people who are insulin resistant.

When your body resists insulin, a hormone that turns blood sugar into energy, sugar builds up in your blood. Even though weight loss and exercise can often reverse the problem, many people can't seem to trim down and shape up. Doctors say that puts them at risk for type 2 diabetes, a disease that is growing at an alarming rate.

High doses of aspirin blocked a particular enzyme in the mice, making them responsive to insulin again and causing their blood sugar levels to drop. Since aspirin is known to fight inflammation, the mice study suggests inflammation could be a source of type 2 diabetes and obesity.

If aspirin therapy does prove successful in people, you must only receive it under a doctor's care. The necessary doses are high enough to cause intestinal bleeding, and liver and kidney damage. Researchers hope to develop a drug similar to aspirin, but without these dangerous side effects.

How diabetics can survive heart disease

Diabetes quietly but steadily damages your heart and blood vessels — and increases your odds of having a fatal heart attack or stroke. In fact, women with diabetes are almost three times more likely to die within a few years of a heart attack than are non-diabetic women.

As a diabetic, defending yourself against heart disease is a matter of life or death.

Get the aspirin advantage. Only one in five diabetics takes an aspirin a day, even though aspirin therapy can significantly lower your risk of a heart attack.

When the American Diabetes Association (ADA) surveyed more than 2,000 people with diabetes, just 1 percent knew aspirin could help them prevent a heart attack. Ask your doctor about this simple therapy that can safeguard your heart.

Slim down. The more you weigh, the harder your heart must work, and the more trouble you'll have with your blood sugar. Lose those extra pounds sensibly and you cut your risk of heart disease and complications from high blood sugar.

Try a low-fat diet with the exercise program your doctor suggests. Even regular walking can help you get in shape. Experts say losing just 10 or 20 pounds can make a big difference in controlling your diabetes. But you'll have to keep it off to see long-term results.

Cut more cholesterol. Even if your cholesterol and triglycerides are in a normal range, you must monitor them carefully and follow a preventive low-fat diet.

The ADA says LDL (bad) cholesterol should be less than 100 milligrams per deciliter (mg/dl) and HDL (good) cholesterol should be more than 45 mg/dl for diabetic men and 55 mg/dl for diabetic women. These guidelines are more strict than the ones for the general public.

Eliminate fried foods from your diet and you'll close the door on a major source of fat. Replace saturated fat like margarine with heart-friendly monounsaturated ones found in canola, olive, and peanut oil. Instead of red meat, eat fatty fish like salmon a few times a week. It can lower your triglyceride levels and keep heart disease at bay.

Patrol your pressure. Diabetics are twice as likely to have high blood pressure. That just means you'll have to be a little more vigilant than others. The ADA recommends you keep yours at or below 130/85. While this is lower than the 140/90 for non-diabetics, you need the extra protection.

If a low-salt, healthy diet doesn't help you hit the target, you might need medicine. Do whatever it takes to keep your pressure in a normal range. Even though you can't see the damage, years of high blood pressure can cause injury to your arteries, setting you up for a heart attack later.

Keep your blood moving. Insulin resistance causes your blood vessels to narrow. That means the blood supply to your brain can be blocked more easily. And that puts you at higher risk for stroke. Aspirin therapy can help keep your blood from forming stroke-causing clots. So can eating a healthy diet high in fatty fish with plenty of fruits and vegetables.

As a diabetic, you'll have to work hard to keep your heart healthy. But the payoff of a longer, healthier life makes those sacrifices more than worth the trouble.

Bring on the workout, but baby your feet

Each year, about 54,000 people have a foot amputated because of diabetic neuropathy — nerve damage from high blood sugar. Although exercise can help control your blood sugar and weight, fear of injuring your feet may keep you on the couch. Learn how to baby your feet and get the benefits of exercise.

Call on your doctor. Get a thorough exam before starting an exercise program. Your doctor should look carefully at your feet to make sure they don't have any problems that could worsen with exercise.

If the shoe doesn't fit, don't wear it. Find an athletic shoe that fits the shape of your foot, without rubbing or pinching anywhere. Your toes should be comfortable, and your heel shouldn't slip. If you wear any sort of insert, bring it with you to get the right fit. Try shoes on with the type of socks you'll wear when exercising. Your best bet is a thick, absorbent acrylic blend that keeps your feet dry. Check for pebbles, tacks, tears, or bumps in your shoes every day.

Focus on your feet daily. If you've lost some sensation in your feet, you might not feel a sore or cut for a few days. That could lead to infection — a serious problem for a diabetic. Check your feet carefully every day after your bath or shower. Look for blisters, scrapes, bruises, swellings, and bumps. Use a mirror to check the bottom of your feet if necessary.

Care for your nails. Cut toenails straight across to keep them from becoming ingrown. Check for sharp corners that could cut into other toes and file them carefully. Use an emery board with rounded edges instead of a metal file.

Fuel up first. Exercise after a meal to ensure plenty of energy and to avoid the low-blood-sugar blahs. Eat light, though, or you won't feel up to a workout.

Start slow. Do five to 10 minutes of easy aerobic exercise, such as pedaling a stationary bike at a leisurely pace. This gets your muscles, heart, and lungs ready for more intense exercise. Follow this with gentle stretching for another five minutes or so.

Arm yourself with strength. Focus on upper body exercises and avoid routines that require stepping up and down repeatedly, like jogging, step exercises, or using a treadmill. Good choices include lifting light arm weights, using a rowing machine, swimming, or bicycling. Try to work out for 30 minutes to an hour, three or four times a week.

Listen to your feet. If you develop a sore, pain, swelling, or any other problem with your feet, call your doctor immediately. The sooner you get the problem treated, the sooner you can get back to exercising.

Reverse diabetes with no-hunger diet

Reverse your diabetes simply by giving up animal protein. That's the message from an exciting new study.

Researchers tried a new diet plan on 51 diabetics who could no longer control their disease with high doses of medicine or insulin. The diet allowed no sugar, and only one serving of animal protein — such as meat or fish — every other day. The participants ate vegetable protein to make up for the missing calories and continued on their usual medicines. Those who stuck to the diet reportedly liked it because they didn't skip meals or cut calories.

After six months, the people who followed the diet had amazing results. Although they didn't lose weight, their blood fats and sugar levels returned to normal or near normal. Some were able to stop taking medicine, and others only needed half as much. The researchers conclude that a diet low in animal protein and sugar can reverse diabetes or improve metabolism so medicines can work.

If you'd like to try the diet, get permission from your doctor first. You'll have to avoid sugar and substitute vegetable protein like tofu, nuts, or legumes for meat at least three nights a week. And remember, eggs count as animal protein. Eat meatless soups, sandwiches, or salads for lunch, and include whole grain cereals in your breakfast menu.

Past periods might predict diabetes

Long or irregular monthly cycles as a young woman could be a warning of future diabetes. Researchers found this unusual link in studies of over 100,000 women.

If, between the ages of 18 and 22, cycles were too erratic to track or lasted longer than 40 days, the women were twice as likely to develop diabetes in middle age. Overweight young women with cycles like this had an even higher diabetes risk.

There may be a link between this phenomenon and polycystic ovary syndrome (PCOS) — a condition that can disrupt your menstrual cycle, cause excess body hair, and make you overweight and resistant to insulin.

If you think you might have PCOS, talk to your doctor about your symptoms. If this condition has already been diagnosed, take extra steps to prevent developing diabetes. Your body could be sending you clues about your future. Shouldn't you listen?

Keep clear of complications

If you have diabetes, there's a good chance you'll develop complications. Here's a list of what to watch for early on, and what you can do to prevent problems. Keep your blood sugar under tight control and you can help prevent all of these conditions.

Watch for	Symptoms	Prevention
diabetic retinopathy	(often without symptoms); floating spots, blurred or impaired vision	yearly checkup with dilation, daily aspirin
kidney disease	(often without symptoms); high blood pressure	yearly urinary micro-albumin test; lower blood pressure with diet and exercise; consider medication
depression	feelings of hopelessness; lack of energy or interest	see your doctor for treatment options
gum disease	red, swollen gums that often bleed when brushed	brush and floss daily; visit dentist twice a year; tell your dentist you have diabetes
osteoporosis	backache; stooped posture; fractures	regular exercise; diet high in potassium, magnesium, vitamins C and D; calcium
carpal tunnel syndrome	numbness, weakness, tingling, or pain in hand or wrist	report pain to your doctor

An action plan for defeating diabetes

When you hit 75, if you want to still remember all your grandkids, be able to finish that crossword puzzle, and recall exactly where you left your glasses, start fighting diabetes now.

Over 2,000 senior women with diabetes performed lower on mental ability tests than women without diabetes. Those who had the disease longest fared the worst. Since diabetes damages blood vessels throughout your body, those in your brain may be affected as well. Plan to keep your brain in tip-top shape with these 10 simple diabetes-fighting tips.

Make breakfast count. Enjoy a low-fat bran muffin or bran cereal for breakfast. The fiber helps slow down the process of converting carbohydrates to glucose — a good thing for your blood sugar. Skip the coffee since there's some evidence it affects your ability to control blood sugar. Instead, down a glass of orange juice for excellent antioxidant protection and help keeping your blood sugar stable.

Snack on strawberries. The vitamin C in these sweet treats can provide powerful protection against many complications of diabetes, like slow-healing wounds and high cholesterol. In addition, it helps destroy free radicals, which can cause cataracts. Why not slice some on your cereal?

Turn off the tube. How much television you watch is related to your likelihood of developing diabetes. This really means, the more you sit in front of the TV, the less physical activity you're getting. And a sedentary lifestyle is one of the biggest risk factors for developing and prolonging diabetes. Walk the dog, pull some weeds, or dance to your favorite music.

Find a reason to smile. Happy people have fewer strokes. Since diabetics are at higher risk for these potentially brain-damaging attacks, it makes sense to avoid them. So figure out what makes you happy and make room for it in your day.

Eat like a rabbit. Munching vegetables on a regular basis could lower your risk of diabetes more than 80 percent. Fresh produce is, of course, loaded with all-round healthy nutrients. But this kind of diet usually indicates a generally healthy lifestyle. So grate carrots, slice tomatoes, and dice cucumbers. You'll enjoy the harvest and clearer thinking.

Brush and floss. Besides ruining a nice smile, gum disease can make it harder for you to control your blood sugar. So keep your pearly whites bacteria-free with daily brushing and flossing.

Exercise in the evening. Good news if you hate getting out of bed in the morning to exercise. Working out this way is certainly good for you, but it doesn't do much for your blood sugar. Exercise in the evening, however, and your sugar levels should drop significantly. Evening exercise produces more of the hormone, cortisol, which helps your body use energy.

Ancient recipe fights dangerous diseases

At Passover, many Jews enjoy a food called charoset, a mixture of fruit, nuts, wine, cinnamon, and honey. This combination forms a delicious, thick paste symbolizing the mortar their enslaved Hebrew ancestors used to build the cities of Egypt.

Charoset contains a wealth of healthy ingredients with cancer-fighting antioxidants. The fruit helps prevent heart disease in general. And specifically, the magnesium and potassium in apples help ward off angina and heart attacks. Cinnamon can stabilize blood sugar and kill bacteria that cause infections. Walnuts pack a powerful punch thanks to omega-3 fatty acids, which reduce inflammation and keep blood clots from forming. That means less chance of hardened arteries, heart attack, and stroke.

To make charoset, peel and grate one-half cup of cooking apples and set aside. Use a food processor to finely chop one-half cup of walnuts. Add a handful of dates, three bananas, two tablespoons of honey, two teaspoons of cinnamon, and one-fourth cup of sweet red wine. Blend until smooth.

Pour the blended mixture over the grated apples and mix well. The charoset should have the consistency of wet cement. Spread on crackers and enjoy.

Indulge in a bedtime snack. For people with mild type 2 diabetes, a small, high-carbohydrate snack before bed can help control your blood sugar during the night. Try a half-cup of tapioca, or a bagel with banana.

Skip the nightcap. A drink before bed is a bad idea for most people, and it can be dangerous for some diabetics, causing a drop in blood sugar the next morning. Use the calories for a small, healthy snack instead.

Spend extra time in dreamland. Experts believe sleep is necessary for your body to process sugar properly. A recent study showed that people who don't get enough sleep are more likely to become resistant to insulin — a direct path to diabetes. Strive for at least eight hours of snooze time. You'll wake up with a refreshed mind and body, ready for another day of good health.

In addition to these natural suggestions, take any medication your doctor has prescribed for your diabetes. According to research, that's another way to offset any mental damage this disease might cause.

Diverticular Disease

Outfox diverticula with 'roughage'

Half of all Americans age 60 or older have it. And almost everyone age 80 or older does, too. That's incredible, considering many health professionals think you can prevent diverticular disease simply by eating more roughage — or fiber.

A low-fiber diet causes constipation, which puts pressure on the walls of your colon. Over time, weak spots in the walls give way and balloon out, forming small pockets in your colon called diverticula.

When you have diverticula, you have a condition called diverticulosis. While most people are symptom free, symptoms can include mild cramps, bloating, constipation, and rectal bleeding.

If food and fecal particles clog the pockets, they can become inflamed or infected. This condition is called diverticulitis, and the symptoms — tenderness on the lower left side of your abdomen, fever, nausea, vomiting, chills, cramping, and constipation — can be severe. Diverticulitis often requires antibiotics, a trip to the hospital, or surgery.

The same simple treatment might prevent diverticulosis and diverticulitis — a high-fiber diet. That equals 20 to 35 grams of fiber every day, according to the American Dietetic Association. To boost your fiber intake, learn to love these foods.

Whole grains. Whole grains are one of the best ways to add fiber to your diet. This roughage softens and bulks up your stools, making them pass easier through your intestines, and it strengthens the colon wall muscles, too. That means less straining and fewer diverticula.

Get off to a good start with a breakfast of bran flakes, which have 5 grams of fiber a serving. For lunch, have a sandwich on whole wheat bread to add 4 more grams. Enjoy a side of brown rice at dinner — one cup has 3.5 grams. That's almost 13 grams of fiber right there.

Fruits and vegetables. Produce contains a special kind of fiber that encourages the growth of healthy bacteria in your intestines. These good bacteria help digestion and keep your digestive tract running smoothly.

To boost your fiber intake, eat at least five fruits and vegetables every day. Just remember — eating whole fruits is better than drinking fruit juice. And lightly steamed or raw vegetables will do your colon more good than soggy, overcooked ones. So skip the mushy, canned vegetables whenever you can eat fresh produce.

Beans. People in Africa and Asia have fewer cases of diverticulosis than people in industrialized countries, particularly England, Australia, and the United States. No wonder. They eat more fiber-filled foods, like beans. Just a half-cup of cooked kidney beans has an amazing 6 grams of fiber. Lima beans are also impressive with 4.5 grams. So toss some into your stir-fries, salads, and casseroles.

Water. Many people are constantly dehydrated and don't even know it. If you are constipated often, even when you eat a lot of fiber-rich foods, you might need more water. Drinking at least six to eight glasses of water every day should make your stools softer and decrease your chances of developing diverticula. If you already have diverticula, water can help the fiber flush out bits of food that could cause problems. And it's especially important to drink plenty of water when you add more fiber to your diet. If you don't, you could end up with a blockage in your intestines — something far worse than constipation.

One thing to remember about fiber — when you add more to your diet, be sure to take it slow. Sudden increases can make you feel bloated and gassy.

Top things to avoid if you have diverticulosis

Steer clear of these potential troublemakers. They can leave your intestines in knots — literally.

High-protein diets. These eating plans call for you to cut your carbohydrate intake. This means losing out on fiber-rich fruits, vegetables, and whole grains.

Refined grains. The refining process strips the fiber out of bread, cereal, and other grain products.

Red meat. Harmful bacteria form in your gut when you digest red meat. They weaken your colon walls and make you more prone to diverticula, pockets in the walls of your colon. In addition, the fat in red meat increases your risk of diverticulosis, too.

Stimulant laxatives. They irritate your colon more than they help. Instead, try natural laxatives like prunes, prune juice, or psyllium.

Nonsteroidal anti-inflammatory drugs (NSAIDs). You risk severe complications if you have diverticulosis and use NSAIDs, such as aspirin or ibuprofen.

Seeded foods. Traditional wisdom says pass up foods like popcorn, strawberries, and tomatoes. The kernels and seeds may get stuck in the diverticula and cause diverticulitis. Yet, many scientists say there's no proof. So ask your doctor what's safe for you.

Dizziness

Simple solution for dizziness

You may worry your blood pressure is too high. But if you get dizzy when you stand up after a meal, you have the opposite problem — a drop in blood pressure. The solution may be as simple as drinking water before, during, and after your meals.

When older people in a study drank about two cups of tap water, their blood pressure rose within a few minutes. This effect did not occur in the younger participants. It increased rapidly over the next 15 minutes and lasted about an hour before it went back down. Drinking more water extended this benefit for another hour.

Experts aren't sure exactly why, but the effect of the water on blood pressure was equal to smoking two unfiltered cigarettes or drinking about 10 ounces of brewed coffee. Water is, of course, the healthiest of these choices for avoiding dizziness.

This same kind of dizziness may occur when you get out of bed in the morning. But water at bedtime or during the night may not be the best solution. Some people experience a dangerous rise in blood pressure when lying down and should not drink water within an hour and a half of retiring. And by limiting water at night you aren't as likely to get up in a hurry to go to the bathroom, risking a fall if you get wobbly.

Here are some other ways to avoid getting woozy when you stand.

★ Eat six to eight small meals a day. More blood can reach your brain since less has to stay in your stomach to help digest your food. Eating also releases insulin, which lowers blood pressure.

★ Get a little extra salt in your diet. It increases water retention, which raises blood pressure. Just don't go overboard.

★ Raise the head of your bed to a 30-degree angle. This causes you to retain more water during the night.

★ Lift yourself up slowly when you wake, and sit on the side of the bed a few minutes before you stand.

★ Stay out of the heat, including hot baths. And avoid strenuous exercise and alcohol.

If these don't help, talk to your doctor about substitutions for any medications that could be causing you to feel faint. She may also suggest wearing special elastic stockings or an abdominal corset to help keep the blood flowing back to your brain.

When dizziness needs a doctor's attention

Dizziness usually isn't serious — whether you have the "room is spinning" variety, called vertigo, or that "woozy, floating, about to faint" feeling. But sit up and take notice if it happens a lot or you aren't sure why it occurs.

And if your dizziness accompanies the groups of symptoms below, you may need medical help for one of these more critical conditions.

Heatstroke or heat exhaustion

★ Faintness and weakness

★ Muscle cramps

★ Rapid or extremely slow heartbeat

If these symptoms follow exposure to hot weather, this is an emergency. Get help quickly.

Carbon monoxide poisoning

★ Faintness

★ Recurring headache

★ Nausea and vomiting

★ Breathing problems

This poisoning may come from exposure to fumes from automobiles, heating systems, or industrial sources.

Concussion

★ Headache

★ Confusion

★ Blurred vision

★ Vomiting

If these symptoms follow a loss of consciousness from a head injury, they're signs of the most severe form of concussion. Get medical help promptly.

Brain tumor

★ Nausea or vomiting

★ Loss of vision or visual disturbances

★ Seizures

★ Severe headache

This is a serious condition, so don't delay in getting a checkup.

Atrial fibrillation

★ Faintness and weakness

★ Breathing difficulty

★ Tiredness

★ Irregular heartbeat that feels like a fluttering in your chest

Although this type of irregular heartbeat may resolve itself, it shouldn't go untreated.

Bradycardia

★   Extremely slow heartbeat (60 or fewer beats per minute)

★   Sudden weakness or fatigue

Bradycardia could be caused by an underlying disease or a heart medicine, such as a beta-blocker.

Transient ischemic attack (TIA)

★   Headache

★   Blurred vision or double vision

★   Weakness in your arms or legs

★   Slurred speech

This is a temporary brain disturbance but may also signify a mild stroke.

Cervical spondylosis

★   Stiff neck

★   Pain in your neck that extends to your shoulders and arms

★   Weakness and loss of sensation in your fingers, hands, and arms

This condition occurs when arthritis or bone deterioration causes pressure on the nerves in your neck.

Labyrinthitis or Meniere's disease

★   Ear noise and hearing loss

★   Uncontrolled eye movement

★   Nausea and vomiting

These diseases are serious disorders of the inner ear.

You should also see your doctor if, in addition to dizziness, you have chest pain, pass black stools or have other signs of blood loss, are taking high blood pressure medicine, or have just started taking any new medication.

Top moves for motion sickness

Don't let dizziness and nausea spoil your trip. Whether you travel by car, boat, plane, or train, these tips for avoiding motion sickness can help.

Keep your eyes on the horizon. You get that dizzy, sick feeling when your body and your eyes send different messages to your brain. By looking into the distance, you help your eyes match the movement.

Don't read and ride. No matter how good the book, it can make you sick in a moving vehicle.

Hold still. Press your head firmly against the headrest, or use a pillow to hold it steady. The less you shake your inner ear, the less motion sickness you'll have.

Take deep breaths of fresh air. Try to avoid smoke and strong food and perfume odors.

Eat light. Don't travel on an empty stomach, and if it's a long trip, nibble a little along the way. Avoid heavy meals.

Leave alcohol behind. Drinking will make a bad situation worse.

Take a natural remedy. Ginger relaxes muscles in your digestive system. And, unlike some medications for motion sickness, it won't make you sleepy.

Food Poisoning

No-nonsense defense against food poisoning

Bacteria grow quickly in foods left too long at room temperature and can make you sick. Since your immune system is probably not as strong as it used to be, you need to be more careful than ever about storing leftovers.

Uneaten food — including home-delivered meals and restaurant leftovers — should go into the refrigerator right away. Don't eat anything left out for more than two hours, and if you haven't eaten refrigerated leftovers within three days, throw them out.

Keep these and the following tips in mind, and you'll help your family avoid a bad case of food poisoning.

Shop with safety in mind. Your grocery list isn't the only one you need to take with you to the grocery store. This food safety list is just as important.

★ Don't buy cans of food that are swollen or leaking, and watch out for jars that have cracks or loose or bulging lids.

★ Check expiration dates on perishable items, especially meats and dairy products. For items you won't use up right away, select those with the latest "sell by" date.

★ Be sure frozen foods are rock-solid and the packages aren't torn or crushed.

★ Buy only refrigerated eggs. Peek inside the carton to be sure they are clean and have no cracks.

★ Save items that spoil quickly — like meats and frozen foods — for last. Put meats in plastic bags so juices don't drip on other items. And if it will take an hour or more to get home, take along an ice chest to keep these foods cold.

Store foods properly. Continue to keep food safety in mind when you arrive home with your groceries.

★ Keep your refrigerator cooled to 40 degrees Fahrenheit or less, and immediately refrigerate or freeze perishable items.

★ Make sure meats are wrapped so their juices don't leak onto other foods.

★ Refrigerate foodstuffs like mayonnaise and catsup after they are opened. Read the labels on any you aren't sure about. It's best to throw out any you leave at room temperature by mistake.

★ Store potatoes in a cool dry place but not in the refrigerator or under the sink. Throw out any that have turned green.

★ Never store food items near cleaning products and other chemicals.

Prepare meats with care. Meats, especially chicken, are a major carrier of bacteria. But with the proper handling and preparation they won't make you sick.

★ Thaw frozen foods in the refrigerator or microwave, not on the countertop.

★ Wash your hands with warm soapy water for at least 20 seconds before and after handling raw meat. Clean cutting boards, knives, and other utensils in warm soapy water as well between uses.

★ Clean up spilled juices with paper towels rather than a dishcloth or sponge that's likely to spread germs. And scrub countertops where meat has been prepared with a mixture of a tablespoon of chlorine bleach to one quart of water.

★ Cook meats thoroughly, and serve them on a clean platter, never on the unwashed dish that held the raw meat.

Most people fail to follow one or more of these precautions. Don't make the mistake of waiting until a case of food poisoning grabs you.

Top tips to dodge dangerous bacteria

Use common sense and take some not-so-obvious steps to avoid bacterial infections.

✪ Cook meat and poultry well. Bacteria can hide in under-cooked portions.

✪ Never eat raw clams, oysters, or other shellfish. Avoid raw sprouts as well.

✪ Use pasteurized eggs in recipes — Caesar's salad, for instance — where the egg is left raw. And drink only pasteurized apple juice and cider.

✪ Wash your hands immediately after petting animals, particularly at a zoo or farm. Also, clean your hands with soap and water after handling reptiles, pet chews, and raw meat — and when you use the bathroom, of course.

✪ Sanitize cutting boards by running them through the dishwasher after you use them. Or put wooden boards, but not plastic, in the microwave for five minutes. Use a separate board just for meats.

✪ Consider tossing the kitchen sponges, which hold a lot of bacteria. If you use them, microwave them on high for 60 seconds to kill germs.

10 most tainted foods — and how to battle the threat

Popcorn, peanuts, and pickles are enjoyed at movie theaters, ball-games, and picnics everywhere. Who would ever dream they could be a threat to your health?

Unfortunately, they're among the most contaminated foods you eat, says a report from the Pesticide Action Network. Most food — whether grown in the U.S. or overseas — contains at least traces of banned chemicals such as dioxin or DDT, the report says. Some experts believe these toxins can build up in your body, possibly leading to cancer or other health problems.

The report lists the 10 most tainted foods — containing three to seven toxic chemicals each — as butter, cantaloupe, cucumbers and pickles, meatloaf, peanuts, popcorn, radishes, spinach, summer squash, and winter squash.

If you find some of your favorites on this list, you don't have to give them up. Just take these steps to lower the effects of their hidden toxins.

Buy organic. You can't be sure organically grown foods haven't been contaminated by the environment. But at least you know they were grown without added chemicals from fertilizers or pesticides. Another bonus — they tend to be more nutritious, especially if locally grown and purchased fresh. The faster they get from the field to your plate, the more vitamins and minerals you get to enjoy.

Clean and cut away chemicals. Always scrub fruits and vegetables thoroughly before eating them. If you have any doubt about the skin's safety, remove it. Take advantage of canned fruits and vegetables as well. They tend to have fewer chemicals, probably because they are peeled before processing.

Broaden your selections. Eat fewer tainted foods by rotating them with others not on the list. Alternate spinach with kale, collards, or turnip greens, for instance. Munch on a rice cake instead of popcorn. Try other melons in place of cantaloupe, and eat a variety of nuts.

Although no food is guaranteed to be chemical-free, you have a better chance of staying healthy if you eat a wide variety of foods.

Fight the danger lurking in your breakfast bowl

You may believe your morning bowl of cornflakes gives you a healthy jump on the day. But in fact, your iron-fortified cereal could make you sick.

"Iron is a double-edged sword," says Mark Failla, a professor of nutrition at Ohio State University. On the plus side, it helps your red blood cells carry energizing oxygen all through your body, and it helps keep your immune system healthy.

But researchers have found that high amounts of iron in the cells of your intestines allow bacteria to enter the cells more easily and live longer. That means you're more likely to get an intestinal infection.

Eating foods with added iron, therefore, may not be such a good idea. "Instead of fortifying everyone's diet with excess iron," says Failla, "we should diagnose iron deficiency and then provide supplemental iron only to those who need it."

Women who still have their monthly periods, for example, might need extra iron to get their recommended dietary allowance (RDA) of 18 milligrams (mg). But men and postmenopausal women, with a much lower RDA of 8 mg, can easily get enough from non-fortified foods. Moreover, they are likely to get too much if they aren't careful.

If you are in this second group, consider these steps to avoid iron-related bacterial infections.

Limit foods high in iron. Choose more fresh fruits and vegetables, and eat less of the foods that are highest in iron — like meats, beans, and dried fruits.

Check labels of fortified foods. Manufacturers add iron to most cereals, along with grain products like breads and flours. Read the labels to see how much iron you get with each serving so you can curb the amount you eat.

Switch supplements. Check your daily multivitamin. If it has added iron, change to one that doesn't.

Give blood. Younger women need more iron because they lose a great deal during menstruation. By the same token, you can lower the amount of iron in your system by donating blood to the Red Cross. You will help someone else while reducing your risk of a bacterial infection.

If you feel sluggish, though, your iron may be too low. As a pre-menopausal woman, you should have your blood tested to be sure you get enough. If you are male or a postmenopausal woman and take aspirin or other nonsteroidal anti-inflammatory drugs (NSAIDS), see your doctor. You could have a problem with internal bleeding.

Drive deadly guest from your dinner table

Guess who's not coming to dinner — botulism. At least not if you are on the lookout for this uninvited guest. It won't be easy to spot since you can't taste or smell this dangerous form of food poisoning. But if you know how it's likely to sneak in, you can destroy it before it makes someone seriously ill.

Botulism is rare these days from foods you buy, so if it does crash your dinner party it will most likely come from food prepared at home. The bacterium thrives in a low-acid, oxygen-free environment. So it shows up mainly in vacuum-sealed jars of home-canned vegetables or other homemade foodstuffs that give it an airtight cover or coating.

Here's how to prevent being poisoned by the most likely culprits.

Beware of homemade flavored oils. Plant ingredients like garlic, chilies, and herbs add delicious flavors to oils you use on salads and breads. But the oil provides the perfect environment for botulism spores to grow. Take these precautions to make sure that doesn't happen.

★ Use thoroughly dried ingredients. Only those that are at least 30 percent water allow the bacteria to grow. Avoid using any that are dried hard on the outside, but soft on the inside — like some sun-dried tomatoes.

★ Add acid to "wet" ingredients before mixing. Crush fresh garlic, onions, ginger, or chili peppers, and then soak them in vinegar for 15 to 20 minutes before adding them to the oil.

★ Make only what you need for one meal — or at least will use up in a few days — and keep it refrigerated until you use it. The bacteria grow slowly below 40 degrees, but left at room temperature the oil can quickly become dangerous.

Take the same precautions with these ingredients in homemade butter or margarine spreads.

Can foods with caution. Heat destroys bacteria during the canning process and seals in the food so no new bacteria can enter. Foods with a lot of acid — pickles and jams, for example — require less heat than low-acid foods, like vegetables and meats.

★ Use only recipes from a source you trust. Don't make up your own or change the recipe in any way, especially if it will change the amount of acid. To be sure the contents reach the required temperature and stay hot long enough, use only the size jar recommended in the recipe.

★ Use a pressure cooker to can low-acid foods, including tomatoes. (The amount of acid they contain can vary.) That's the only way to get the temperature high enough to kill the bacteria that cause botulism.

★ Toss out any canned food if the lid bulges or you see gas bubbles inside. If, when you open a jar, the food smells or looks spoiled, throw it out as well. Never taste canned food to determine if it's ruined. If in doubt, throw it out. Place the food, jar and all, in a plastic bag to be sure it doesn't drip and spread the poison.

★ Even if it looks and smells OK, when you are ready to eat home-canned food, boil it for 20 minutes to be sure it's safe.

Bake potatoes without the foil. Potatoes in an airtight foil wrap can harbor botulism bacteria. To be safe, microwave or bake them in a conventional oven without foil. If you do use foil, be sure the potatoes are fully cooked, and refrigerate any you don't eat right away.

Don't give honey to babies. Botulism is rare in adults because of the high acid level in their stomachs. Infants, however, don't start out with enough stomach acid to protect them. Honey is a dangerous food during their first year.

Don't let poisonous bug cloud your drinking water

You think you can avoid *Escherichia coli* (*E. coli*) by cooking meats thoroughly and washing vegetables carefully before you eat them. But what about that glass of water you are about to drink? It looks clear, but is it really safe?

Maybe not. You can get *E. coli* poisoning — and become extremely ill — if animal or human waste gets in your water supply, possibly after heavy rainfall or melting snow. Children under five, older people, and anyone with weak immune systems, perhaps from cancer or AIDS, are most at risk. Symptoms include severe diarrhea and stomach cramps.

You probably don't have to worry if your water comes from a local water system. If it isn't safe, you'll hear about it. After some serious cases of water-borne *E. coli* a few years ago, the law now requires your public water department to notify you of any contamination.

If you have a private well, though, you'll need to keep an eye on it yourself. Here are some tips for making sure it's safe.

★ Have your well water tested from time to time. Contact your local health department to find out the best way to do it.

★ Boil water for drinking if you think it may be infected. Keep it at a rolling boil for one full minute, longer if you live at a high altitude. Or buy bottled water. Just don't count on your home filter system to catch this deadly bug.

★ If your water tests positive for *E. coli*, follow local health department procedures for disinfecting your well. Continue drinking boiled or bottled water until tests give you an "all clear" message.

★ Monitor your water to be sure *E. coli* doesn't recur. If it becomes an ongoing problem, consider drilling a new well. You may also want to think about replacing your current pipes with copper ones. A test found copper pipe has 10 times more antibacterial power than plastic or stainless-steel pipe.

Water you don't intend to swallow — maybe when swimming in a pool or lake — can also be an *E. coli* risk. So be sure to keep your mouth closed when in the water. And to protect others, don't swim or bathe with other people or prepare food for them if you have diarrhea.

Forgetfulness

15 fool-proof tips for a youthful memory

Christy Jordan's family was forever leaving the laundry room door open. "The dogs would get into the clean clothes and chew their way through everything," she remembers. So Christy hung a sign on the door that read, "Close the door," and another on the way out that asked, "Did you close the door?" The results — no more paw prints on her clean towels.

These kinds of cues work like an anti-aging cream for your brain. Experts at Washington University in St. Louis tested the memories of 20-year-olds and 70-year-olds. They gave the seniors tricks to help them recall lists of words and numbers, and surprisingly, these tips shaved years off aging memories. The seniors were able to remember almost as much as the younger adults.

Try these memory tricks that can work for you, too.

Talk with your hands. Science may have proven Mom wrong. A study at the University of Chicago shows that gesturing while you talk actually improves your memory. Explain with your hands and you free your mind to remember other things like a grocery list or phone number.

Put your senses to work. Use the sights, sounds, smells, and feelings of a moment like keys to unlock certain memories. Try to remember the scent of a place, the color of a room, the surrounding sounds, and how you felt in that moment. Concentrating on these parts can bring the whole memory into better focus.

Jazz it up. Music may soothe the savage beast, but it also boosts your memory. Listening to background music helped some people with dementia remember more facts from their life. And who could forget the ABC's singsong rhythm? Try adding your own tune and beat to everyday lists to make them more memorable.

Post reminders. Take Christy's approach. Hang sticky notes around the house to help you remember certain chores. "Take out the garbage." "Pick up cat from vet." "Get clothes from the dryer." Don't feel silly. It's worse if you forget to pay the bills.

Beat the lost and found blues. Choose a home base for things you lose often, and always put them there. For instance, if you constantly misplace your keys, put a peg or hook in the wall by the door, and hang your keys on it as soon as you walk inside.

Track down lost items. Don't panic if you forget to put an item in its place. Go back to where you used it last, and retrace your steps. Also, checking your path mentally could lead you to the lost item. Close your eyes, and picture what you were doing with it.

When in doubt, write it out. Some facts are too important to forget. Keep a pen and paper near the phone so you can jot directions and phone numbers. Keep a calendar handy to record appointments as soon as you make them. Take a tiny notepad with you on doctor's visits to write down information about your tests and medications.

Crunch those numbers. Numbers can foil even memory experts. Unfortunately, you probably have many to remember — phone, social security, and insurance policies, just to name a few. Your short-term memory can only hold about seven items at a time, the length of one telephone number. But you can put the squeeze on long numbers by chunking them together. So instead of trying to remember 2-5-6-1-8-2-7, think of it as two-fifty-six and eighteen-twenty-seven. You've just turned seven items into two simpler ones.

Master the name game. Forgetting someone's name can be an embarrassing experience, but a few quick tricks can make any name stick.

★ **Focus.** Pay full attention to a new acquaintance. Listen closely as she says her name, and look at her face. People in the Washington University study remembered faces better than words — even without memory hints.

★ **Say it again, Sam.** Repeat a name as soon as someone says it. Speaking it out loud makes it stick in your memory better than just hearing it.

★ **Spell it.** Ask how to spell a name if you need more reinforcement. Just hearing the name again may fix it in your mind.

★ **Visualize it.** Picture the letters in your head as she spells her name. You could even imagine black letters appearing on a white sheet of typing paper.

★ **Associate it.** Some names match the person. Maybe Julia is wearing a lovely jewel on a necklace. You can use visualization here, too, and see the jewel next to Julia's face in your mind's eye.

★ **Comment on it.** Strengthen the association in your mind by verbalizing it. "My, Julia, that's a lovely necklace you're wearing. What kind of jewel is it?"

★ **Use it.** One of the best ways to remember someone's name is to say it often. So don't be shy — practice makes perfect.

Perk up your recall with caffeine

The hot java that gets you going in the morning could keep you on the ball all day long. Caffeine is more than a morning wake-up call — it can be an afternoon brain booster, too.

As you age, memory and mental alertness begin to peak early in the day and slow down in the afternoon. Researchers at the University of

Arizona found that caffeine, a natural stimulant, can counteract that late-day mental slump.

Here are some tips to make the caffeine kick work for you.

Grab a late-day cup of joe. That morning coffee stays in your system for three or four hours. You can brew another cup in the afternoon when you start to slow down, or turn to another source of caffeine, instead, like cola, tea, or chocolate. Most teas contain less than half the caffeine of coffee, so their effects will be milder.

Don't fill to the rim. Too much caffeine can leave you shaky and unable to concentrate. Try not to drink more than 300 milligrams of caffeine a day — that's about two to three cups of coffee. And make sure you drink plenty of water. Caffeine can dehydrate your body, causing confusion, disorientation, and other attention problems.

Sweeten with the original. Studies continue to link the artificial sweetener aspartame with memory problems. Sugar, on the other hand, may actually perk up your memory. So skip the fake sweetener, and stick with the real thing.

Caffeine isn't for everyone. If you don't normally drink coffee, for instance, the caffeine can make you jittery and mentally unfocused. Luckily, other stimulants can give you an afternoon lift. Get your blood pumping by stretching or taking a brisk walk. Or engage in a lively conversation. Fight mental fatigue a variety of ways, and stay on your toes all day long.

Prescription drugs can steal your memories

You're not losing your mind. It could be that your medication is making off with your memories. Before you blame age or Alzheimer's, check this list of popular drugs. Talk to your doctor about changing your prescription if you think one is causing your memory loss.

Condition	Generic drug	Brand name
High blood pressure	Atenolol	Tenormin, Tenoretic
	Betaxolol hydrochloride	Kerlone
	Bisoprolol fumurate	Zebeta
	Bisoprolol fumurate and Hydrochlorothiazide	Ziac
	Fosinopril sodium	Monopril
	Labetalol hydrochloride	Normodyne, Trandate
	Lisinopril	Zestril, Prinivil
	Lisinopril and Hydrochlorothiazide	Zestoretic, Prinzide
	Losartan potassium	Cozaar
	Losartan potassium-hydrochlorothiazide	Hyzaar
	Metoprolol succinate	Toprol-XL
	Propranolol hydrochloride	Inderal, Inderide
	Timolol maleate	Blocadren
	Timolol maleate-hydrochlorothiazide	Timolide
Heart disease or High cholesterol	Fluvastatin sodium	Lescol
	Pravastatin sodium	Pravachol
	Simvastatin	Zocor
Anxiety or Depression	Alprazolam	Xanax
	Bupropion hydrochloride	Wellbutrin
	Lorazepam	Ativan
	Nefazodone hydrochloride	Serzone
Ulcer	Hyoscyamine sulfate	Levsin
Nausea	Scopolamine	Transderm Scop
Sleeping disorders	Triazolam	Halcion
	Zolpidem tartrate	Ambien
Parkinson's disease	Benztropine mesylate	Cogentin
	Selegiline hydrochloride	Eldepryl
Smoking habit	Bupropion hydrochloride	Zyban

Top foods that maximize your memory

A trip to the grocery store could leave you with lasting memories. Not that you'll always cherish your time in the canned food aisle — but you could boost your brainpower by putting certain items in your cart. Start out with this "memorable" dinner menu.

- ✪ Serve up some salmon. It's full of protein, omega-3 fatty acids, and vitamin B12, all linked to better brain function.

- ✪ Season that salmon with easy-to-grow rosemary. Its antioxidants will keep your memory sharp as a tack.

- ✪ Bake a potato — and eat the skin. The carbohydrates enhance short-term memory, while the iron-rich skin keeps your brain alert.

- ✪ Toss a spinach salad for some fast brain-boosting folate. Sprinkle with almonds for boron, an amazing mineral that affects everything from hand-eye coordination to long- and short-term memory. Dress it with olive oil loaded with memory-saving monounsaturated fat and vitamin E.

- ✪ End with a fruit salad. Combine watermelon for thiamin and B6, mangoes for vitamins E, C, and beta carotene, and blueberries, a sweet antioxidant treat that keeps your mind sharp and helps reverse the effects of aging.

Eat a variety of healthy foods and make each meal a mental powerhouse.

Defeat diseases that cause forgetfulness

Lost your keys again? Get your blood pressure checked. If it's high, you may not be getting a healthy amount of blood to your brain. This can affect your brain tissue and as a result your memory. In fact, there are a number of health problems that can lead to forgetfulness — all of them preventable.

Get the drop on high blood pressure. The damage high blood pressure causes in your brain can start in middle age, although you may not notice memory problems until your 60s. Left untreated, high blood pressure puts you at almost six times the risk for mental decline. Fight back by managing your blood pressure with regular exercise, a healthy diet, and, if necessary, medication.

Don't be smitten by stroke. Guarding against strokes could save your memory. A 6-year study of over 10,000 people found that those who were stroke-free did up to nine times better on memory tests than people who had suffered strokes. Start protecting yourself now — eat right, control your blood pressure, and walk or work out daily.

Reign in runaway diabetes. Control your diabetes and you're more likely to keep your memory. Let it go untreated and Harvard University researchers think you'll double your risk for mental decline. The longer you wait, the higher your risk.

Like high blood pressure, diabetes can begin affecting blood flow to your brain in middle age. You may not notice the changes at first, but over the years the damage adds up. Work with your doctor to develop a treatment plan that includes moderate exercise and a diet rich in whole grains, fruits, and vegetables. And stick with it — your mind is worth it.

Slow down after surgery. The anesthesia from surgery can leave your mind confused and your memory cloudy. Once it wears off, your memory should bounce back. Until then, give yourself time to recover. Discuss concerns with your doctor before and after surgery.

Do away with depression. Unhappiness is one of the most common and, thankfully, reversible causes of memory loss. Beat those blues by spending time with friends, getting plenty of exercise, and filling your plate with a variety of healthy foods.

Take the sting out of stress. Illness, losing a loved one, even financial woes can pile on stress. Not only will this increase your forgetfulness, but you can also develop other memory-stealing health problems like high blood pressure and depression as a result. Activities like walking, gardening, and even writing about your worries in a journal can help you battle stress.

Beef up your B's. Up to one-fourth of all people don't get enough vitamin B12. This deficiency tends to mimic what most think of as typical signs of aging — memory loss, fatigue, weakness, and depression. The truth is, you could be B12 deficient and never know it.

You need about 2.4 micrograms of B12 each day, but seniors, especially, have a hard time absorbing it from regular foods. Eat fish, chicken, eggs, and red meat, but also get plenty of fortified foods like milk and cheese. Your doctor can test you for a B12 deficiency, and prescribe supplements and a special diet.

Huddle against hypothermia. You don't have to be outdoors in the snow to get hypothermia. Even slightly low body temperatures cut the blood flow to your brain enough to cloud your thinking and memory. So when the cold sets in, add blankets to your bed, and wear extra layers of clothing — indoors and out. If you get soaked in a sudden rain, change into dry clothes as soon as possible.

Ration the alcohol. You probably know that alcohol kills brain cells, but having more than two drinks a day also cuts the blood flow to the part of your brain that makes memories.

A faulty memory doesn't have to be a fact of life. Take steps now to keep your mind sharp. Healthy living can even reverse memory loss, recapturing some of those lost moments. If your ability to remember gets worse, see your doctor. She can work with you to find the cause and develop a healthy treatment plan.

Experts reveal secrets to a super memory

Older adults today are aging better than ever, and with fewer memory problems than just 10 years ago. Although forgetfulness is often associated with aging, only about 4 percent of adults over 70 have serious trouble remembering. And that number could continue to drop, especially for women. A Dutch study found that women over age 85 typically had a better memory than men.

Get smart with ginkgo

Ginkgo biloba can improve your memory and help you think faster. This amazing herbal remedy widens your blood vessels, and can increase the blood flow to your brain by a whopping 70 percent. It could also knock out twelve other age-related illnesses.

★ Slashes your risk of heart attacks by widening your arteries and protecting them from cholesterol damage.

★ Strikes out at strokes by preventing blood clots and reducing brain damage after a stroke.

★ Slows down the course of Alzheimer's disease by opening up blood vessels in your brain.

★ Prevents varicose veins by strengthening the walls of your blood vessels.

★ Soothes the pains of intermittent claudication by improving blood flow to your legs.

★ Helps heal vision problems like macular degeneration and glaucoma.

★ Relieves Raynaud's syndrome by increasing circulation to your fingers and toes.

What's more, ginkgo could help you shake problems with depression, anxiety, confusion, poor concentration, vertigo or dizziness, and tinnitus.

Just make sure your supplements are made from the plant's leaves, not the seeds. And don't take ginkgo along with blood-thinning medicines such as aspirin or warfarin.

The key to mental energy — lifestyle. That's what top aging experts declared in a landmark report sponsored by the National Institute on Aging. After looking at over a hundred studies from the last 20 years, these researchers drew up a set of guidelines to help you get the most mental mileage out of your Golden Years.

Make learning a lifelong adventure. Mental challenges can help keep your brain sharp all the way into your 90's. Even late in life, your brain can rewire itself, grow new cells, and learn new activities. But you have to give your mind a regular workout to keep it in shape. Pick up a hobby, like woodworking or quilting, or learn to play thinking games like chess and cards. Crossword puzzles are brain boosters that go great with your morning coffee. You'll enjoy making new memories, while saving the ones you have.

Stay active after retirement. Ready for a quiet retirement? Not so fast. According to the aging report, an interesting, rewarding workplace may safeguard your brain. Part-time jobs can help you stay busy, but also consider traveling, or volunteering with people in need. And if you're hooked on learning, do it with a group of people. Join a quilting circle instead of studying a book, or teach your grandchildren to play chess. Your gifts of time and wisdom let everyone benefit from your long life.

Look after the inner you. Emotionally stable older adults tend to have more brainpower and be more self-sufficient. Unfortunately, feelings of depression, grief, and loneliness are all too common for some seniors. As you age, it's especially important to build a community of supportive friends and family. Spend time with the significant people in your life, perhaps through family gatherings or church activities. And don't be afraid to ask your doctor for help overcoming the blues.

Take a hike. A long walk may clear your head more than you know. Exercise keeps your body fit, but it's good for your brain, too. Even basic aerobics like walking increase blood flow to your brain, improve your thinking, and speed up your reaction time. A daily bike ride can give you a brain-body workout, but so can gardening and housework. Do something you enjoy, and you'll be more likely to stick with it.

Find time to unwind. Constant stress does more than affect your ability to think. It actually changes your brain's structure over time. Experts recommend relaxing with meditation and yoga. On the other hand, simply enjoying a few quiet minutes at the end of the day can reduce anxiety. Find what works for you, whether it's reading or running, and take time to enjoy it.

Get plenty of shut-eye. Sleep, especially the dreaming kind, is essential to clear thinking and an airtight memory. Cut back on sleepless nights by cutting out disturbances. Move the television out of the bedroom, and try wearing earplugs at night to muffle odd noises or a snoring partner. If you have trouble going to sleep, relax before bedtime. A warm bath or a good book can ease you into more restful slumber.

Kick those bad habits. Smoking and heavy drinking are both associated with memory loss in old age. Studies show that smokers and former smokers are at a higher risk for mental decline than nonsmokers. What's more, too much alcohol can leave you with a cloudy memory and damaged brain cells. Considering their other health risks, think twice about cigarettes and alcohol.

In addition to these lifestyle recommendations, the experts say managing other health issues — like nutrition, illness, and safety — can lead to a longer, more satisfying life.

Gallstones

4 ways to steer clear of gallstones

You've finally lost those extra 20 pounds you've been gaining and losing for years. But this time you don't feel like celebrating. All that crash dieting has created gallstones, and you're in terrible pain.

Your gallbladder is a pouch-like structure near your liver. It stores a digestive substance called bile, which travels from your liver to your small intestine by way of tiny tubes called bile ducts. Sometimes cholesterol from the food you eat crystallizes and forms a tiny stone in your gallbladder. This is not a problem unless it gets too large or blocks a duct. When that happens, you'll likely experience agonizing pain high above your stomach on the right side.

Gallstones develop for a variety of reasons. If they run in your family, your chance of getting them is higher than average. Fortunately, you can make lifestyle changes to cut your risk other ways.

Maintain a healthy weight. If you're overweight, even slightly, you have nearly twice the risk of gallstones. Very overweight, or obese, people are six times more likely to form stones. To lose weight safely, your best plan of action is to make moderate changes in your diet. Decide how many calories you are presently consuming, on average, each day. Then reduce that amount by 500 to 1,000 calories. Experts usually recommend you lose no more than a pound or two a week.

Don't go overboard. Very low-calorie dieting slows your body's production of bile acid, which normally helps prevent stones from forming. In addition, if you don't eat about 10 grams of fat at a meal, your gallbladder gets sluggish, and stones can form.

Don't toy with yo-yo diets. A new study shows that people who continually lose weight and put it back on are up to 70 percent more likely to get gallstones. For your gallbladder's sake, lose weight slowly and keep it off.

Reconsider hormones. Women get two-thirds of all gallstones, probably because of higher levels of estrogen in their bodies, especially during pregnancy. Your risk goes up when you add estrogen-containing hormone replacement therapy (HRT) or birth control pills. If you have a family history of gallstones, think carefully before taking birth control pills or HRT. Ask your doctor about other options.

Give yourself a sporting chance. Just as a rolling stone gathers no moss, a moving person is less likely to get gallstones. Take up a sport or exercise vigorously several times a week — with your doctor's approval. Researchers found that exercise, such as playing a sport, lowers your risk of gallstones.

So pick up your tennis racket or lace up your jogging shoes and get going. You can outrun your risk of painful stones with simple lifestyle changes that can keep your gallbladder running smoothly.

Strengthen your body for gallbladder surgery

Each year more than 500,000 people have their gallbladders removed. Called a cholecystectomy, the operation sounds scary, but it's not. Unlike your heart, kidneys, and other vital organs, you can usually do just fine without a gallbladder.

A gallbladder's only job is storing bile from your liver before it goes to your small intestine to help digest food. After the operation, your liver will simply connect directly to your intestines.

As with any surgery, how you treat your body before and after can affect your recovery. Follow these tips so you can get back to your normal routine as soon as possible.

Choose healthy food. Eat a well-balanced diet for as long as possible before surgery. Nutritionally weak people don't recover as fast as those who eat well. So skip the junk food and reach for nutritious fruits and vegetables, whole grains, and lean meat for protein. If gallbladder pain makes you too nauseous to eat, ask your doctor what foods are best for you before surgery.

Avoid grease. When your gallbladder isn't working properly, your body has a harder time digesting food. You've probably noticed how uncomfortable a large, fatty meal can make you feel. Avoid fried foods, anything with butter or a cream sauce, and fatty meats. Certain other foods, like cabbage and pickles, might also give you trouble. Wait until after your surgery to eat them.

Pop a multivitamin. Cover your bases by taking a daily multivitamin with minerals. If you're a bit low in something essential, it could help raise your levels before the operation.

When your gallbladder needs help fast

Symptoms of gallbladder disease can appear suddenly. You might easily mistake the intense pain for appendicitis, irritable bowel syndrome, or even a heart attack. If you experience the following symptoms, contact your doctor immediately.

★ constant pain high above your stomach on the right side

★ pain radiating to your right shoulder or between your shoulder blades, especially after eating or at night

★ nausea and vomiting

★ fever

★ yellow skin or yellowing of the "whites" of your eyes

Don't delay getting help. If a gallstone completely blocks a bile duct, it can severely damage your gallbladder, liver, or pancreas.

Speak up about supplements. Many people take supplements, but they don't mention it to their doctors. The most popular ones are echinacea, ephedra, garlic, ginkgo, ginseng, kava, St. John's wort, and valerian. Some of them work like drugs and can interfere with anesthesia and medicine. To safeguard your health, you might have to slowly taper off or discontinue them several weeks before surgery. For your own safety, you must tell your doctor in advance about any herbs you take, even if you have already stopped taking them.

★ **Echinacea.** Although you might take it to boost your immunity, it can suppress your immune system if you take it long term. That could slow down healing after surgery. Stop taking it as early as possible.

★ **Ephedra.** This herb can increase your heart rate and blood pressure. Don't take it for at least 24 hours before surgery.

★ **Garlic and ginkgo.** These inhibit blood clotting. If your doctor gives you an anti-clotting drug after surgery, the combination could cause uncontrolled bleeding. Stop taking them for at least a week before your operation.

★ **Ginseng.** This ancient herb inhibits clotting and lowers blood sugar, but it might make your blood sugar too low during surgery. It can also interfere with anti-clotting drugs, such as warfarin. Stop taking it at least one week before surgery.

★ **Kava.** Since this is used for its sedative and anti-anxiety effect, it can add to the power of anesthesia. Give it up at least 24 hours before your procedure.

★ **St. John's wort.** This popular mood-altering herb can affect your reaction to other drugs. Stop taking it at least five days before your operation.

Get well soon. You probably won't be given any dietary restrictions after your surgery, but good nutrition is still important. Eat well-balanced meals and stay away from empty calories, like junk food, no matter how hungry you feel. Several small meals each day might be best as you recover.

Choose foods high in vitamin C, such as orange juice, broccoli, sweet red peppers, and strawberries. This super vitamin is loaded with antioxidants to fight cell damage. In addition, it helps form collagen, which your body needs to make scar tissue.

Gallbladder surgery shouldn't slow you down for long. If you eat right and only take prescribed medicines, you should be back on your feet in no time.

Gingivitis

Top-notch techniques for fighting gingivitis

Transform your toothbrush and floss into potent weapons against gum disease. All it takes is good teeth-cleaning technique.

Bad technique, on the other hand, can do the opposite. Food particles and germs build up in your mouth and form a sticky film called plaque. This leads to gingivitis — swollen, red gums that bleed easily. Over time, it develops into a serious condition called periodontitis, which puts you at risk for tooth loss and even heart disease.

Say goodbye to all this — and say hello to healthy gums — when you learn these expert dental tips.

Brush like a champ. Most people spend only a few seconds brushing. This doesn't cut it. Experts recommend you scrub your ivories for two minutes.

According to the American Dental Association (ADA), however, an extra minute at the sink is no substitute for good form. So take your time, but also follow the ADA's steps to good brushing.

★ Angle your brush 45 degrees against your gums.

★ Brush back and forth with short, gentle strokes.

★ Clean the front, back, and flat chewing surfaces of your teeth.

★ Sweep up and down with the brush's top edge to hit the inside of your front teeth.

Floss to fight plaque. Next, reach for either waxed or unwaxed floss.

★ Break off about 18 inches and wrap the ends around your middle fingers, leaving a few inches in between.

★ Hold this part with your thumbs and forefingers.

★ Rub the floss between two teeth with a gentle sawing motion.

★ Pull it into a "C" around the bottom of one tooth and slide it carefully inside your gum line.

★ Scrape the floss up and down the tooth, away from your gums.

★ Repeat for every tooth, including your back ends.

If you have problems handling the string, talk with your dentist about floss threaders, special toothbrushes, and other dental tools that can reach your mouth's tight spots.

Treat your tongue. Plaque doesn't just attack your gums and your teeth — it targets your tongue, too. So brush your tongue for at least 30 seconds each time you clean your pearly whites. Be gentle. And aim especially for the back part, where most of the bacteria hide.

If this makes you gag, try a child-sized brush or a special tongue scraper. These are available at your pharmacy. Or say "ahhh" when you gargle with antiseptic mouthwash. That allows it to douse the back of your tongue.

Swish some water. Simply gargling with plain water may reduce mouth bacteria by one-third, according to researchers. This could come in handy when you can't brush right after a meal or snack.

Take care of your dentures. Denture wearers — you're not off the dental hygiene hook. Here's how to take care of your gums and clean your dentures.

★ Rub your gums, tongue, and mouth with a soft toothbrush every morning before you put in your dentures.

★ Rinse all loose food off your dentures after each meal.

★ Clean them next with a soft brush and denture paste or mild soap.

★ Soak them every night in a glass of denture cleanser.

Following all these tips can save you the agony and frustration of gum disease. So now that you know the proper way to do it, take a bite out of plaque.

Whip up homemade gum guardians

Some of the best mouthwashes and toothpastes can't be found at your pharmacy. Open your kitchen cupboard instead.

★ **Lemon mouth rinse.** Combine the juice of half a lemon with one cup of water, and rub it on your gums. The acid in the lemon juice will help kill off bacteria that form in your mouth.

★ **Herbal mouthwash.** Boil one teaspoon each of chamomile and sage in one cup of water. Let it simmer for 10 minutes. After it cools, use it to gargle.

★ **All-natural toothpaste.** Mix together equal parts salt and baking soda. Shake well. Then moisten your toothbrush, sprinkle some on, and scrub away.

Brush up on how to buy the best toothbrush

A good toothbrush is your gums' best friend. So it's important to know the how, what, and when of buying a new one.

Time your purchase. Your toothbrush is a bacteria zoo. It houses millions of gingivitis-causing germs, which multiply after every use. Fortunately, the American Dental Association (ADA) believes toothpaste kills the bugs before they harm you. It recommends replacing your brush every three to four months — sooner if the brush gets frayed.

But researchers think it's better to be safe and replace your tooth-brush every month. Consider once or twice a week if you have a serious medical condition. It's a good idea to switch to a fresh one after any dental procedure or round of antibiotics, too.

Grab the right one. Choosing the new brush is a simple decision. First, find a brush with at least four to five rows of bristles. Pick soft ones because hard bristles can actually hurt your gums. Then find a size that fits your mouth and easily reaches your back molars.

Store it properly. Leave your new brush out in the open between uses. The bristles will dry quicker, giving germs less chance to roost. On the other hand, if you keep your brush in an airtight case, it will stay wet. And that's exactly what bacteria like.

Dunk your brush. One thing bacteria don't like is a bath in Listerine or a similar antiseptic mouthwash. Soak your bristles in it for 20 minutes after every use. It's proven to keep the bugs in check.

Retool your original. Arthritis and other hand-related conditions can make brushing difficult. But a few minor adjustments to your toothbrush can solve the problem.

★ Slide a ball made of rubber, sponge, or Styrofoam onto the brush handle.

★ Push the handle through a sponge hair curler.

★ Attach a bicycle grip.

★ Strap the brush to your hand with a rubber band, elastic strip, or tape.

Go electric. To make brushing easier, you can also upgrade to a power toothbrush. These hi-tech gizmos blast away bacteria with super fast bristles, pulsing sound waves, or laser-accurate shots of water. Some even alert you when you've brushed long enough or scrubbed too hard.

They can be expensive, though. And according to the ADA, old-fashioned brushes may do just as good a job as long as you brush for two minutes. So before you invest in one of these gadgets, talk it over with your dentist.

Look for the seal. No matter what toothbrush you buy, look for the ADA seal on its package. It's a mark of quality you can count on.

Top 10 ways to safeguard your gums

You can fight gum disease, tooth loss, and bad breath in one fell swoop. Or actually 10.

Brush regularly. Using fluoride toothpaste twice a day makes for excellent dental hygiene.

Floss often. Do it daily to remove plaque from spots your brush can't reach.

See your dentist. Visit her twice a year.

Switch snacks. Eat at least five fruits and vegetables every day, instead of sugary junk foods.

Cash in on calcium. Don't forget three or more foods rich in this tooth-strengthening mineral, like yogurt, milk, and cheese.

Drink water. Shoot for six to eight cups a day. Your mouth needs it to make saliva, which washes away harmful bacteria.

Chew sugar-free gum. This is another great way to boost your saliva flow.

Quit smoking. Tobacco is one of your smile's worst enemies.

Gargle. Ask your dentist which mouthwash will work best for you.

Control stress. It wears down your immune system, leaving you at the mercy of germs.

How to beat dentist-chair dread

Jon Wilkins suffered through 24 cavities and six caps growing up. Now 56 years old, he hasn't forgotten. "If I had my choice," Wilkins says, "I'd never set foot in a dentist office again."

That would be a big mistake. Regular dental exams are essential for healthy gums and teeth. So if you dislike the dentist as much as Wilkins, follow these tips from the American Dental Association. They can help you rest easy in the dentist chair while your mouth gets the care it needs.

Pick the right time. Avoid feeling rushed or pressured at the dentist. Set an appointment that's convenient and comfortable for you. Mornings may work, or maybe Saturday afternoons will do.

Open up to your dentist. Your dentist hopes to make your visit a pleasant experience. So tell her if you're upset or nervous. She'll take that into account and then give you the best treatment possible.

Tune out anxiety. To drown out the drill and other nerve-wracking sounds, bring your portable music player and headset. Turn on your favorite soothing cassette, CD, or radio station. Ask your dentist first, though.

Take yourself away. When you feel trapped in the dentist chair, close your eyes and imagine yourself someplace else. A sunlit beach, a mountain lake, or your grandkids' backyard may do the trick.

Smell relief. Aromatherapy also could calm you down, according to an exciting new study. People who sniffed a floral scent during dental appointments, the researchers found, left the experience more at ease.

To try it, dab a handkerchief with three to four drops of an essential oil such as lavender. Sniff it at arm's length whenever you're tense in the dentist office.

Rest easy with anesthesia. Depending on your procedure, the doctor may need to give you an anesthetic drug. If you're anxious, he may also give you an anti-anxiety medicine. Research has shown these options to be safe and effective, and they should provide a more relaxing and pleasant dental experience.

However, it's smart to tell your dentist beforehand if you take over-the-counter or prescription medications. Speak up about serious medical conditions, too.

With these tips in mind, your next trip to the dentist will be a cinch. You probably still won't go more than you have to, but at least you'll have a more positive experience.

Gout

Dethrone the 'disease of kings' with new diet

A new diet has challenged all the old beliefs about gout prevention. In just three months, the revolutionary eating program reduced gout attacks by two-thirds. The men in this small but groundbreaking study also lowered their uric acid levels by nearly 20 percent. Plus, they lost an average of 17 pounds.

People once called gout the "disease of kings" and blamed it on excessive eating and drinking. Now, scientists know it's a form of arthritis. Your body produces too much uric acid, or it has problems flushing out this natural waste product.

Either way, the uric acid builds up in your system and overflows into your joints. There, it turns into needle-like crystals, which make the joints red, swollen, and tender. You usually inherit this condition, but it may develop because of certain medications. And even though food doesn't cause gout, what you eat still can affect your condition.

The new 40-30-30 diet was originally designed for people with insulin resistance. Scientists now believe this carbohydrate-protein-fat ratio could lower gout risk, too. That's because insulin resistance seems to affect how well your kidneys filter out uric acid. Follow these steps to make this diet work for you.

Cut calorie intake. Being overweight is a major risk factor for gout, experts agree. So cut your calories to 1,600 a day — the amount recommended in the study — and divide them among three to five meals. You should lose weight on this plan, which will help you control your uric acid levels.

Prop up your protein. Slimming down is not the only secret to guarding against gout. The diet also calls for you to punch up your protein intake to 30 percent of your daily menu.

That's a big jump when you look at the usual anti-gout diet, which recommends much less. Protein-rich foods, the old reasoning goes, are packed with purines. These compounds break down into uric acid in your body and may ignite a gout flare-up.

In the recent study, however, added protein seemed to do the opposite. It helped lower uric acid. Try to eat 120 grams of protein a day to meet your 30-percent requirement. One 6-ounce chicken breast can put you on your way with 53 grams. Or munch a cupful of black walnuts for 31 grams.

Switch fats. Don't eat just any kind of protein, though. Cut back on sources high in saturated fats, like dairy foods and red meat. Replace them with the "good" fats — mono- and polyunsaturated fatty acids. And make these 30 percent of your diet, which roughly equals 50 to 55 grams a day.

To get these beneficial fats, the study participants ate four servings of fish a week. Mind you, fish are rich in purines. It may be a safer bet to try other great sources, like peanuts, olives, olive oil, avocados, almonds, and canola oil.

Change your carbs. Get the remaining 40 percent of your calories from carbohydrates. Once again, be picky about which kinds. Forget those refined sugars from processed foods, sodas, and candy. Meanwhile, load up on complex sugars from fruits and vegetables.

This special combination of carbohydrates, proteins, and fats may provide lasting protection against gout. After a year on this diet, the men in the study kept their uric acid count down and their weight off.

Nevertheless, these results are preliminary, and more research needs to be done. Before you attempt this eating plan, talk with your doctor. She'll be able to steer you toward the right decision.

Top gout triggers

Arthritis experts finger these foods for their high levels of purines. They can spark a new flare-up if you've had gout in the past.

Before dropping any foods from your diet, however, talk with your doctor.

Foods to cut

They're loaded with purines, so eat them as little as possible, if at all.

- alcohol
- organ meats, like liver and kidneys
- anchovies, sardines, herring, codfish, trout, and haddock
- fish roe (eggs)
- mussels and scallops
- gravy and consommé
- turkey
- bacon
- veal

Foods to watch

You can eat these in moderation since they contain medium amounts of purines.

- other meats, seafood, and poultry
- beans, lentils, and peas
- whole grain cereals
- asparagus
- mushrooms
- spinach
- cauliflower

Wash away joint pain

A glass of refreshing water is a cheap way to take the edge off gout and other arthritis pain.

The pure beverage keeps your body's machinery running in tip-top condition. It's especially important for lubricating your joints, which helps you fight all types of arthritis. On top of that, it washes pollutants and waste chemicals out of your system. This includes uric acid, a gout sufferer's worst enemy.

Amazingly, you lose up to 10 cups of water a day through your sweat, urine, and breath — even more if you exercise. So it's essential to drink the right amount of water — at least six to eight glasses every day. If you sip some only when you're parched, you don't drink enough. Your thirst is not always accurate, especially as you get older. You could already be dehydrated by two cups before you have the urge to drink.

Instead, make water your drink of choice and a regular part of your daily routine. Have a cup with each meal, for instance. Bring a bottle of water with you in the car. Or finish off a glass after you brush your teeth and gargle. Your joints will thank you. And the rest of your body will, too, since water also eases dry skin, kidney problems, and a world of other hurts.

By the way, don't think caffeinated or alcoholic beverages will work just as well. They actually act as diuretics and take out more fluid than they put in. Go with herbal teas or juices if you want something other than water.

Brew your own anti-gout remedy

Your morning pick-me-up could be the easiest and tastiest way to keep your gout at bay.

A study of more than 2,200 men showed coffee might lower uric-acid levels. In fact, the men's uric-acid count dropped with every cup of joe they drank. And in this case, lower is better. Having high levels of that substance in your system puts you at greater risk for a gout flare-up.

Researchers thought caffeine might have something to do with it because of its diuretic effects. But when they tested green tea, which also has caffeine, they found it did not lower uric-acid levels.

They now think the organic chemicals in coffee may act like prescription anti-gout medication. These compounds seem to stop your body from making too much uric acid. Both brewed and instant java appear to have these gout fighters.

It's important to be cautious with these findings, however. This study was the first of its kind, so more research needs to be done. Even the researchers warn their findings could have been just a coincidence.

Still, arthritis experts list coffee as a low-purine food. In other words, your one or two mugs in the morning won't increase your risk of gout. But if you plan to raise your daily coffee intake beyond that, weigh the pros and cons with your doctor first.

A sweet substitute for pain medications

Life without gout is like a bowl of cherries. Then again, a bowl of cherries may give you a life without gout.

That's because these delicious, vitamin-packed fruits are proven to relieve arthritis pain at least as well as aspirin, ibuprofen, and other nonsteroidal anti-inflammatory drugs (NSAIDs). And cherries work without triggering stomach upsets or other side effects.

These amazing powers stem from compounds called anthocyanins. Not only do these plant chemicals give cherries their beautiful red color, they also stop your body from pumping out hormone-like chemicals and enzymes that cause inflammation and pain.

To benefit from anthocyanins, experts recommend eating 20 cherries a day during a bout of gout. That "dosage" is enough to neutralize the swelling and ache.

If that's too many for you to stomach, try dried cherries instead. One of these raisin-like snacks has the anti-gout strength of eight fresh fruits. So just three can do the trick.

Of course, always see your doctor first before you treat yourself for a gout attack.

Headache

Surprising ways to headache-proof your life

Going to sleep or soaking in a hot bath can mean excruciating pain for a small group of people.

These are two, little-known triggers for cluster headaches which, according to the National Headache Foundation, affect less than 1 percent of the population. Considered the most painful kind, these headaches start with a stabbing, almost unbearable pain behind or around one eye. The pain can move to your forehead, temple, or cheek, but usually stays on one side of your head. You can develop a watery, bloodshot eye or runny nose on that side as well.

A typical cluster headache lasts about 30 to 45 minutes, then goes away — only to return later in the day. During a cluster "cycle," you can get up to four headaches a day. A cycle can linger for weeks or months, then disappear for months or even years.

Quit smoking and limit alcohol to reduce your risk of cluster headaches. But you can also protect yourself from those other, more surprising triggers.

Suspect sleep apnea. If you have cluster headaches, you probably have sleep apnea, as well. It's a disorder where you temporarily stop breathing several times during the night. This limits the amount of oxygen in your blood, and could explain your headaches.

A recent study of people with cluster headaches found that 80 percent of them had sleep apnea — and none of them knew it.

If painful cluster headaches disrupt your night or you often wake up with one, you should see your doctor about sleep apnea. Treating it should help your headaches, too.

You can help relieve sleep apnea with a few lifestyle changes — quit smoking, limit alcohol, lose weight, and sleep on your side instead of your back. You can also wear a special mask that forces air into your nasal passages while you sleep. Surgery to open blocked airways should be a last resort.

Keep cool. Here's a hot tip to avoid cluster headaches — watch your body heat. Exercising, taking a hot bath, or just being in a hot room or outside on a hot day can trigger a cluster headache within an hour. Like alcohol or sleep, increased body heat causes your blood vessels to dilate, a possible cause of headaches.

To counter the heat, go outside, turn up a fan or the air conditioner, or apply a cold compress to your face. Keep your bedroom cool to prevent nighttime attacks.

Take care of your teeth. Having a tooth pulled is never pleasant, but it could be more painful than you expect. In two cases, people who had their molars taken out began experiencing severe cluster headaches two weeks later, despite never having them before.

Experts believe the surgery may have affected the surrounding nerve tissue — even led to changes in their brain processes. A head injury can do the same thing, and also cause cluster headaches.

Brush and floss regularly so a toothache won't turn into a headache.

Headache relief that's good to the last drop

Next time a tension headache strikes, head straight for the coffee pot.

Downing a big cup of "joe" might loosen that tense pain in your scalp, and soothe those sore, knotted muscles in your neck. In fact, your symptoms should start to improve within an hour.

A recent study by Chicago's Diamond Headache Clinic found that caffeine provided faster pain relief than ibuprofen. Both were equally effective at getting rid of headaches, but caffeine did the job half an hour sooner.

Tension headaches are often caused by dilated blood vessels in your head. Caffeine probably works because it constricts — or narrows — your blood vessels.

Pick your favorites. The amount of caffeine used in the Chicago study was 200 milligrams (mg). You could get that much from a large mug of brewed coffee or two regular-sized cups of java. But if you don't want a slug from the mug, check out these other sources of caffeine.

	Serving size	Amount of caffeine
Mountain Dew	12 oz	55 mg
Diet Coke	12 oz	45 mg
Dr. Pepper	12 oz	41 mg
Pepsi	12 oz	38 mg
Hot tea (black, brewed 3 min)	6 oz	36 mg
Coca-Cola Classic	12 oz	34 mg
Hershey's dark chocolate bar	1.5 oz	31 mg
Nestea with lemon & sweetener	12 oz	16 mg
Hot chocolate (sugar-free powdered mix)	1 packet in 6 oz water	15 mg
Hershey's milk chocolate bar	1.5 oz	10 mg
Chocolate ice cream	1 cup	4 mg

Give pain a double punch. If you really want to knock out your tension headache, try combining 200 mg of caffeine with 400 mg of ibuprofen. This dynamic duo proved the fastest and most effective method of headache relief in the study — beating either treatment used alone.

Caffeine also boosts the effectiveness of aspirin and acetaminophen. Read the ingredient labels on over-the-counter pain relievers since many already include caffeine.

Too much is too much. Remember, caffeine is a drug — one that you can grow to depend on. The National Headache Foundation recommends limiting yourself to two caffeinated beverages a day. If you drink a lot more than that, cut back gradually to avoid headaches from caffeine withdrawal.

In addition, you can develop "rebound headaches," nervousness, dizziness, or an upset stomach from too much caffeine.

Top ways to topple a tension headache

They're not all caused by tension, but you can often treat tension headaches by reducing your body's stress level.

Take a nap. Sometimes a short snooze is the only way to lose a nagging headache.

Cool off. Hold an ice pack on your forehead or run cold water over your head to soothe the pain.

Warm up. Place a warm compress on your neck or the back of your head. Sometimes heat works better than cold.

Soak your toes. Rest your feet in a tub of hot water for 15 minutes. Try this with an ice pack on your head at the same time.

Hit the showers. Standing under a hot spray can really wash away the ache.

Rub out the pain. Massage your temples, forehead, shoulders, and neck.

Breathe deeply. Ease the tension by relaxing your shoulder and neck muscles and taking slow, deep breaths.

Stop the clock. Find a comfortable spot, dim the lights, and think of something peaceful.

Send pain packing with these travel tips

Traveling can be a real headache, even if you're going on vacation. With all the planning, rushing around, and waiting in lines, don't be surprised if a tension headache invites itself along for the ride.

Take precautions to avoid a headache, and be prepared in case one sneaks up on you during your next trip.

Plan ahead. You can prevent headaches by doing a few simple things before and during your trip.

★ Cut down on stress, a major cause of headaches, by being organized. Make lists of what you need to do or what you need to bring. Plot routes and make reservations in advance, and account for airport delays or heavy traffic.

★ Stick to your regular sleep schedule. Getting too much or too little sleep can bring on a headache. Avoid the temptation of staying up late or sleeping in.

★ Eat at normal times. Skipping meals can leave you with an empty stomach — and a head full of pain. Pack some snacks if you need a boost between stops.

★ Drink water. It's a smarter choice than alcohol, especially during a flight. Celebrate your vacation — but go easy on the alcohol or you might spend the next day nursing a hangover.

Pack appropriately. When you go to the beach, you pack a bathing suit. When you go to the mountains, you pack a sweater. Why not be just as practical when it comes to headaches? Bring the following items along, and your headache won't stand a chance.

★ Bring all your medication, including over-the-counter or prescription pain relievers. Pack it in your carry-on for easy access and label it clearly to avoid customs and security hassles.

★ Put together a list of foods that trigger your headaches. It's a good reminder of what to avoid when dining out.

★ Pack sunglasses and a wide-brimmed hat for shade from the sun's glare.

★ Bring a portable tape or CD player with headphones so you can listen to soothing music.

★ An eye mask is handy to shut out bright light when you need to nap.

★ Don't forget that comfy pillow from home. You'll sleep better in unfamiliar places.

★ A small heating pad or portable ice pack can soothe your aching head.

★ Herbal tea bags will let you sip away stress. Try chamomile, valerian, or ginseng.

Follow this healthy itinerary, and you'll enjoy a headache-free vacation. Bon voyage!

Hearing Loss

Don't turn a deaf ear to hearing loss

Four out of five people with hearing loss don't get help. If you are one of them, you're missing out on more than the world's soundtrack. Healthy hearing could also mean better family relationships, more self-esteem, and more independence and security, according to a study by the National Council on the Aging.

So take the first step — discover and accept your hearing loss. Listen to these suggestions from the National Institutes of Health to learn how.

Keep your ears peeled. Straining to understand conversations is one of the clearest warning signs of a problem. For instance, you may:

★ ask people to repeat themselves.

★ think everyone is mumbling at you.

★ give answers that don't match the questions asked you.

★ have particular trouble listening when women or children talk.

★ get lost when two or more people speak at the same time.

The next time you chat with family or friends, pay attention to whether you have any of these problems.

Test the phone and crowds. Hearing loss could also be to blame if a mobbed restaurant, shopping mall, or any other crowd makes listening

---

Top ways to shield your ears

Stop smoking. Surprisingly, it can damage your ears, along with your heart and lungs.

Plug your ears. Many activities — like hunting and lawn mowing — are dangerously loud. Keep earplugs on hand for emergency protection.

Nix on-the-job noise. If you have to yell to talk to your colleague, bring out the earplugs again.

Turn down your stereo. Loud music can be deafening — literally. Be especially careful when wearing headphones.

Avoid harsh chemicals. Certain solvents, like styrene, and some drugs, like aminoglycoside antibiotics, may damage your hearing.

Rent a movie. Hollywood flicks can be as earsplitting as rock concerts. Consider a video instead.

Eat in peace. Restaurants with bare floors and walls trap noise. Try an eatery with carpets and curtains, which absorb sound.

Quiet your appliances. Attach vibration silencers to large noisy appliances. Place foam mats under smaller ones.

Seal your home. Caulk cracks in walls and windows to keep outside racket where it belongs.

---

near impossible. The same is true for telephone calls, which can be a difficult chore when your ears aren't 100 percent.

Listen to what other people say. Don't ignore it when people complain about your television being too loud. And take notice if people get annoyed because you can't understand them. These comments from others may signal you need help.

Sound the alarm. If you hear a ringing or buzzing sound in your ear, that's a telltale sign of hearing damage. It's called tinnitus, a condition that often results from noise-related ear damage. Sometimes it goes away, but sometimes tinnitus stays for good.

Get a hearing checkup if you have tinnitus or if you recognize any of the other warning signs. Visit an ear, nose, and throat specialist (an otolaryngologist) or a hearing loss expert (an audiologist). He can help you decide whether you need treatment or not.

The latest buzz on hearing aids

Be glad your doctor recommended a hearing aid. That means you'll soon hear things you've been missing — raindrops, bird songs, and especially, your friends' voices.

And don't worry about embarrassment. Today's hearing aids aren't the clunky hardware from your parents' day. They're smaller, less noticeable, and better at what they do. They pose one problem, though — there are so many to choose from. Here's how to buy the one that suits you.

Consider the design. Talk with your audiologist about the different types of earpieces. She can help decide which is best for your budget and your condition.

★ In-The-Ear (ITE). These small models fit inside your ear. Their size, however, can make them difficult to adjust.

★ Behind-The-Ear (BTE). You wear a BTE device behind your ear. It's more visible than an ITE piece.

★ Canal Aids. They sit in your ear canal, so these appliances are probably the most hidden. But they can be difficult to adjust and remove.

★ Body Aids. These aids are best for people with severe hearing loss. They are bigger and easier to see, since they attach to your belt or pants pocket.

★ Disposable. Just like contact lenses, these hearing aids work for about a month, then you throw them away and insert a new pair. They're a great match if your hearing loss is only mild to moderate.

Choose a model. Once you choose your design, pick from the two main choices in hearing-aid technology.

★ Analog. Like microphones, these hearing aids pick up noises and amplify them in your ear. More pricey varieties have several settings for a variety of social situations.

★ Digital. These latest and greatest gizmos can be computer programmed on an individual basis. They provide the most flexibility, but they are also the most expensive.

Ask about buying options. It's important to find out about the warranty, free trial offers, cost of repairs, and the training you'll receive with your hearing aid.

Also, ask your audiologist if you need two hearing aids. After all, having one in each ear can make your listening experience twice as clear. Consider an add-on called a telecoil, too. It makes talking on the phone much easier.

Find a free one. If even a basic hearing aid is too expensive, don't give up hope. Many organizations, such as Lions Clubs International, offer free ones to folks who qualify. For more information on your local chapter and its hearing aid opportunities, contact:

Lions Clubs International
300 W. 22nd Street
Oak Brook, IL 60523
630-571-5466, ext. 287
E-mail: executiveservices@lionsclubs.org

Uncork earwax for clear hearing

Earwax, believe it or not, may be making you deaf.

It's normally good for you — it keeps out dirt, bacteria, and other foreign matter. But too much wax can block sounds before they reach your inner ear. So use one of these tried-and-true natural remedies to sweep away excess earwax and restore your hearing.

★ **Oil bath.** Drip a little warm mineral or vegetable oil in your ear with an eyedropper. Wait about 15 minutes. Then pour in warm water. Turn your head sideways to drain out the wax.

★ **Fizzy wash.** Add one teaspoon of baking soda to two teaspoons of water and shake well. Leave a few drops in your ear. The wax will dissolve in about an hour.

★ **Vinegar soak.** Mix vinegar and warm water and apply a few drops to your ear. Hold it in with a cotton ball. After a few minutes, wipe away the leakage. The wax will break up in a day or two.

Test it out. Once you have your hearing aid, you'll need to get used to it. Make sure you're comfortable putting it in and taking it out. Learn the difference between the right and left one. And try changing the batteries.

Then wear your hearing aid as frequently as your audiologist recommends. It's essential to keep it in even when you get frustrated with it. Practice focusing on different sounds in crowds, and test the device in different situations. You'll need to get accustomed to your voice, which will sound loud at first.

Get it fixed. Report any problems with your hearing aid. Return it to your audiologist if you're not pleased with the overall listening experience. It could need adjusting, for example, if background noises or whistling sounds interfere with your listening.

Care for it. To make it last, clean your hearing aid daily. Your audi-ologist can show you how. Also, follow these guidelines.

★ Keep it from heat and moisture.

★ Replace spent batteries right away.

★ Turn it off when not in use.

★ Don't apply hairspray or any hair products while it's in your ear.

★ Keep it and its batteries away from children and pets.

In no time at all, your hearing aid will improve your life. By then, you'll forget you even have it in.

Heartburn and Indigestion

Turn out the light on acid stomach

Eight out of 10 people who get heartburn say it bothers them at night. Most find it keeps them from falling asleep or wakes them up with that burning feeling in their chest. This can have a huge impact on your ability to function the next day.

"Nighttime acid reflux is a serious, widespread, and often undertreated health problem," says Donald Castell, M.D., chairman of the Department of Medicine at The Graduate Hospital in Philadelphia. Although there has been a lot of focus on daytime heartburn, he thinks more attention should be paid to nighttime occurrences.

The consequences of nighttime heartburn can be far more serious than just feeling tired and sleepy after a restless night. In fact, according to one study, it means you're 11 times more likely to develop cancer of the esophagus than other people.

With such a critical side effect, it's important to see your doctor if you have ongoing heartburn. He'll probably prescribe a medication to calm your acid reflux. In a recent survey, however, about half of those who take medicine said they still have some symptoms. So consider these ways to help yourself to a better night's sleep.

Rest on your left. Your esophagus angles a bit to the left where it connects to your stomach. If you sleep on your right side, stomach acid is more likely to flow into your esophagus and stay there.

Lying on your back brings on more frequent reflux, but the acid tends to clear out faster than when you are on your right side. You might want to use a sleeping wedge behind your back to keep you facing left.

Prop up. Raise the head of your bed about 6 inches with wooden blocks. Or sleep with a foam wedge under your upper body. At this angle gravity helps keep the juices in your stomach. Pillows don't work as well because they make you bend at the waist, putting even more pressure on your stomach.

Make dinner light. Try five or six small meals throughout the day rather than three heavy ones. If you stretch your stomach with a lot of food, you practically force acid back into your esophagus. And wait a few hours after your last meal before you go to bed. You'll have less acid in your stomach to cause problems.

Chew acid away. Skip dessert and pop a piece of gum instead. Chewing increases the flow of saliva, which helps neutralize stomach acid.

Wear loose clothing. Choose a nightgown rather than pajamas. Elastic around your middle can put pressure on your stomach and increase your chances of heartburn.

Calm down at bedtime. Worries can bring on heartburn, so try to set aside any problems and relax before you turn in for the night. Professional counseling, relaxation techniques, and regular exercise can all help.

Lose some weight. Extra fat presses on your stomach and forces acid into your esophagus.

Stop smoking. Nicotine relaxes the valve between your stomach and esophagus, allowing the acid to back up. Getting a good night's sleep is one more reason to drop this bad habit.

If symptoms continue, it's important to see your doctor. Keep a diary of the foods you eat, when you eat them, and when your heartburn occurs. Take it with you to help your doctor better understand your particular situation. And discuss any medications you're taking as well. Some — including aspirin — may contribute to your heartburn.

Top 10 hidden heartburn hazards

Spicy and acidic foods can irritate the lining of your stomach and esophagus. Others — like chocolate — cause the valve between your stomach and esophagus to relax, allowing acid to move back up and trigger that burning feeling in your chest.

Although not everyone is bothered by the same foods, if you have frequent heartburn, try eliminating these from your diet:

- Alcohol
- Carbonated beverages
- Chocolate
- Citrus fruits and juices
- Coffee
- Ketchup and other tomato products
- Mustard
- Pepper
- Peppermint
- Vinegar

Fatty foods may not cause heartburn as much as experts once thought. One study found meals high in calories, but not necessarily high in fat, increased the risk of severe heartburn. Since a high-fat diet is usually a high-calorie diet as well, it's still a good idea to avoid those fatty meats and dairy foods.

Is it heartburn or heart attack?

More than 5 million people show up at hospital emergency rooms with chest pains each year. For one out of four there's good news — it's not a heart attack.

"We often find people in the emergency department frightened that they are having a heart attack when they are actually experiencing severe heartburn," says Robert W. Schafermeyer, M.D., president of the American College of Emergency Physicians.

Most people experience heartburn when lying down after a heavy or spicy meal. It's a major symptom of gastroesophageal reflux disease, or GERD. Stomach acid flows back into your esophagus, causing a burning sensation in the center of your chest. You may also experience nausea, gagging, coughing, or hoarseness.

While heartburn is quite common, it's not always serious. But heart attacks are. So don't take any chances. Seek immediate help if you feel sudden, severe pain in your chest. For that matter, get help if you experience any chest pain along with sweating, light-headedness, and nausea.

"It is right for anyone with severe abdominal or chest pain to seek immediate, emergency medical treatment," says Schafermeyer. But you could avoid a lot of fear and anxiety, he adds, by preventing GERD emergencies.

Talk to your doctor if you have frequent heartburn that diet and lifestyle changes mentioned in this chapter don't relieve. If left untreated, GERD can seriously erode the lining of your esophagus — possibly leading to cancer.

Sniff out surprising source of acid reflux

It's another restless night with heartburn. Stop wondering what you ate to cause this agony — it's just something in the air.

According to Dr. Marc E. Rothenberg of the Children's Hospital Medical Center in Cincinnati, "What a person breathes in can actually affect the gastrointestinal system."

It's proven that people with acid reflux get more upper respiratory symptoms — stuffy nose, coughing, and hoarseness — than others. "And we know that people who develop reflux often have asthma," Rothenberg adds.

Now, based on his experience and his research, Rothenberg sees a direct link between the pollen and molds you breathe in and your abdominal pain, difficulty swallowing, and sore throat. He also believes his research can help adults who don't find reflux relief with current medications.

"A significant number of those," he says, "may have an allergen-driven process; they have a different form of reflux that we're calling eosinophilic esophagitis."

Rothenberg says new drugs that are being developed for asthma may help people with this new kind of reflux as well. Meanwhile, here are some things you can do to reduce your contact with the allergens that could be causing your reflux symptoms.

★ Stay inside when pollen levels are high in spring and fall — especially in the morning.

★ Wear a mask that covers your nose and mouth if you have to cut grass or do other yard work.

★ Take a quick shower and shampoo your hair when you come indoors.

★ Close your windows and use air-conditioning.

★ Wipe away household mold with bleach and water.

If the reflux continues, talk to your doctor about any allergy treatments that might help.

Go bananas to cool the burn

That stubborn cough you can't quite shake could be caused by heartburn. So before you down a medicated cough syrup, consider a natural alternative — eating a banana — to both calm your chronic cough and soothe your burning indigestion.

Let the air out of belching and burping

Burps and belches can be embarrassing, but they are normal ways to get rid of the air you swallow when you eat or drink. Although generally harmless, you may want to curb these noisy eruptions — and that related bloated feeling. Try these tips for cutting down on the amount of air you swallow. Most will help keep your heartburn in check as well.

Don't gulp your food. Take small bites and chew with your mouth closed. Since you are more likely to eat faster and swallow more air if you are hungry, consider eating more frequent — but smaller — meals.

Watch what — and how — you drink. You'll naturally have more stomach gas after drinking carbonated beverages, like colas and beer. You may also burp more if you use a straw or drink from a narrow-necked bottle.

Close your mouth. Chewing gum or sucking on hard candy increases saliva, which helps neutralize stomach acid. But you'll often swallow extra air without noticing. Simply try to keep your mouth closed.

Don't smoke. You'll also swallow air if you suck on a cigarette, cigar, or pipe.

Select the best supplement. Calcium carbonate tablets, like carbonated beverages, can release carbon dioxide in your stomach. Switch to calcium citrate for a gentler — and quieter — way to build bone.

Change your habits. When you feel bloated, you may be tempted to force yourself to belch. But you'll just swallow more air in the process.

And if you belch a lot even when you're not eating or drinking, swallowing air may be a nervous habit. Try to reduce stress on your own, but don't hesitate to get professional help.

Heat Exhaustion and Heatstroke

How to stay healthy when temperatures soar

When you think of summer, you probably think of beaches, cook-outs, and family vacations. But summer, with high heat and humidity, is not all fun and games. It's also a prime time for heat exhaustion and heatstroke, a potentially fatal condition.

Older people are especially at risk. When you get older, you don't sweat as much or get as thirsty as you used to. That means your body doesn't cool itself as efficiently, and you're probably not drinking enough fluids.

Symptoms of heat exhaustion include heavy sweating, dizziness, fatigue, rapid heartbeat, headache, muscle cramps, nausea, and cold, clammy skin. Heat exhaustion can progress to heatstroke.

With heatstroke, your body temperature skyrockets to 104 degrees or higher. Symptoms include shallow breathing, fast pulse, confusion, slurred speech, and loss of consciousness.

During the next heat wave, follow these tips to prevent heat-related illness.

Dress comfortably. Wear light, loose-fitting clothes. Put on a wide-brimmed hat or carry an umbrella to provide shade when you're outside.

Top tips for handling the heat

Here's what to do if the heat is getting to you.

Halt. Stop what you're doing. Pushing yourself can only make it worse.

Rest. Find a cool place and lie down with your feet propped up. Remove any tight clothes.

Drink. Water works best, but you can also drink fruit juice. The important thing is to replenish lost fluids.

Chill. Take a lukewarm bath or shower. Or just sponge yourself off with cool water. Turn on your fan or air conditioner.

If you suspect someone is suffering from heatstroke:

Dial. Call for medical help immediately. Heatstroke can be fatal.

Move. Get the person to a cool place, whether it's an air-conditioned room or just a spot in the shade.

Cool. Pour cold water on the person's skin or wrap the person in wet sheets.

Drink up. Drink lots of water — even if you don't feel thirsty. You need to replenish the fluids you lose. But avoid caffeine and alcohol, which dehydrate you.

Reschedule your workout. Limit any strenuous activities to the early morning or late evening when it's cooler, or exercise indoors.

Eat regularly. Don't skip meals. Food helps keep you hydrated. It also makes you thirsty, so you drink more fluids. Eat light meals — not hot, heavy meals. Avoid using your oven as much as possible.

Check your pills. Ask your doctor about your medication. Some drugs cause dehydration. These include antihistamines, beta-blockers, calcium channel blockers, diuretics, and antidepressants.

Avoid crowds. Big crowds mean big heat. Stay away from busy places overflowing with people, and plan trips to avoid rush hour.

Chill out. Stay indoors where it's cool. If your home isn't air-conditioned, go to the mall, public library, or movie theater to cool off. Ask a friend or family member for a ride if you don't have a car.

Open and shut. Open windows at night if you don't have air conditioning. During the day, crack windows at opposite ends of your house or apartment to get the air moving. Keep the shades drawn to keep out hot sunlight.

Freshen up. Take frequent cool baths to ease the discomfort.

Be a pal. Develop a buddy system during hot spells. Check on friends, relatives, and neighbors who live alone — and make sure someone will check on you.

With a little bit of effort, you can give heat waves the cold shoulder — and put the fun back into summer.

Hemorrhoids

Change habits to prevent painful veins

When the commercial for a hemorrhoid preparation comes on television, you might have to stifle a giggle. But painful, bulging veins around your anus are no laughing matter.

Although hemorrhoids plague about 40 percent of adults in the United States, many people are not comfortable seeking treatment. Luckily, simple lifestyle changes can often chase them away. If the following home remedies don't bring relief within seven days, or if bleeding occurs, see your doctor.

Eat some prunes. Constant constipation can be the beginning of hemorrhoids. Straining to pass hardened stool puts too much pressure on the veins in your rectum, causing them to bulge. But don't rely on harsh chemical laxatives, which could backfire by making you dependent on them and even more constipated. Instead, use natural laxatives, like prunes, prune juice, or psyllium.

Some health professionals think chronic diarrhea can also trigger hemorrhoids, especially in alcoholics. If diarrhea lasts more than a few days, make an appointment to see your doctor.

Give fiber a chance. Fiber is plant material you can't digest. Although it doesn't provide fuel for your body, it helps move things quickly through your digestive system. Unfortunately, many people eat highly processed, low-fiber foods, like white bread and white rice, instead of high-fiber fruits, vegetables, and whole grains. Get back to a healthier, old-fashioned diet with whole-wheat bread, brown rice, and plenty of fruits and vegetables. You'll be healthier, better nourished, and — best of all — regular.

Drink more water. Softening your bowel movements could be as simple as sipping a few extra glasses of water each day. Take a quick inventory of how many glasses of liquid you drink on a typical day. Because caffeine pulls water out of your body, subtract one glass of water for every caffeinated drink, such as coffee or cola. If your total is less than six to eight glasses, you're not drinking enough water to keep your bowel movements soft. Add a twist of lemon or lime to make water more interesting, or keep a pitcher of decaffeinated iced tea in your refrigerator.

Keep moving. Regular exercise can help prevent hemorrhoids by keeping your bowels in good working order. In addition, it gets you off the couch. Constant sitting can put pressure on your rectal veins.

Relocate the bathroom library. Some people have time to read *War And Peace* while using the bathroom. Recent research suggests that staying on the toilet too long can cause hemorrhoids. That's because your rectum and its veins don't get any support from a toilet seat. So get rid of the books and magazines and wait until nature calls to sit down.

Shed some weight. Extra weight puts added pressure on veins, often causing varicose veins in your legs. Hemorrhoids are simply varicose veins of the rectum. Slim down to save yourself from both conditions.

If your hemorrhoids are extremely painful, or you pass blood during a bowel movement, see your doctor at once to rule out a more serious problem, such as a blood clot or colon cancer.

With all the options available to you, there's no need to suffer. If home treatments don't work, your doctor can remove or reduce your hemorrhoids using a variety of procedures.

Instant relief for hemorrhoid pain

Don't let itching, burning, swollen hemorrhoids keep you on the sidelines. Get back in the action with these tried and true remedies.

Take a mini-bath. Most drugstores sell tiny tubs called Sitz Baths that can be placed on an open toilet seat. Fill it with a few inches of warm water. Soak for 15 minutes, three times a day.

Chill out. Retire to your bedroom and put your feet up. Place a cold pack over your hemorrhoids and rest for a few hours.

Visit the drugstore. Check the ingredients on over-the-counter products for hemorrhoids. Those with hydrocortisone relieve swelling. Benzocaine and pramoxine have a numbing and cooling effect on inflamed skin.

Find natural relief. The following natural products have been used for centuries to relieve pain and swelling.

★ Witch hazel. This astringent helps shrink blood vessels, which means less pain and throbbing.

★ Myrrh. Use this natural antiseptic to keep bacteria away from tender skin.

★ Aloe vera gel. The juice from the aloe plant reduces skin irritation. Look for it at a natural foods store.

If home treatment doesn't produce good results within seven days, see your doctor.

High Blood Pressure

Simple strategy mines salt from your diet

There's no arguing — exercise will make you healthier. The sad truth, however, is that alone it will probably only lower your blood pressure a couple of points. But don't throw away your sneakers. Combine the two therapies — restrict salt and stick to a good workout plan — and you'll take an even bigger bite out of high blood pressure.

Search out the sodium. About half the U.S. population is salt sensitive. If you fall in this category, your blood pressure reacts more drastically to the amount of salt you eat — the less salt, the lower your blood pressure. Because it's hard to test for salt sensitivity, the National Heart, Lung, and Blood Institute recommends everyone cut back on salt.

It's not always easy, however, to stay under the 2,400-milligram (mg) sodium daily limit these experts advise — that's equal to about one and one-fourth teaspoons of salt a day. In fact, researchers believe most Americans take in about 4,000 mg of sodium every day. Simply hiding the saltshaker is not enough. Here's where most people get their daily quota of salt.

Natural salt content of foods	10%
Salt added at the table or during cooking	15%
Salt added to foods during processing and manufacturing	75%

For your heart's sake, stay away from particularly salty culprits like these.

Food	Example	Sodium content	Alternative
Processed meats Most are pumped full of sodium to keep them moist and fresh.	2 slices of bologna	536 mg	Cook lean cuts of meat and slice them thinly for sandwiches.
	4-inch sausage link	517 mg	
	turkey hot dog	785 mg	
Store-bought baked goods Nearly a third of the sodium you eat likely comes from baked goods and cereal.	plain bagel	379 mg	Compare nutrition labels and buy the low-sodium varieties whenever you can.
	5 medium pretzel twists	486 mg	
Dairy products Foods made from milk tend to be high in salt.	1/2 cup low-fat cottage cheese	459 mg	Use liquid vegetable oils in recipes instead of salted butter. Check labels and opt for low-salt versions.
	1/4 cup cheese sauce	299 mg	
Fast food Most restaurants add salt and salt-rich sauces for flavor.	fish sandwich	615 mg	Eat at home and cook healthy, low-salt meals. Eat less salt at other meals if you're planning a fast food run. Avoid fried dishes, mayonnaise, and other sauces. Downsize — don't "supersize."
	chocolate shake	273 mg	
	egg and bacon biscuit	999 mg	
	baked potato with cheese sauce & chili	701 mg	
	2 bean & cheese burritos	1166 mg	

Lick salt cravings. Salt is an acquired taste. If you grew up in a country without much processed food, salty food would probably taste unpleasant to you. But you can retrain your taste buds. Gradually cut back on salt until you're down to the 2,400-mg daily limit. When post-menopausal women did this in a clinical study, their blood pressure dropped an average of 16 points. Try it yourself and finally taste your food — not just the salt. Eventually, salted foods will turn your taste buds off, and that will be good news for your blood pressure.

---

10 top tips for measuring bp at home

To get an accurate blood pressure reading at home, you need to know what you're doing.

First, select a blood pressure monitor — or sphygmomanometer — recognized by the Association for the Advancement of Medical Instrumentation (AAMI). Make sure you can read the numbers easily. Take it to your pharmacist for instructions and inspection — make sure the bulbs, valves, and hoses aren't broken or leaking air.

- ○ Test yourself at different times of the day. Blood pressure often varies — it's often higher in the morning and lower at bedtime.

- ○ Don't smoke or drink caffeine for half an hour before testing.

- ○ Choose a comfortable chair that supports your back.

- ○ Sit quietly for about five minutes.

- ○ Rest your arm at chest level using the armrest and a pillow if necessary.

- ○ Be sure the cuff fits your arm. If it's too small you could get a false high reading, and if it's too big, a false low one.

- ○ Inflate the cuff so that it's snug, but not painful.

- ○ Don't deflate it too rapidly.

- ○ Take two readings twice a day.

- ○ Keep a record of your readings to show your doctor.

Quench your thirst without raising your pressure

It's not only what you eat, but also what you drink that can affect your blood pressure. Learn which beverages help lower blood pressure and which ones spell trouble.

Go for guava juice. This delicious tropical fruit packs more than twice the vitamin C found in an orange and is loaded with potassium. Research shows this winning combination is able to lower blood pressure several points. Vitamin C keeps your small blood vessels springy and healthy. And potassium helps your heart beat steadily.

Make room for milk. The more calcium from dairy you get, the lower your blood pressure. At least that's what researchers in Norway discovered when they studied more than 15,000 people. They found a small and largely unexplained link between drinking milk and lowering blood pressure.

Talk to your doctor before you increase your dairy. And remember the recommended amount of calcium for seniors is about 1,200 milligrams (mg) every day.

Choose low-fat dairy products to avoid damaging your arteries with saturated fat. If you don't already drink skim milk, try a glass with any meal. Just avoid high-sodium dairy drinks like chocolate shakes. A 10-ounce shake contains 273 mg of sodium. That will hurt — not help — your heart.

Fill your glass with fiber. High-fiber drinks, such as Metamucil, not only keep you regular, they help regulate your blood pressure, too.

A group of people with high blood pressure added 12 grams of psyllium — a natural plant fiber found in many remedies for constipation — to their daily diet. Their blood pressure dropped a couple of points while the group who didn't get extra fiber saw no benefit.

Those taking a protein supplement along with a high-fiber drink fared even better. Their blood pressure dropped an average of 10 points. The moral to this story — add a high-fiber drink to your daily routine, and don't skimp on the protein.

Cut back on coffee. Now there's an upscale coffeehouse on every corner, it's harder to pass up a cappuccino or latte. However, if you want to keep your blood pressure down, you've got to limit your java.

The problem is how caffeine narrows your arteries. According to research, even one cup of coffee can raise your blood pressure for up to two hours. If you already drink several cups a day, cut back gradually to avoid a withdrawal headache. And then switch to herbal tea or another decaffeinated drink.

Say no to soda. Besides all those empty calories, many sodas also contain as much as 100 mg of caffeine — about the same as a 5-ounce cup of percolated coffee.

But that's not the only problem. If you're munching salty snacks with your soda, as many people do, you're making even more trouble for your heart. Skip the soda and the salt.

Look out for licorice. Some herbal teas contain licorice for flavoring, and if it's the real thing — not its taste-cousin anise — your arteries will quake with fear.

Real licorice, containing glycyrrhizic acid, causes your body to retain sodium and fluids, and lose potassium. This double whammy raises blood pressure and puts a strain on your heart.

Most teas and candies contain artificial flavoring, but check the ingredient list before you buy.

5 drug-free ways to hold down high blood pressure

Here's one way to lower your blood pressure: Lounge on the sofa with a beloved pet at your feet. Put Frank Sinatra on the stereo and think of all you have to be thankful for.

As you can see, helping your heart doesn't have to be all work and no play. Make some pleasant lifestyle changes and watch your blood pressure drop.

Make time for music. Listening to enjoyable music can not only relax your body but lower your blood pressure, too. Try to spend time each day soaking up the sounds of your favorite tunes. Occasionally replace dinner and a movie with a concert. If the price of tickets is too daunting, check the paper for freebies. And don't forget to ask about senior discounts.

Find a furry friend. Just having a pet nearby can help keep your blood pressure down when you're stressed. And it's no wonder. Cats and dogs, especially, offer unconditional love that can buffer you and your blood pressure from the hazards of everyday life.

If you don't have a pet, try pet-sitting for a few weeks. You might discover they make great companions. Then visit your local animal shelter to adopt one of your own. Just be sure you have the resources to care for a pet before you bring one home.

Program your breathing. Take 15 minutes a day to relearn how to breathe and you could lower your blood pressure an average of 10 points.

A new device called RESPeRATE claims to be the first medical treatment approved by the Food and Drug Administration (FDA) to lower high blood pressure without drugs.

You wear a sensor belt and a headphone set connected to a small processing device. The gadget measures your breathing and emits a sound pattern that guides you to inhale and exhale at a slower, healthier rate.

Recent studies showed dramatic results. People using the device at home for 15 minutes every day for eight weeks, lowered their systolic blood pressure (the top number) an average of 15 points, and their diastolic pressure (the bottom number) an average of 10 points.

Ask your doctor about this revolutionary therapy that has no side effects. You can also get more information about the device from the Web site at www1.resperate.com, or call toll-free 877-988-9388.

Talk to someone special. Quality time with your spouse is good for your heart — perhaps because you're at ease with someone you know so well. It's even scientifically proven that interacting with your partner lowers your blood pressure.

Even after many years of marriage, make time to be together. Go out for a leisurely meal or take a stroll. Don't read the newspaper or watch television during dinner. Instead, use mealtime to discuss pleasant subjects.

If you are widowed or divorced, spend regular time with a close friend who enjoys conversation. Your life will be more enjoyable and your blood pressure could benefit as well.

Get off the warpath. Anger can send your blood pressure soaring. And if you're the type of person who is constantly wound up, even an angry memory will cause your blood pressure to climb higher and stay high longer.

Get counseling to find out why you're often angry. With help, you might be able to sort things out and say goodbye to your hostility. In the meantime, try these tips for anger management.

★ Count to 10 before you speak.

★ Put an upsetting incident in perspective. Don't ruin your health over something you won't remember next week.

★ Look for the positive. Whether it's a person or an event, there's always some redeeming quality.

★ Avoid negative people. If you surround yourself with other hostile people, you'll find more things to be angry about. Seek out people with a positive outlook on life.

Heal your heart with healthier sleep

Take a moment to examine your sleep habits. If you're like some women who can't keep their eyes open during the day, you may be 66 percent more likely to die from heart disease. Your blood pressure — even your total health — could depend on when and how well you snooze.

Be wary of nap attacks. The need to nap is not a normal part of aging. An occasional afternoon snooze doesn't always spell trouble, but if you're so sleepy during the day that it interferes with your normal routine, you're at risk of heart disease.

When you sleep, your blood pressure and heart rate drop. On the other hand, as soon as you wake up, they rise dramatically. That's why more people have heart attacks first thing in the morning. And for the same reason, a daytime nap is linked to double the risk of dying from a fatal heart attack. Don't stop taking naps, just talk to your doctor about why you need them.

Listen to your breathing. A study of over 70,000 women found that those who snored were more likely to have high blood pressure, high cholesterol, or diabetes. They were also twice as likely to die from a heart attack or stroke.

If you snore, you may have a condition called sleep apnea. This means you stop breathing many times while you sleep. As a result, you wake up often and usually feel sleepy during the day. Ask your doctor about treatment options.

Drop a dress size. Experts believe extra body weight changes how you breathe during sleep. In fact, obesity is strongly associated with sleep apnea — and sleep apnea increases your risk of heart attack, high blood pressure, stroke, and even death.

Lose even a little of that extra weight and you may sleep better and live longer.

Don't sabotage your sleep. If you're not sleeping well at night, examine your lifestyle choices. You could be affecting your shut-eye and your heart health.

Drink caffeine late in the day, and chances are you'll sleep poorly that night. It also stimulates your heart and can cause palpitations and tachycardia. If rapid heartbeat is a problem for you, it's better to stay away from caffeine. Avoid alcohol in the evening, too, which can raise blood pressure and keep you awake.

Regular, moderate exercise throughout the week will not only help you sleep better, but strengthen your heart and lower your blood pressure. Just don't get too much activity right before bedtime. Your body will be too wound up to relax.

Faith can fix a failing heart

Religious convictions keep many people on a spiritual path. But your heart also benefits when you take part in activities like church services and prayer.

If you're religious, clinical studies say you probably have lower blood pressure than other people. And, again according to research, blood pressure drops significantly after religious practices like prayer.

Stay connected with your church family especially during stressful times. St. Paul knew what he was talking about when he told the Philippians that prayer would give them peace that would guard their hearts.

High Cholesterol

4 can't-miss herbs get tough on cholesterol

You can beat high cholesterol without prescription drugs. In fact millions of people around the world do it with simple herbs.

Fight back with fenugreek. This bittersweet herb is best known as an ingredient in curry powder and chutney, but it's also used to flavor imitation maple syrup. Besides having an interesting taste, fenugreek is also a good source of fiber. This could explain its ability to reduce your cholesterol.

In one study, researchers found that about one-half teaspoon of fenugreek, taken twice a day for three months, lowered cholesterol and blood sugar levels in diabetics. Another study showed it could lower bad cholesterol and triglycerides while raising good cholesterol.

Use either whole or ground fenugreek seeds in cooking. A good place to find them is a market that specializes in Indian foods. If you have diabetes, consult with your doctor before adding fenugreek to your diet.

Let ginseng give you the edge. In the Far East, people have used this root for thousands of years to treat a variety of ailments ranging from low energy to heart problems. Ginseng contains potent chemical compounds called saponins, which can fight atherosclerosis, and sitosterol, which your intestines absorb to help lower cholesterol.

You can find the root in many grocery stores, but it's expensive. Supplements cost less, but choosing a product can be confusing. There's Siberian, American, and Korean ginseng in various strengths. Look for a reputable manufacturer with the word "standardized" on the product. Make sure it contains 4 to 7 percent ginsenosides. If you have high blood pressure or diabetes, don't take ginseng without first discussing it with your doctor.

Get good-for-you ginger. That spice you mix into cookies or your stir-fry can help your heart. Not only are you adding zest, you're also reducing your risk of blocked arteries and lowering your cholesterol by helping your body digest fat.

To get those results, however, you'd have to eat quite a few cookies and stir-fry meals. Luckily, ginger supplements come in 500-milligram capsules. A typical dose is three capsules, taken twice daily.

Ginger can increase the potency of some heart medicines, so don't combine it with any. It can also keep your blood from clotting, which is good if you're worried about cholesterol, but bad if you're planning to have surgery. As always, check with your doctor.

Hit hard with hawthorn. This member of the rose family is loaded with flavonoids, natural elements that control the amount of LDL or bad cholesterol in your body and increase the amount of HDL or good cholesterol. These flavonoids also widen blood vessels around your heart, resulting in a better supply of blood, oxygen, and nutrients.

You need a prescription for hawthorn in Europe and Asia, but in the United States, you can usually buy it wherever supplements are sold. Because the herb works slowly, it might be several weeks before you see any benefit. Large doses can be toxic, so ask your doctor before trying it.

Antioxidants A-C-E heart disease

Colorful vegetables can do more than brighten up your dinner plate. Because they're packed with antioxidants, they can also keep your cholesterol in check and generally fight heart disease.

Choose A-plus protection. Cell-damaging free radicals are constantly roaming through your heart and blood vessels. They attack LDL cholesterol and make it worse. That's bad news for your heart. But here's some good news. Vitamin A fights free radicals and minimizes their damage.

While it comes in supplements, experts say don't overdo it. Too much A and you can permanently damage your liver — even die. On the other hand, your body makes vitamin A from beta carotene. Eating lots of fresh fruits and vegetables is a nutritious way to get beta carotene in safe doses.

Compared to those who skimped on beta carotene, senior women who ate more than 15 milligrams of beta carotene a day had a 22 percent lower risk of heart attack and a 40 percent lower risk of stroke.

Eat deep orange and dark green produce like spinach, carrots, apricots, and sweet potatoes. Since vitamin A is stored in body fat, you don't have to eat these foods every day. Just be sure to include them in your diet on a regular basis.

'C' your way to a healthy heart. Like vitamin A, vitamin C helps fight free radical damage. As a bonus, it also increases your good HDL cholesterol. But that's only what it does in its spare time.

Mostly, it helps lower blood pressure and keeps small blood vessels from becoming stiff and unhealthy. Men who consumed high amounts of vitamin C cut their death rate from heart disease in half.

Because C can't be stored in body fat, you need a daily dose for maximum benefit. That's easy to do since a cup of orange juice supplies a full day's requirement. For variety, try cantaloupe, grapefruit, tomato juice, and kiwi fruit.

Ease your arteries with E. When free radicals attack LDL cholesterol, your immune system steps in and, basically, makes matters worse. White blood cells hook up with the cholesterol and create what is known as foam cells. These stick to your artery walls, making them stiff and narrow.

Luckily, vitamin E acts as an antioxidant to disable the free radicals before there's too much damage. According to a study done at Harvard School of Public Health, men who took at least 100 international units (IU) of E a day for at least two years had 37 percent fewer heart attacks. Daily vitamin E seems to protect people who already have heart disease, too.

Good food sources of E are sweet potatoes, sunflower seeds, peanuts, olive oil, canola oil, and wheat germ oil. You won't be able to eat the high amounts of vitamin E used in the studies, though. One tablespoon of canola oil, for example, only equals 2 IU of vitamin E. Talk to your doctor about supplements before you try them. Although generally considered safe, they can interfere with certain heart medications such as Coumadin.

Eat foods rich in these three basic vitamins and you'll ace heart disease now.

Cholesterol supplement ruled a drug

Most people only use yeast to make bread rise. But experts say a certain red yeast that grows on rice can lower something — your cholesterol. That's because it contains statins similar to those in cholesterol-lowering drugs.

Widespread use of the popular supplement Cholestin led the Food and Drug Administration (FDA) to examine the product and determine that its main ingredient — red yeast rice extract — should be classified as a drug and therefore could not be sold as a dietary supplement.

Red yeast rice appears to keep the liver from making as much cholesterol. But its active compound — mevinolin — is chemically identical to lovastatin, which is sold as the prescription drug Mevacor. Because of that, the FDA ruled it has the properties of a drug and needs to be regulated.

The company that makes Cholestin has removed red yeast rice from its products. You may still see Cholestin on store shelves, but it has been reformulated with plant sterols and stanols, which may also help your cholesterol level.

You should still check with your doctor before trying a supplement, and never replace a prescription medicine without his approval.

Top 10 foods to keep your arteries happy

Looking for something out of the ordinary that's heart-healthy, too? Here's a list of weird and wonderful foods that can help keep your arteries open for business.

Artichokes. The juice from this vegetable can lower cholesterol and blood fat levels as well as some prescription drugs.

Cocoa. Both cocoa powder and dark chocolate boost good cholesterol and lower bad. Try cocoa bran breakfast cereal.

Guava. Packed with soluble fiber, guava carries cholesterol out of your body.

Nuts. Grab some pecans, walnuts, and macadamias for monounsaturated fat. In addition, walnuts can thin your blood and help prevent dangerous clots.

Oranges. Eat several for cholesterol-busting fiber and for folate, which fights artery-damaging homocysteine.

Pomegranate juice. An antioxidant superstar, it can keep cholesterol from building up in your arteries.

Prunes. Eat 12 of these fiber-packed gems a day, and your cholesterol level could fall in just four weeks.

Pumpkin. Rich in beta carotene, pumpkin protects against heart attacks and pumpkin seed oil helps reduce cholesterol.

Rhubarb. This fiber-rich vegetable lowers your bad cholesterol without affecting the good.

Yogurt. Fermented milk, the basis for yogurt, may keep cholesterol from piling up in your arteries.

Veggies key to new cholesterol cure

If Bugs Bunny had to worry about LDL and HDL, he'd butter his carrots with a cholesterol-lowering spread.

Margarine substitutes, like Benecol from McNeil Consumer Products Co., are made from plant substances called stanols and sterols. They keep your body from absorbing cholesterol in your intestines. Unfortunately, they also keep your body from absorbing important fat-soluble nutrients, like beta carotene and vitamin E.

That's where Bugs Bunny's recipe comes in. Researchers say you can easily remedy the vitamin deficiency these spreads can cause by eating five or more servings of vegetables daily. Just be sure you include one food high in beta carotene such as carrots, sweet potatoes, tomatoes, apricots, spinach, or broccoli.

Here are the fast facts, good and bad, about cholesterol-lowering spreads.

* These products are most helpful for people with borderline high cholesterol (200-239 mg/dL).

* To see any benefit, you must eat about 2 grams of the spread every day for at least two years.

* You must use them to replace fats you normally eat. Otherwise you'll gain weight and cancel out any benefit.

* Don't use the spreads to replace medication.

If you don't normally eat margarine, look for the "Take Heart" line of products by Altus Foods. These include cereals, snack bars, and fruit juices — all made with plant sterols. Who would have thought you could enjoy a tasty Chocolate Chunk or Raisin Spice bar and lower your cholesterol at the same time.

Hypothermia

How to wrestle the cold — and win

Greco-Roman wrestler Rulon Gardner shocked the world by upsetting three-time Olympic champion Alexander Karelin of Russia to win the 2000 Olympic gold medal. But his toughest challenge was yet to come.

In February 2002, Gardner was stranded while snowmobiling with some friends in Wyoming. After spending 17 hours in temperatures that dipped to 25 degrees below zero, Gardner was hospitalized for hypothermia and frostbite. Eventually, he needed to have a frostbitten toe amputated. But, unlike many hypothermia victims, he survived.

Hypothermia kicks in when your body temperature drops below 95 degrees. (When he was found, Gardner's temperature was 88). It's usually associated with prolonged exposure to cold weather, like in Gardner's case. But you can also get it in 50-degree weather if it's wet and windy enough. You can even develop hypothermia indoors during the winter.

Older people who live alone are especially at risk. About half of all hypothermia-related deaths occur in people 65 or older. When you get older, you become less sensitive to cold weather and no longer shiver effectively, which is one of your body's ways to keep warm. Certain medications can also affect how your body warms itself.

Symptoms of hypothermia include confusion, low blood pressure, shallow breathing, sleepiness, slow reactions, slurred speech, and a weak heartbeat.

Top ways to respond to hypothermia

If you suspect someone you're with is suffering from hypothermia, it's no time to freeze up. Hop into action with these life-saving tips.

Call for help. Contact a doctor or a medical facility right away. Without medical attention, someone with hypothermia can develop frostbite, slip into a coma, or even die.

Warm up. Until help arrives, get the person out of the cold and out of any wet clothes. Provide dry clothing and wrap the person — including the head and neck — in warm blankets. However, do not run a warm bath. It's safer to warm up gradually.

Get cozy. You can lie close beside the person and cover both of you with thick blankets. Sharing your body heat will help.

Drink warm fluids. Soup, coffee, or tea will do the trick. But don't try to warm up with a shot of alcohol. It only speeds up the loss of body heat.

Stay awake. Talk, play music, or make noise. Whatever you do, don't let the person lose consciousness.

Follow these tips to prevent hypothermia.

★ Bundle up to go outside. Dress in layers, including a waterproof jacket. Don't forget gloves or mittens and a hat.

★ Keep your thermostat set at 70 degrees in the winter. Saving money is great, but saving your life is more important.

★ Eat and drink regularly. Don't skip meals. Your body needs fuel to stay warm. Eat hot, nutritious meals all winter.

★ Ask your doctor about your medications. Some drugs make it hard for your body to stay warm. Drugs that interfere with your body's natural heat-regulating mechanism include barbiturates, tricyclic antidepressants, and benzodiazepines.

★ Play it safe. Don't risk going outside in severe storms. Keep emergency provisions in your car during the winter.

★ Avoid alcohol and smoking. Although both make you feel warm, they actually hamper your body's ability to control your temperature.

★ Get enough sleep. If you're tired, your resistance is lower.

★ Ask a friend, relative, or neighbor to check on you during cold weather. You can return the favor. Just call or visit someone who lives alone every once in a while to make sure everything's OK.

Take these precautions, and you'll conquer the cold this winter. You won't win a gold medal for it, but beating hypothermia is still an Olympian feat.

Insomnia

Super sleep solutions

Cell phones may or may not cause brain cancer, but researchers suggest they could contribute to another health problem — insomnia. If you make late-night phone calls, you may be powering up your brain just when your body's trying to power down.

Researchers from England found that's what happened when they exposed men to cell-phone-like amounts of electromagnetic radiation for 30 minutes. Afterward, their brains kept "talking," churning out high levels of brainwave activity for up to 50 minutes.

Although experts aren't sure exactly how this affects your brain, it's probably a good idea to keep the cell phone in its charger when you get ready for your own recharging. Try talking through a headset, or use your old-fashioned home phone.

Of course, cell phones are only one obstacle to a good night's sleep. Here are some other sleep stealers along with super solutions for chasing them away.

Shake off stress. Sometimes your mind won't quiet down after your head hits the pillow even if you don't use a cell phone. It's a safe bet to assume stress is behind this kind of insomnia. That's where stress management comes into play. You can try one of the many relaxation techniques, like prayer, meditation, yoga, or tai chi. Or start at home with this simple exercise, called progressive muscle relaxation.

★ Sit in a quiet and comfortable room.

★ Pick one group of muscles, like your right leg muscles, and tense them.

★ Keep these muscles tightened for 15 seconds.

★ Relax them while exhaling.

★ Rest, choose another muscle group, and repeat.

After practicing this exercise in a chair, you'll learn how to calm all your muscles when it matters — in bed. Whether you use it or another stress reliever, you'll get the best results if you do it every day.

Scare off nightmares. You may have a bad dream you just can't shake. But if you've suffered a traumatic event, your scary dreams could be a form of sleep disorder. You may not think anything can help, but experts say your nightmares are a habit you can unlearn. While you should discuss disturbing dreams with a doctor or therapist, you can also try these five nightmare-soothing steps on your own.

★ Write down your recurring bad dream.

★ Imagine next how you want to change this dream.

★ Write down this new and improved dream.

★ Play out this new dream in your imagination for at least 15 minutes every day.

★ Repeat these steps for each of your bad dreams.

Forget trouble foods. If you've experienced heartburn or the jitters, you probably already know which foods you should not eat or drink right before bedtime. Here are the most common culprits to avoid.

★ Any type of caffeine, including coffee, tea, chocolate, or cola.

★ Spicy or super-sized suppers or late-night snacks that could bring on heartburn.

★ Sugary snacks that could "wire" you.

★ Alcohol or tobacco products.

All of these tips sound simple enough, but they still take dedication. Don't give up on your sleep problems without a fight. If these solutions don't give you relief, work with your doctor until you find ones that will.

Fight off fatigue

Your insomnia probably makes you feel tired and sluggish all day. But you don't have to be defeated by drowsiness. Try these fatigue-fighting tips to restore your energy.

Get a boost at breakfast. One bowl of high-fiber cereal could really wake you up. A Welsh study showed that eating cereal with at least 5 grams of fiber could reduce fatigue by about 10 percent. So browse the labels in your supermarket's cereal aisle, and find one in that range. Then enjoy about one cup's worth every morning for an energy boost that lasts all day.

Exercise to build energy. According to the latest research, 10 minutes of exercise may give you all the lift you need. A brief workout seems to foil fatigue by releasing chemicals in your brain that improve your mood. It may also perk you up by giving you a sense of accomplishment.

Fitness experts recommend 30 minutes of moderate activity each day, but this study shows you can break it into quick, 10-minute sessions and still benefit. Choose any activity you enjoy — walking, biking, or gardening, for instance — as long as it gets your pulse up and leaves you a little flushed.

Power up with a peppy potion. To combat sudden afternoon slumps, drink this delicious smoothie from the National Honey Board.

6 ounces frozen, concentrated orange juice

2 cups green tea

1 pint ripe strawberries

1/4 cup honey

Brew the green tea and let it cool. Meanwhile, stem and clean the strawberries. Mix the berries and the honey in a blender or food processor until they're smooth. Add the orange juice and blend well. Stir in the green tea. Serve over ice.

The honey in this recipe boosts your blood sugar gradually to help you make it through a long day. The other ingredients contain nutrients and antioxidants your body needs for peak performance. And the green tea adds a little caffeine to boot.

Find other tasty, energizing treats at the National Honey Board's Web site at <www.honey.com>.

Build good sleep habits. Nutritious food and exercise are great ways to boost your daytime energy, but you're better off preventing fatigue in the first place. Get a good night's rest with these healthy bedtime habits.

★ Quit daytime napping.

★ Save your bedroom for sleep and sex, and leave all other activities, like watching television or reading, for another room.

★ Keep your bedroom dark and quiet.

★ Relax for 30 minutes before you turn in.

★ Wear comfortable, loose clothes to sleep.

★ Get out of bed if you don't drift off after a half hour.

★ Wake up the same time every day, no matter what time you fall asleep.

Not everyone needs eight hours of slumber. But everyone feels the effects when they don't get enough sleep. This snooze "debt" adds up and wears down your body. So follow good bedtime practices, and keep your fatigue at bay.

Top anti-insomnia herbs

Whatever way you take these herbs, they'll send you to dreamland quicker than you can say "Rip Van Winkle."

Valerian. It may work as well as prescription sleep aids — without the side effects.

Chamomile. Not only does this flower fight colds, chamomile makes a great sleepy-time tea.

Lavender. Add five to 10 drops of this essential oil to a steamy bath, or burn a candle made from the oil.

Hops. Stuff hops into a sleep pillow for a quick visit with Mr. Sandman.

Lemon balm. This tasty tea is guaranteed to calm your nerves and bring on sweet sleep.

Marjoram. The same herb you use in your kitchen can work in your bedroom to bring on restful sleep.

Orange blossom. Leave a vase of these calming flowers on your nightstand.

Juniper. This tree's essential oil can calm your frazzled nerves.

California poppy. Get the power of prescription sleep aids without the prescription.

Just remember — herbs can act like drugs, so don't overdo them. And if you take antidepressants, check with your doctor first.

Wake up to the signs of sleep apnea

Eight out of 10 people with sleep apnea don't even know they have it. That's downright dangerous, considering you actually stop breathing when you have an apnea attack. Your windpipe gets blocked and you wake up gasping for air — sometimes hundreds of times a night. This start-stop breathing puts you at greater risk for stroke and heart disease.

It might not be easy to tell if you suffer from sleep apnea, but it's more likely if you're a heavy snorer. Experts have pieced together several clues to help you figure out if you have a problem.

Look for telltale sounds. One of the best ways to uncover sleep apnea is to listen for its distinctive noises. At first, an attack sounds just like the typical rattling snore. But without warning, you start to gag and choke, as you struggle to breathe. After several moments, you catch your breath and return to snoring like nothing happened. Ask your loved ones if they've heard this pattern during the night. Or, if you sleep alone, tape yourself for a few nights, and see if you hear it.

Be mindful of morning headaches. In a recent study from Dartmouth University, two-thirds of people who frequently had morning headaches also had sleep apnea. And eight out of 10 headache sufferers who also snored turned up with the sleep disorder. Sleep apnea seems to cause these headaches by cutting off oxygen to your brain, so it's important to treat the problem and get your breathing back to normal.

Keep an eye on cluster headaches. If your headaches come at night, that might be another clue, particularly if they're cluster headaches. These excruciating headaches that pierce one side of your head could be another symptom of sleep apnea's oxygen cutoff. Cluster attacks usually wake you up in the middle of the night, but they can strike in the morning, too.

Count your trips to the toilet. Stumbling to the bathroom late at night is not always a side effect of getting older. It could mean you have sleep apnea. A small study at the University of Alabama at Birmingham found a strong association between sleep apnea and nocturia, the urge to urinate at night.

Make sure it's not menopause. Twice as many postmenopausal women have sleep apnea as do premenopausal women. If you are postmenopausal and spot one of the other sleep apnea signals, you have a doubly good reason to talk with your doctor. She could recommend treatments geared just for you.

If you suspect you have sleep apnea for any of these reasons, start your recovery by trying one of these simple lifestyle changes.

★ Lose weight.

★ Avoid alcohol and other sedatives before bedtime.

★ Quit smoking.

★ Sleep on your side instead of your back.

At the same time, talk with your doctor about the best way to proceed. Since sleep apnea is a potentially dangerous condition, you may need to be tested in a sleep center for an accurate diagnosis.

Silence snoring with new treatment

You still have reason to hope even if other snoring remedies haven't worked. A new procedure called "injection snoreplasty" is less painful and expensive than other surgery. And it may work better, too.

Surgery is always a last resort, but in this case, it may be worth it. This minor operation only takes a few minutes in your doctor's office. Your doctor injects the loose muscles of your throat with a solution that causes scarring. The scarring hardens those muscles, makes them flap less, and quiets your snoring. That makes for a better night's sleep for you and everyone else within earshot.

Ask your doctor whether this procedure is an option for you.

When snoring becomes deadly

People may joke about snoring, but it's not as harmless as they think. Sleep experts know it not only causes insomnia but also may be a sign of more serious health problems, including type 2 diabetes.

Incredibly, researchers have found frequent snoring may double your risk for this serious condition.

Being overweight puts you at risk for both snoring and diabetes, so it makes sense they may be linked. A Swedish study of more than 2,500 men supported this connection. It found obese snorers were more likely to develop the disease within 10 years.

But if your weight is normal, you're still not in the clear. Data from the 25-year Nurses' Health Study suggests snorers have a higher risk of diabetes no matter how much they weigh. Researchers think you get less oxygen when you snore, triggering a chain reaction that leads to insulin resistance and, eventually, diabetes.

Snoring may lead to other major health problems as well, such as sleep apnea, high blood pressure, heart disease, and stroke. Obviously, then, it's not something to ignore. You could try fixing your problem with an over-the-counter drug or device, but why not try something natural first?

Sing in the shower. About 20 minutes of singing a day could be all it takes to cure your snoring, according to a small but innovative British study. Researchers found that daily singing exercises seem to tighten the throat muscles and reduce snoring. After three months, study participants who followed the recommended program snored less than before.

The researchers believe these exercises could silence your snoring for good and even save you from surgery. To see if you might benefit, try to create your own "throat toning" exercises, and practice them each day.

Sleep upright to fight gravity. In a study of astronauts and sleep problems, zero gravity appeared to help them breathe easier and enjoy a heavenly night's slumber. This leads researchers to believe gravity has a hand in snoring, especially when you lie on your back.

You don't have to launch yourself into orbit to benefit from this discovery. Just avoid sleeping on your back, and try to raise yourself up by propping your back or head with pillows. You can also raise the bed by putting blocks of wood under the headboard.

Get some rest with ginger. This snore-silencing remedy comes from Central America. Steep two teaspoons of grated ginger in cinnamon tea. Then add honey and milk for flavor. Drink a cup each night before you go to bed. The theory here is that ginger makes you produce more saliva, and the added moisture helps soothe your throat muscles.

Don't just roll over and close your eyes (and ears) to a snoring problem. If you and your partner suffer through nightly "buzz saw" serenades, it's time to do something about it. Talk to your doctor about other solutions before this "harmless" problem leads to a deadly disease.

Banish jet lag with the ideal meal plan

Business travelers beware — chronic jet lag may make it harder for you to remember where you left your keys. When you make long flights a regular habit, you suffer more than just the normal jet-lag grogginess. Your brain gets stressed, which, over time, affects your memory and responses. One area of your brain may even get smaller.

So say researchers who studied brain MRIs (magnetic resonance imaging) from two groups of airline flight attendants. One group rested two weeks between transatlantic flights. The other group got less than a week off. According to the findings, the flight attendants who rested least seemed to have smaller temporal lobes, the part of the brain in charge of memory. They also performed worse on memory and reaction tests. It's important to know, though, that the flight attendants flew those grueling shifts for five years or more.

Even if you only travel once in a blue moon, you may be bothered by another symptom of jet lag — indigestion. To help your system adjust, you might want to change your meal times to match your new time zone a few days before you leave. And once you arrive, try to space your meals apart the same number of hours you would at home. Keep your meals light, and always make your first meal of the day a healthy breakfast.

To help you sleep better once you get there, fill your travel diet with these snooze-friendly compounds — B vitamins, the hormone melatonin, and the amino acid tryptophan. They'll help you sleep sounder so you can wake refreshed and ready to face the world.

Here's an example of one day's menu.

* **Breakfast.** Wake up to a bowl of oatmeal, a banana, and a glass of milk. The cereal will give you a big dose of melatonin, the helpful sleep hormone. The milk's calcium and the banana's B6 help your body fill up its fuel tanks with its own supply of the hormone. With all that melatonin on standby, you'll fall fast asleep when the lights go out.

* **Lunch.** Chow down on turkey on whole wheat with a side of cottage cheese. The tryptophan in the turkey and cottage cheese, along with the carbohydrates and B vitamins in the bread, will give your body what it needs to make melatonin later.

* **Snack.** Treat yourself to dried apricots or low-fat yogurt. The niacin in apricots will keep your melatonin-manufacturing pineal gland healthy. The calcium in the yogurt will help, too.

* **Dinner.** Feast on salmon filet, a baked potato, and spinach salad. Then you'll have B vitamins, carbohydrates, and tryptophan all on one plate. Plus, the potato and the spinach are chock full of magnesium, another important weapon against jet lag.

* **Bedtime snack.** Close the day with a bowl of cherries an hour before you hit the sack. Out of all fruits, they seem to have the most melatonin.

While they will help with an upset stomach and insomnia, these foods won't save your brain from the effects of frequent flying. The best way to do that, according to researchers, is to get as much rest as possible between long flights.

Irritable Bowel Syndrome

Ease stress to calm digestion

If you are like most people with Irritable Bowel Syndrome (IBS), you've learned to control your symptoms with diet. What you may not know is that your colon, which is part of your large intestine, is partially controlled by your nervous system. In fact, doctors once thought IBS was a psychological condition because they couldn't find anything physically wrong with the colon.

When you have IBS, your colon is oversensitive to triggers — ranging from pockets of gas to medication, hormones, and even chocolate. These triggers stimulate the smooth muscles lining your intestines, causing them to contract sharply resulting in painful cramping, bloating, diarrhea, constipation, and gas.

One thing is certain — stress makes IBS worse. If you can control stress in your life, chances are your digestive system will settle down. Try these simple coping skills to minimize tension.

Read all about it. Learn everything you can about IBS. Consider joining a support group. Knowing your options will help give you peace of mind that can calm your digestive system.

Write it down. Keep a diary of everything you eat and how it makes you feel. After a few days, you will be able to pinpoint problem foods and avoid these triggers.

Practice problem solving. If you detect a recurring pattern in your diary that ends in pain, come up with a plan of action to root out the source. If you are uncomfortable after eating high-calorie, high-fat meals, switch from meat and dairy to vegetables and rice.

Make your voice heard. You might be stressed because you have trouble speaking up, expressing anger, or voicing a preference. If so, take a course in assertiveness. A trained counselor can help you speak openly about your condition and defuse stress.

Prioritize your activities. Sometimes squeezing too much into your day can be overwhelming. Make a list of your daily tasks. Rate how important each activity is. Do only those things you rate highly, and don't feel guilty about the rest.

Eat by the clock. Eat modest meals at set times. Big meals can cause cramping and diarrhea. Try smaller portions, more frequently, to regulate your digestive system.

Catch up on Zs. Sometimes you don't feel rested even after sleeping for eight hours. As if that's not enough, a restless night can cause your IBS to flare up the following day. To improve the quality of your sleep, many doctors recommend going to bed and waking up at the same time every day.

Take in some air. Breathe in deeply through your nose. Fill your lungs with air until your abdomen pushes out. Slowly exhale. Deep breathing can slow your heartbeat and relax your abdominal muscles.

Listen to your body. You can teach yourself to control your gut reactions using biofeedback. First, you'll need to find a trained professional to teach you what to do and to hook you up to the appropriate monitor. This will track your body's response to various conditions. Notice what makes you relax so you can reproduce this response at home.

Relax your muscles. Try this simple exercise to discover how much stress is trapped in your body. Tighten and hold a group of muscles, like your neck and shoulder muscles, for about 15 seconds. Now relax them as much as you can. Notice the difference between this relaxed state and the way you usually hold yourself. Continue tightening and releasing other muscle groups until you have relaxed your entire body. Once you learn how to relax, you'll find it easier to detect tension and deal with it.

Tap into touch. A soothing massage can rub the tension right out of your muscles. Like massage, acupuncture can relax your muscles and may offer IBS relief. Some people report that acupuncture lessened their muscle spasms and helped regulate their bowel movements. Check your telephone directory or the Internet to find certified practitioners in your area.

Although IBS is a chronic condition, it won't damage your digestive system. You'll also be glad to know you are not at high risk for intestinal bleeding or colorectal cancer.

Extinguish gas with simple changes

Everybody breaks wind occasionally, but if passing gas gets painful, it's time to take action. You can eliminate this ill wind, and the bloating that comes with it, by making a few changes to your diet and lifestyle.

The main cause of gas is swallowed air. You suck it in when you chew, smoke, gulp, and even sigh. The air you swallow mixes with the gasses your stomach produces while it digests food. All this air has to escape with the rest of your waste.

Normally, gas is nothing but a minor embarrassment. But if you have Irritable Bowel Syndrome (IBS), any little pocket of gas can cause severe pain in your colon.

The good news is you can control your gas by making these simple changes:

Throw out the clock. Don't rush through your meal — eat slowly and chew carefully. Not only will you swallow less air, you will also curb stress, an underlying cause of IBS.

Pass on the meat. If you eat a diet rich in fat, you may want to cut back. Fat triggers contractions in your colon while it's being digested. You also digest it slowly, which can make you feel painfully bloated. Eat less meat and other high-fat foods and more fruits and vegetables to keep your digestive system running smoothly.

Downplay dairy. If you notice milk products bring on gas, you may be lactose intolerant. This means you don't have enough lactase, an enzyme normally found in the small intestine. It's needed to digest lactose, the sugar in milk and other dairy products. Many health professionals suggest eating yogurt with live cultures to help you digest lactose.

Choose solid over airy. Stay away from foods with air whipped into them, like soufflés, milkshakes, whipped cream, carbonated drinks, and whipped butter and yogurt.

Be wary of sugar free. Read labels and avoid foods with the artificial sweeteners sorbitol or mannitol. Your gut may not be able to process these products, and they can give you gas.

Shun gassy veggies. Avoid gas-producing foods, like cabbage, broccoli, and legumes. These vegetables aren't completely processed until they reach your colon, where they ferment. If you can't kiss your beans goodbye, eat them with a product called Beano, which cuts down on gas.

Add fiber slowly. Fiber does wonders for your digestive system by helping move waste along. But too much fiber, too fast, can produce excessive gas. If you are beefing up on fiber, make sure you do it gradually, over the space of a few weeks. And to help fiber do its job, make sure you are drinking enough water — at least six to eight glasses a day.

Exercise, exercise, exercise. Moving your body speeds up digestion and helps gas pass quickly through your digestive system. It can also strengthen your abdominal muscles to ease bloating.

If you are worried about passing gas in public, keep in mind that the average person breaks wind 12 or more times a day. So unless your gas is causing you discomfort, don't worry about it. It's a normal byproduct of life.

10 ways to make peace with your colon

★ Start your day with a steaming cup of herbal tea instead of coffee.

★ Choose honey over artificial sweeteners. Honey helps clear up constipation and diarrhea.

★ Crunch down on a bowl of multi-grain cereal with raspberries. Both are full of fiber.

★ Try a flaxseed muffin or add flaxseed or wheat germ to your cereal for more fiber.

★ Snack on an apple. It's a rich source of pectin, a type of fiber.

★ Forget soft drinks. Drink at least eight to 10 glasses of water every day to keep your digestive tract running smoothly.

★ Ask for whole wheat bread instead of white. Breads should be rich in fiber, not air.

★ Add fiber-rich beans to your salads and soups.

★ Trade high-fat meals for delicious entrees loaded with vegetables and brown rice.

★ Eat fruit with every meal. A delicious fruit salad is a great way to add fruit to your diet.

Tropical cure for diarrhea

Hit the produce section next time you get diarrhea. A green cooking banana, native to Africa and Asia, can regulate your bowel movements in just days.

One to two green cooking bananas, boiled in water and mixed with rice flour, helped children conquer persistent diarrhea in less than a week. Without this tropical aid, the children took three-and-a-half weeks to recover. That's because bananas are a rich source of a soluble fiber called pectin, which firms your stool.

Normally, food passes through your digestive tract in liquid form, eventually reaching your colon where the water and nutrients are absorbed. If the lining of your digestive tract is infected with unfriendly bacteria, viruses, or parasites, your food travels too quickly through your colon and remains watery.

Just like it does in gelatin and jelly, pectin absorbs water and congeals. It hardens your stool enough to slow it down so you can absorb more nutrients.

To try this remedy for yourself, pick up some green cooking bananas in the imported fruit section of your local grocery store. You can cook them either in their skin or without it. Cut the fruit into chunks and drop them in a pot of boiling water. Cook them until they turn yellow, about seven to 10 minutes. Mash the cooked banana and serve it warm over rice.

It's not surprising that green bananas mixed with rice can help you fight diarrhea. A similar remedy — the BRAT diet — is often recommended to ease your transition back onto solid food. This combination of Bananas, Rice, Applesauce, and Toast is rich in fiber but gentle and bland enough to pass through your weakened digestive tract without stirring it up.

To help keep your intestines running smoothly, work pectin-rich apples, bananas, citrus fruits, and strawberries into your diet.

Although diarrhea is a common symptom of IBS, if you have persistent cramping, bloody stool, or a low-grade fever, see your doctor to rule out a more serious condition.

Tip your cup to natural remedies

You can soothe the discomfort of IBS with one of these natural remedies:

★ **Peppermint.** By far the most effective, this mint can relax the smooth muscles lining your intestines. To make a strong tea, pour two-thirds of a cup of boiling water over two table-spoons of freshly dried peppermint leaves. Let it steep for about five to six minutes and strain. You can also take enteric-coated capsules half an hour before eating. Don't try this with small children. The strong scent can make them gag.

★ **Chamomile.** Like peppermint, chamomile tea soothes muscle spasms. Drink freshly brewed tea three to four times a day for fast relief. Use dried flower heads or buy extracts from rep-utable companies for best results. If you have allergies to rag-weed or daisies, try peppermint instead.

★ **Ginger.** For cramping and indigestion, add fresh ginger to your diet. You can eat it raw, candied, or make a tea. Just steep two teaspoons of grated root in boiling water for about 10 minutes. Strain and sip slowly.

Other herbs that may help IBS are anise seed, caraway, fennel, and coriander.

Kidney
Stones

Destroy kidney stones with diet

Eating the right foods may keep you from experiencing the excruciating pain of kidney stones. The wrong foods, on the other hand, could put you more at risk.

Imagine having a golf ball stuck in your kidney, and you'll get an idea of the seriousness of this condition. Kidney stones form when certain compounds, like calcium, oxalate, and uric acid, collect in your urine. Normally, these substances simply pass through your body. But, in some people, they harden into crystals of all shapes and sizes, some as large as golf balls.

Small stones may cause no symptoms, but others could bring on sharp pains in your back or side. Your urine may become bloody, smelly, or cloudy. You could also have fever, chills, vomiting, and a burning feeling during urination. If you experience these symptoms, you need to see your doctor immediately.

Once you suffer through one kidney stone, you're more likely to have another. That's why prevention is so important. By swapping the dangerous foods in your diet for kidney-friendly foods, you'll help fight off this potentially painful condition.

Kidney foe	Negative effect	Kidney friend
Animal protein • meat • fish • poultry	• increases calcium in urine • decreases citrate, an anti-stone compound • boosts uric acid levels	Plant protein • bulgur • barley • rice • beans
Salt	• increases calcium in urine • decreases citrate	• herbs • lemon juice
Calcium supplements	• increase oxalate levels	Calcium-rich foods • low-fat dairy foods • sardines • fortified juice

Last but not least, load your diet with foods high in magnesium, potassium, and vitamin B6. Both magnesium and B6 help your body control its oxalate levels, while potassium decreases the amount of calcium in your urine. That means they lower your risk of a stone.

So feast on bananas, avocados, beans, potatoes, prunes, figs, and broccoli. They're all packed with these three kidney-caring nutrients. By treating your body with the right foods, you'll have one less painful condition to worry about.

Fight kidney stones in your sleep

Nighttime may be the most dangerous time of the day for your kidneys, according to a recent study. It's when your urine is the most concentrated so you're more at risk to develop kidney stones. You're also more likely to wake up with renal colic, the excruciating back pain caused by stones.

So don't take the night off from kidney stone prevention. Instead, follow these bedtime habits.

Load up on liquids. To prevent renal colic and new stones, fill up on water before you hit the hay. And start sipping again as soon as you wake up. Drink as much as three to four quarts of fluids throughout the day — more if it's hot outside, or if you exercise.

Water dilutes your urine and prevents crystals from building up. You'll know it's working when your urine becomes nearly clear.

Include other stone-stifling liquids in your menu, too, like coffee and lemonade. Coffee waters down your urine and flushes your kidneys before stones can form. Lemonade is high in citric acid, which will help your body dissolve kidney stones.

Meanwhile, stay away from grapefruit and apple juice. They seem to increase your risk of kidney stones.

Roll away from a stone. Protecting your kidneys from stones may be as easy as turning over in bed. Recent research shows people with stones in their left kidney tend to sleep on their left side, and vice versa. This pattern appears to happen because the kidney in question gets less blood. That makes it harder to filter out harmful substances.

So roll over if you always sleep in the same position. Try sewing a tennis ball in the side of your pajamas to help you remember. This old trick works for snoring, and it may banish kidney stones, too.

Popular painkillers may damage your kidneys

Your kidneys may not be able to handle your daily dose of acetaminophen and aspirin. These analgesics ease the pain of chronic conditions like headaches and arthritis. But they also seem to increase your risk of kidney failure if you take them every day.

Your kidneys clean your blood of waste chemicals, including painkillers. Over time, these drugs can wear down your kidneys. The organs lose the power to filter your blood. They never recover from this kidney failure, and you need dialysis or a kidney transplant to survive.

Experts used to believe only blended analgesics were to blame. These drugs are usually a mixture of aspirin, acetaminophen, and caffeine. However, aspirin and acetaminophen appear to be harmful by themselves, too, according to a study in *The New England Journal of Medicine.*

The research shows you may have five times the risk of kidney failure if you take about 1.5 grams of acetaminophen a day. The same amount of aspirin seems to triple your risk. That's an extremely high dosage, so it may not apply to your situation. Still, if you use these painkillers on a regular basis, talk with your doctor. She may want to check you for kidney damage and possibly recommend a more kidney-kind analgesic.

Top kidney enemies

Stay away from soy if you're prone to kidney stones. It's loaded with oxalate, a plant compound that's a major building block for those painful crystals. Play it safe and avoid soy milk, tofu, miso, tempeh, and other soy products. And pass up these other oxalate sources, too.

- Spinach
- Rhubarb
- Beets
- Nuts
- Chocolate
- Tea
- Wheat bran
- Strawberries

The list may include some of your favorite treats, but if you're prone to stones, you'll be happier without them.

Lyme Disease

Take aim at Lyme disease

If you're looking for a bull's-eye to identify Lyme disease, you might be off the mark.

New research contradicts conventional wisdom about one of the classic telltale signs of Lyme disease — a spreading rash shaped like a bull's-eye, red on the outside and pale in the center.

In a study conducted by the Maine Medical Center Research Institute, only 9 percent of people who got Lyme disease had a bull's-eye rash. By contrast, 59 percent had uniformly red rashes, while 32 percent had red rashes that were a darker shade of red in the center.

The people in the study were on the lookout for any early sign of Lyme disease, so it's possible their rashes just didn't have time to develop the classic pattern. Even so, it might be a good idea to look for any type of rash — not just one shaped like a bull's-eye.

Here are some other tips for identifying and dealing with Lyme disease.

Know your enemy. Named for Lyme, Connecticut, where the disease was originally described, Lyme disease is spread by deer ticks carrying the bacterium *Borrelia burgdorferi*.

Your risk varies depending on where you live and the time of year. While Lyme disease has surfaced in nearly every state, you're far more

---

Top tips to thwart ticks

The best way to prevent Lyme disease is to avoid ticks. Here's how.

Cover up. Wear long pants and sleeves. Tuck your shirt into your pants and pull your socks over your pant legs to seal off as much of your skin as possible. If you have long hair, pull it back. And wear a hat.

Spray it on. Apply an insect repellent to your clothes and exposed skin. Look for brands containing DEET.

Play it safe. Walk in the center of trails to avoid brushing up against shrubbery. Don't sit on the ground.

Protect your property. Put up fencing to keep deer out. Get rid of brush, trees, leaves, and woodpiles — all good hiding spots for ticks.

Protect your pets. Talk to your vet about how to keep ticks off your cats and dogs. Although they don't transmit Lyme disease to people, house pets bring ticks within biting distance of you.

Be alert. Check for ticks often. Wear light-colored clothing so you can spot them easily.

Remove them right away. If you find a tick attached to your skin, don't panic. Gently pull it out with tweezers, grasping it close to the head. Then swab the bite area with an antiseptic.

---

likely to encounter it in the Northeast, upper Midwest, and the Pacific coast. High-risk months are May through October.

Even if an infected tick bites you, chances are you won't get Lyme disease. A tick must be attached to your skin for at least 24 hours to transmit the disease.

Recognize the symptoms. Besides a rash, other early signs of Lyme disease include fever, headache, a stiff neck, chills, weakness, fatigue, and muscle aches. Later symptoms include severe headaches, chronic arthritis, and joint swelling — even heart problems and mental disorders.

Act quickly. Prompt treatment is key. If you suspect you may have been infected, see your doctor right away. He can run blood tests to determine if you need antibiotics. Early antibiotic treatment helps tremendously and prevents painful arthritis symptoms later on.

Get vaccinated. The FDA recently approved a vaccine that can reduce your chances of getting Lyme disease by about 80 percent. If you're between the ages of 15 and 70, live in a high-risk area, and spend a lot of time outdoors, this might be a good option. Ask your doctor about this new preventive measure.

Watch for symptoms of Lyme disease, see a doctor if you think you've been infected, and protect yourself with a vaccine. It's a simple strategy that's right on target.

Macular Degeneration

Attack AMD with antioxidants

Bugs Bunny enjoys chomping on carrots. He also doesn't need glasses. Coincidence? Doubtful.

Carrots are chock full of beta carotene, which your body changes to vitamin A. Antioxidants like vitamin A help get rid of dangerous free radicals that can damage the retina in your eye.

Scientists have long suspected antioxidants help protect your eyes from age-related macular degeneration (AMD). Now there's new proof — and new hope for people who already have the condition.

Fill up on antioxidants. Although it's best to get your nutrients from whole foods, you may need supplements to get enough helpful antioxidants to combat AMD. The National Eye Institute's Age-Related Eye Disease Study (AREDS) recently showed that high doses of antioxidant vitamins plus zinc helped slow down AMD before it reached an advanced stage.

Each day, people in the six-year study took 500 milligrams (mg) of vitamin C, 400 international units (IU) of vitamin E, 15 mg of beta carotene, and 80 mg of zinc. Those with intermediate macular degeneration who supplemented their diet this way lowered their risk for advanced AMD by 25 percent. They also slashed their risk of vision loss by 19 percent.

"The nutrients are not a cure for AMD, nor will they restore vision already lost from the disease," says Dr. Paul Sieving, director of the National Eye Institute. "But they will play a key role in helping people at high risk for developing advanced AMD keep their vision."

The doses used in the study were very high, so be careful about taking those amounts yourself. As always, talk to your doctor before trying any supplements.

Binge on bright-colored veggies. Your diet may not provide megadoses of antioxidants, but it can still offer some help in the fight against macular degeneration.

Several previous studies have found links between AMD and antioxidants in foods. One group of antioxidants — carotenoids — seems especially important. Carotenoids like beta carotene give fruits and vegetables their bright colors. In one study, people who ate the most carotenoids were 43 percent less likely to develop macular degeneration than those who ate the least.

Beta carotene, although the most famous carotenoid, may not be the best for protecting against AMD. Two others, lutein and zeaxanthin, seem to help the most. They are highly concentrated in your retina, where they fight cell damage caused by ultraviolet light and free radicals. Foods containing large amounts of these important carotenoids include spinach, kale, turnip or collard greens, broccoli, zucchini, corn, peas, and brussels sprouts.

Dark, leafy greens are also good ways to get vitamin C and vitamin E into your diet. For other sources of vitamin C, choose red or green peppers or citrus fruits. Vitamin E is also found in nuts, seeds, wheat germ, and vegetable oils. Look for beta carotene in sweet potatoes, cantaloupes, pumpkins — and, of course, carrots.

Eat the right fat to save your sight

Eating too much fat puts you at risk for all sorts of health problems, including heart disease, diabetes, and cancer. But your eyes are safe,

A-plus way to protect your eyes

When it comes to helping your vision, vitamin A gets an A-plus. In fact, if you don't get enough of this important vitamin, you can go blind.

Because it acts as an antioxidant, vitamin A shields your retina from free radical damage that can lead to macular degeneration. It also fights cataracts, night blindness, and other vision problems.

But that's not all vitamin A does. Its antioxidant powers make it a valuable weapon against cancer and heart disease. It helps control your insulin levels if you have diabetes, protects you from ulcers, and guards your mental abilities as you age.

Folks over 55 have two more reasons to take this potent vitamin. It boosts your immune system and counteracts damage to your liver and muscles caused by years of heavy drinking.

Don't go overboard on vitamin A, though. Too much can be toxic. It's probably not a good idea to take supplements, especially when you can get plenty of vitamin A through your diet.

Good natural sources of vitamin A include liver, eggs, milk, and other dairy products. You can also get carotenoids, which your body converts to vitamin A, from fruits and vegetables. Look for dark green or bright orange produce.

---

right? Fat chance. Because it clogs up the blood vessels in your eyes, fat can lead to vision loss through a disease called macular degeneration.

With macular degeneration, you lose your central vision — the kind you need for driving, reading, and seeing objects clearly. Also called age-related macular degeneration (AMD) or age-related maculopathy (ARM), it's the leading cause of blindness in people 65 and older.

Obviously, this condition is not something to take lightly. But you can help protect your eyes by changing what you eat. Read on to discover which fats do the most damage — and how to defend your vision.

Sidestep snacks. While the amount of fat you eat certainly affects your health, the type of fat you eat might make an even bigger difference.

You probably think saturated fat causes the most trouble because it raises cholesterol and clogs blood vessels. And you're right, studies have linked saturated fat — found in meat and dairy foods — and macular degeneration.

But other fats might be to blame as well, say researchers at the Massachusetts Eye and Ear Infirmary in Boston. They recently discovered that vegetable, polyunsaturated, and even heart-healthy monounsaturated fats all increase the risk of macular degeneration. Linoleic acid, an omega-6 fatty acid found in vegetable oils, had the same effect in their study.

Your best defense is to cut down on processed foods, which contain these types of fats. Some of the worst offenders include potato chips, cookies, chocolate, and French fries. If you need a snack, you're better off grabbing a piece of fruit.

Go fishing. Feeling glum? Rejoice — not all fat is bad. Omega-3 fatty acids, the kind found in fish, may actually help lower your risk for macular degeneration.

That's because a certain omega-3 fatty acid in fish called docosahexaenoic acid (DHA) also appears in the retina, the part of your eye affected by macular degeneration. Eating fish may help repair damage there. Fish may also help by keeping your arteries clean.

Several studies have examined the power of fish. One study found that eating more fish — particularly tuna — significantly lowers your risk for macular degeneration. In fact, eating more than four servings of fish each week gives you a 35 percent lower risk compared to eating three or fewer servings of fish a month. Another study found that eating fish once a week provided the most protection, but even a monthly fish dinner offered some help.

In the Massachusetts Eye and Ear study, fish and omega-3 fatty acids seemed to lower your risk for macular degeneration, but only if your diet does not include much linoleic acid. So put away the margarine, the corn oil, and soybean oil, and start eating more fish. Fatty fish like salmon, mackerel, herring, and tuna offer the most omega-3, but all seafood contains some.

If you can't stand fish, try getting your omega-3 through flaxseed, walnuts, and mustard, turnip, or collard greens. Dark green leafy vegetables like spinach, Swiss chard, arugula, and kale also give you some omega-3.

Take your medicine. If you're already battling high cholesterol by taking statins, you may be battling macular degeneration, too. In a British study, people taking these prescription drugs were 11 times less likely to have age-related macular degeneration. Statins may protect against macular degeneration because of their anti-cholesterol or antioxidant powers.

You don't need to start taking statins to defend your vision, but ask your doctor about them if you're worried about your cholesterol levels. You may end up helping your eyes as well.

Watch your weight. Being too fat is bad for your eyes — but so is being too lean. Researchers at Boston's Brigham and Women's Hospital found obese men were twice as likely to develop macular degeneration — but the leanest men also had a 43 percent greater risk.

They have no explanation yet for this surprising result, but in the meantime, don't put on weight just to avoid macular degeneration. There are too many health benefits to staying slim.

7 top tips to prevent macular degeneration

Improve your eyesight without glasses — and without contact lenses, surgery, drugs, or medicine of any kind. Just take these simple steps to avoid eye problems.

Serve spinach. Eat this green, leafy vegetable four to seven times a week, and you may improve your vision. That's because it's packed with the carotenoids lutein and zeaxanthin.

Wear shades. Exposure to sunlight creates free radicals that can damage your eyes. Sunglasses are a stylish way to protect your vision.

Start your day with some OJ. Orange juice gives you a good dose of vitamin C, an antioxidant that helps protect your eyes from harmful free radicals.

Feast on fish. Because of its omega-3 fatty acids, fish can be a valuable — and tasty — weapon against AMD.

Propose a toast. Drinking an occasional glass of red wine — even once a month — can help lower your risk for macular degeneration.

Get some ginkgo. This versatile herb probably helps fight AMD because of its antioxidant effect.

Kick the habit. Smoking increases your risk for AMD — not to mention a long list of other health problems ...

Menopause

Be cautious of hormone therapy

It's true that hormones can help relieve symptoms of menopause — hot flashes, dry skin, and fatigue — but at what cost? Hormone replacement therapy (HRT) has come under fire lately for some worrisome side effects. In fact, researchers stopped a large HRT study because they were concerned about health risks. Five years into the study, they were startled to see a significant increase in heart disease risk as well as invasive breast cancer. Their research showed: (bullets)

★ A 26 percent rise in breast cancer

★ 22 percent more cardiovascular disease

★ A 29 percent increase in heart attacks

★ A 41 percent jump in stroke

★ Twice the rate of blood clots

That translates into seven to eight more cancer or heart disease cases per 10,000 HRT users each year. That may not seem like a lot, but when you look at the population as a whole, it could mean thousands more health problems over time.

The Food and Drug Administration (FDA) now advises doctors to prescribe estrogen only when benefits clearly outweigh the risks, just long enough for successful treatment, and at the lowest effective dose. If you are considering taking estrogen, be sure you discuss the risks with your doctor first.

First-rate fixes for frustrating flashes

Many menopausal women can have hot flashes for up to five years. Fortunately, there are natural ways to cool down your "power surges."

Breathe into your belly. Experts say slow, calming breaths — so deep they push your stomach out — can cut your hot flashes in half.

Eat to lower the heat. Choose foods high in calcium, like yogurt, cheese, and spinach. And get vitamin E from nuts, seeds, canola oil, and avocados. Just stay away from spicy-hot and salty foods.

Sip something cold. Pour a tall glass of iced tea, or simply hold ice cubes in your mouth. But say no to coffee and alcohol. They can bring on flushes or make them worse.

Try an herbal remedy. Black cohosh, a traditional Native American cure, reduces levels of a hormone that causes hot flashes. You'll find capsules in health food stores. Just don't take this herb for more than six months.

Put out the fire. Take cool baths and showers. And stay out of saunas.

Slow down your pace. Do lighter workouts. Just do them more often.

Some experts suggest a natural eating plan may help you survive menopause and control the related risks of heart disease, osteoporosis, and cancer. That means you should make a nutritious diet your first line of defense. Lifestyle changes — such as a high-fiber, low-fat diet rich in antioxidants — may help lower menopause risks and symptoms, suggests the American Academy of Family Physicians.

Generally, focus on foods that come from plants. Many contain substances that may help regulate hormones. And you'll be less likely to add weight at the waist — a common complaint with menopause.

Choose whole grains. Rich in hormone regulators and nutrition, whole grains include oats, whole wheat, rye, millet, barley, and corn. Read nutrition labels on breads and cereals to make the healthiest purchase.

Add vitamin A. During menopause, vitamin A can help counteract dry skin and fight bothersome yeast infections. Also a powerful antioxidant, it helps prevent cancer. You get it naturally in the form of beta carotene in foods. Dark green and yellow-orange vegetables are good sources.

Count on calcium. Even though one study suggests bone loss can reach 1 percent per year during menopause, getting more calcium may fight this. Remember, you also need vitamin D because it plays an important role in how much calcium your bones actually absorb. Pour some low-fat or nonfat milk on vitamin-D-fortified cereal for a double dose of protection.

Depend on E. Vitamin E can reduce hot flashes and keep your skin soft and younger looking. If you drink lots of water while loading up on E, you might ease vaginal dryness, too. Add E to your diet with nuts, seeds, avocados, canola oil, and low-fat creamy salad dressings.

Build up your Bs. Vitamins B2, B6, and B12 are water-soluble vitamins your body flushes out daily. That means you need to replace them often. They help you turn food into energy; fight migraines, osteoporosis, and depression; and keep your heart healthy. Eat liver, mushrooms, whole grains, bananas, nuts, seeds, eggs, fish, and cauliflower.

Opt for healthy oils. Include extra-virgin olive oil in your diet. Snub hydrogenated oils, partially hydrogenated oils, and trans fatty acids, such as those in margarine. If a food includes a partially or fully hydrogenated oil in its label, try to find a substitute.

With this healthy arsenal of nutrition, you can minimize menopause symptoms now while building a healthier body for the years to come.

Migraines

Track down triggers for migraine relief

Your trip to the amusement park has been fun — until your grand-kids beg you to join them on the roller coaster.

If you accept their challenge, consider yourself lucky if you get off the ride only feeling a bit wobbly. With all the jostling and jarring your head went through during the ride, you could have ended up with a migraine.

You know the pain — it usually starts on one side of your head, but can spread to include your whole head. Light and sound bother you, and you might feel dizzy and sick to your stomach. With a migraine, you could be out of commission for days.

If you're a migraine sufferer, you have a particularly sensitive nervous system. Certain circumstances, or triggers, can spark your agony. Riding a roller coaster is one of the more unusual ones, but there are many. Here are some ways to avoid the most common triggers.

Edit your diet. Did you ever eat ice cream too fast and feel a sharp pain in the middle of your forehead? If you're a woman who gets migraines, you're twice as likely as other women to experience this "head freeze." Anything cold that hits the roof of your mouth could set off a migraine.

Experts believe specific foods trigger at least 30 percent of all migraines. While different foods may trigger migraines for different people, here are some items that may cause you pain.

- ★ Cheese
- ★ Chocolate
- ★ Red wine
- ★ Peanuts
- ★ Caffeine
- ★ Citrus fruits
- ★ Pizza
- ★ Pickles
- ★ Hot dogs
- ★ Avocados
- ★ Bacon
- ★ Bananas

It's unlikely that all these will give you a migraine. To find out what foods affect you, keep a headache diary. Track what you eat each day and note when you get headaches. You'll be able to detect patterns. For example, if you get a headache every time you eat a chocolate bar, you might have to give up that sweet treat.

Change your lifestyle. You have more control over migraines than you think. Besides a woman's hormonal changes during her period or around menopause, you can avoid most triggers. Minimize your migraines by watching out for the following lifestyle factors.

- ★ Stress at work or at home
- ★ Too much or too little sleep
- ★ Fasting or missing a meal
- ★ Overdoing it — especially on a hot day or when you're out of shape

It's easy to counter these triggers. Begin by sticking to a regular sleep schedule — go to bed and wake up at the same time every day. Eat regular meals, exercise often, and either avoid stressful situations or learn to cope with them.

Alter your environment. A vacationing medical professor recently shared an odd story. His wife was suffering from a migraine during a tour of Europe. As they entered a subway station, they were mugged. The professor lost his wallet, cash, and credit cards. The wife, however, miraculously lost her migraine.

This is an unusual example of how the environment can help your migraine. Normally, it works the other way around. Factors in the world around you are more likely to trigger head pain. Keep an eye out for these:

★ Weather changes, such as extreme heat or cold

★ Bright office lighting

★ Smog

★ Perfume

★ Flashing lights

Just as with food triggers, a headache diary can help track environmental factors. All it takes is some careful observation. Once you pinpoint your triggers, make an effort to avoid or minimize them.

Trim the fat to prevent migraines

You might be watching your fat grams to look better, feel better, and live longer. Now there's another good-for-you reason to keep reading those nutrition labels — fewer migraines.

When you eat a low-fat diet, you not only cut down on the number of migraines you get, but you can have shorter and less painful headaches, too. That means less medication.

Researchers at the University of California at Irvine tracked the diets of 42 women and 12 men with migraines. Their findings could change your life.

Halt headaches. During the first month of the study, they all stuck to their usual eating pattern. Those who ate fewer than 69 grams of fat a day suffered, on average, five migraines. Those who ate more fat had twice that many migraines.

When they limited their fat to 20 grams a day — equal to one McDonald's Quarter Pounder — everyone had fewer migraines.

Not surprisingly, they also lost weight, lowered their percentage of body fat, and slashed their cholesterol.

Make smart substitutions. You don't have to turn into Jack Sprat, but a low-fat diet might be worth a try. Even if you can't get down to 20 grams a day, cut some fat and leave those migraines behind.

Here are some easy ways to shave fat grams during a typical day.

★ Use a cup of skim milk instead of whole milk on your breakfast cereal and you'll slash 8 grams of fat from your morning meal.

★ Instead of a double-bacon cheeseburger, fries, and a shake for lunch, eat a turkey sandwich on whole-wheat bread, skim milk, and an apple. You just cut your fat intake by nearly 60 grams.

★ For dinner, a batter-dipped fried chicken breast might sound yummy, but a skinned and roasted chicken breast has 31 fewer grams of fat.

In general, aim for more fruits, vegetables, and legumes and less meat, cheese, and chocolate.

When cooking, steam, poach, roast, broil, grill, or microwave your food rather than sauté or pan-fry it. Use herbs, spices, and chicken broth for flavor instead of butter and sauces.

Get the big picture. Experts believe migraines are just a signal that you have a type of imbalance going on in your body.

High levels of blood lipids — or fats — along with free fatty acids in your blood lead to changes in your body that cause your blood vessels to dilate. This change in blood flow contributes to migraines. Researchers think reducing dietary fat could help reduce migraines.

While this theory seems sound, keep in mind that other factors might be involved. When the people in the study changed their diet, they didn't only eat less fat. They also consumed different nutrients, while eating fewer calories. So fat might not be the only thing affecting their headaches.

It's still a good, healthy strategy — for your head and the rest of your body — to trim some fat from your diet.

Top foods that give head pain the heave-ho

Certain foods can trigger migraines, but others might actually help fight them. Add these items to your regular menu, and maybe you'll subtract migraines from your life.

Spinach. If you get migraines, chances are you have lower magnesium levels than others. Give yourself a magnesium boost with Popeye's favorite vegetable.

Milk. Calcium and vitamin D help premenstrual and post-menopausal women fight migraine pain. Get both with a glass of vitamin D-fortified milk.

Mushrooms. Cook some shiitake, portobello, or plain old button mushrooms and reap the benefits of riboflavin. This nutrient is just as effective as aspirin in relieving headache pain. However, the best source of this B vitamin is beef liver.

Salmon. Fatty fish like salmon provide plenty of omega-3 fatty acids, which fight inflammation that can lead to headaches.

Ginger. This spice wards off nausea and may also help erase migraine pain. Sip a soothing cup of ginger tea or add fresh ginger to your favorite recipes.

Green apples. The scent of green apples sometimes helps lessen the pain of a migraine. Plus, apples are an all-around healthy food.

Osteoarthritis

Stand up to knee pain

Your achy, arthritic knees need tender loving care. But turning into a couch potato is the worst thing you can do. Instead, here's your line of attack against osteoarthritis.

Keep moving. Fight the urge to sit still because your knees hurt. Experts say exercise can ultimately reduce your pain and improve movement. If you get the thumbs up from your doctor, choose gentle, aerobic exercise such as swimming, brisk walking, raking leaves, and playing golf. Try to vary your activities throughout the week so you don't get bored or overwork the same joints.

Slowly work up to 20 minutes per day three or four days a week. Less than that could mean you're not getting enough exercise — more could mean you're overdoing it.

Get strong. Want healthier knees? Then strengthen the muscles around them. You can slash your risk of OA of the knee by 20 to 30 percent just by increasing the strength of your leg muscles. Practice these exercises three to five times a day if your doctor approves. Breathe normally and repeat each one five to seven times. Take a break between sets if you need to.

★ **Buttocks squeeze.** Do this lying in bed, sitting, or standing. Squeeze your buttocks tightly and hold for six or seven seconds.

★ **Leg lift.** Lie on your back and prop a firm pillow under your bent knee. Slowly raise your foot into the air until your leg is straight. Hold for six or seven seconds, and then slowly lower your foot.

★ **Thigh toner.** Straighten your legs while lying or standing, then squeeze the muscle on top of your thigh for six or seven seconds. Your kneecap should feel like it's tightening and moving upward.

★ **Knee extension.** From a sitting position, squeeze your thigh muscle and straighten out your leg until it is parallel to the floor. Hold for six or seven seconds, then slowly bend your knee and lower your foot back to the floor.

Once you start an exercise program, don't quit — otherwise, in a matter of months, you'll lose all the benefits you gained.

Slim down. You've got lots of good reasons to lose weight, but saving your knees from extra wear and tear is one of the best. However, you must focus on losing fat and gaining muscle. Being lean and strong will do your knees more good than just being skinny. So watch what you eat and stick to your exercise program.

Wrap it up. Bandaging an arthritic knee can help ease the pain, but not just any bandage will do. Buy one a size larger than you normally would. According to research, looser bandages work better than the standard-sized ones. Ask your doctor or pharmacist about selecting and using them.

Check your hormones. Some experts think changes in hormones cause more older women to suffer from OA. However, postmenopausal women who took estrogen for at least five years had more knee cartilage than women who didn't. Since cartilage helps protect your joints from OA, you might benefit from hormone replacement therapy. But there are risks. Discuss the pros and cons carefully with your doctor.

Change your surroundings. You don't have to move, just move things around at home. Every time you perform a task, think about

---

Tip-top menu outsmarts OA

Start your day with an orange. Your joints will weaken faster without enough vitamin C.

Pour milk on your cereal. The vitamin D in your fortified milk protects cartilage and bones. Don't like milk? Mix cereal into yogurt, instead.

Sip water all day. This wonder drink helps cushion your joints and is a main ingredient in cartilage.

Snack on an apple. Boron is a trace element in apples that might help prevent arthritis and relieve morning stiffness.

Make a lunch date with a salad. Brightly colored vegetables like carrots and broccoli contain the antioxidant beta carotene that fights inflammation.

Add a splash of dressing. Vegetable oils contain vitamin E, which can reduce the risk of OA. Sprinkle on wheat germ and sunflower seeds for even more E.

Pick low-fat poultry. Keep your weight down with a baked, skinless chicken breast for dinner. Your knees will say, "Ahhh."

Curry some rice. Turmeric, an ingredient in curry, fights inflammation.

Pass the pineapple. This tropical fruit contains manganese, a trace mineral needed to build bones and connective tissue.

Wind down with ginger tea. Ginger also fights inflammation for less joint pain. Relax with a soothing cup.

---

ways to avoid straining your joints. Too much stress on your knees can almost double your risk of developing knee osteoarthritis.

★ Don't squat. This position is particularly hard on your knees. So relocate books on low shelves to higher ground, and use a cushioned kneepad for gardening instead of resting on your haunches.

★ Choose the right chair. You can spend a small fortune on an easy chair that automatically lifts to help you in and out. But if that's not an option, choose a straight-backed chair over a recliner. And try sitting on a pillow or two so you don't have to struggle to stand up.

★ Use a firm mattress. Getting up from a soft mattress can feel like trying to get out of a bowl of mashed potatoes. Buy one that's a bit firmer instead.

Rest is just as important to your knees as exercise, so don't stay on your feet all day. And if the pain just won't quit, discuss anti-inflammatories with your doctor.

Get sweet relief with a sour remedy

Arthritis has been around much longer than modern medicine. And so has this home remedy. While there's no scientific proof it helps osteoarthritis, some people insist it works for them.

Mix two teaspoons of apple-cider vinegar in a glass of water, and then add two teaspoons of honey. Stir until the honey has dissolved. Drink this sweet-and-sour solution with meals. This natural prescription just might work for you.

Alternative exercise plan eases OA

Try these two feel-good ways to gently work and strengthen arthritic joints.

Hurry to hydrotherapy. This is simply a fancy way of saying water exercise. Pool water is usually heated to 85 to 98 degrees Fahrenheit. This will get your circulation going and keep you limber. Water "resists" movement more than air, so your muscles get a powerful workout. At the same time, water supports your limbs — a real plus for people with sore joints.

Look for classes led by a trained hydrotherapist. The Arthritis Foundation offers a six- to 10-week warm-water exercise program. Contact your local AF office for details.

If you have your own pool or spa, you can practice some exercises at home. Check with your doctor first to make sure you don't have any medical conditions that would make hydrotherapy unwise. And get a referral for a professional who can help customize your program.

The Arthritis Foundation says to always relax in the pool or tub first for a while to let the warm water loosen your muscles. Then follow these guidelines.

★ Submerge the body part you are exercising.

★ Move slowly and carefully.

★ Start with just a few easy exercises.

★ Never force your joints into unnatural positions. Gentle stretching is the key.

★ Stop if you become overheated or feel weak.

★ Scale back your routine if you experience pain more than two hours after your workout.

If your doctor recommends long-term hydrotherapy, you might be able to deduct some or all of the cost of your own pool or spa from your income taxes. Talk to a reputable accountant or tax attorney to find out more about medical expense claims.

Try tai chi. This ancient Chinese form of conditioning, pronounced "tie-chee," emphasizes gentle, circular movements to loosen muscles and increase flexibility.

Older adults who took 12 weeks of classes reported feeling calmer and more in control of their arthritis pain. Testing after the classes showed they could walk faster, balance on one foot better, and get up from chairs more easily. Not surprisingly, when the study ended, more than half the participants wanted to continue with tai chi.

Hospitals, fitness clubs, and private instructors offer classes. Look for a program designed for people with arthritis.

Save your knees with the right shoes

Whether you're living with painful knees or trying to avoid them, you must shoe shop carefully.

★ **Analyze your arches.** Wet your feet and stamp your foot-prints onto a piece of paper. If you can see the shape of your whole foot, you have low arches — sometimes called flat feet — and you need a shoe that will stabilize them. If there is only a thin line connecting your toe area and your heel, you have high arches and need shoes with plenty of cushioning. Somewhere in between means you need average support.

★ **Size it right.** Shop in the evening when your feet are their largest. Measure both feet. Bring the type of socks you'll probably wear with your new shoes and allow a thumb's width of extra room past your toes.

★ **Choose the right features.** Walking or workout shoes should be lightweight and flexible, with rounded soles and a wide landing area for your heel. Dress shoes should have low heels — no higher than 2 inches. And remember, wide heels are just as hard on your knees as skinny stiletto heels.

Periodically inspect the backs of your shoes on a level surface. If they lean, it's time to start over.

---

4 natural secrets to pain-free joints

Throughout the years, man has tried to cure his joint pain. Many remedies have been sensible, some were dangerous, and a few just plain odd. One age-old therapy — leeches — recently proved to actually have some merit. Other studies show acupuncture gaining ground as a respectable arthritis treatment.

But if leeches and needles are a little too creepy for you, consider these less alarming, natural ways to battle your OA pain.

Bolster your Bs. Many experts believe diet can beat arthritis pain. If that's true, B vitamins look like a strong contender.

One study found that people with arthritis of the hand had fewer tender joints when they took a daily supplement of 6,400 micrograms (mcg) of folic acid (B9) and 20 mcg of cobalamin (B12). Separate studies showed B vitamins could help arthritis in other parts of your body, too.

Natural sources of B12 include meat, fish, dairy foods, and eggs. You can get folic acid in dark leafy greens, legumes, seeds, and enriched breads and cereals. Of course, you can't get the test doses strictly from foods, so ask your doctor about a prescription for B vitamins. And only take high doses of vitamins under a doctor's supervision.

Get an edge with glucosamine. Your body's natural store of glucosamine strengthens and builds cartilage. The supplement made from clamshells simply helps your body repair damaged cartilage faster, thereby reducing joint pain.

If you decide to supplement with glucosamine, you may not feel the full effect for two to three months. But once it kicks in, glucosamine can be as powerful a pain reliever as nonsteroidal anti-inflammatory drugs (NSAIDs). And you won't have any of the worrisome side effects you often get with NSAIDs, such as intestinal bleeding and liver damage. If your doctor approves, take 500 milligrams (mg) of glucosamine three times a day.

Supplement with SAM-e. It's easier to say "sammy" than to pronounce S-adenosylmethionine, but whatever you call it, this dietary supplement has arthritis sufferers rushing the health stores.

Your body normally makes this biochemical, which helps build cartilage. But as you age, your levels of SAM-e drop. Research shows SAM-e supplements can reduce the pain of mild cases of OA, perhaps, some experts say, by promoting joint repair.

You can usually find SAM-e wherever supplements are sold, but it's not cheap. Depending on how much you take, it can cost between $50 and $250 a month. Be sure the label says SAM-e butanedisulfonate, and that it's packaged in an airtight, lightproof container. The tablets should be coated so they don't dissolve until they reach your intestines.

Take between 800 and 1,600 mg of SAM-e per day, divided into two doses. Not everyone responds to the supplement, so don't waste your money if you feel no better after a month or so. B vitamins — specifically folate and B12 — help SAM-e work better.

Don't take this supplement without talking to your doctor first. You'll need to discuss side effects, possible drug interactions, and the dose that's right for you.

Arm yourself with arnica. For many years, people in Europe have used this herb to treat pain. Although it's poisonous if swallowed, you can buy a gel or make a poultice to place on achy joints. Dilute a tablespoon of arnica tincture in two cups of water. Then soak a piece of sterile gauze in it and place it over the sore spot.

Arnica works like a painkiller and increases circulation in tiny blood vessels. Studies show it can lessen the pain and stiffness caused by arthritis. If it gives you a rash, stop using it and see your doctor. Look for arnica gel and tincture at herb shops and some pharmacies.

You don't have to live with arthritis pain when simple solutions are available. However, if you have bone or joint pain that lingers, or comes and goes, see your doctor for a checkup. Early treatment of OA could keep it from progressing and keep you dancing the cha-cha for many more years.

Emergency aid for joints that ache

When your knees hurt on a chilly day, warmth may help ease the stiffness and pain.

★   Baby your joints with a hot water bottle — just place a towel between it and your skin.

★   Dampen a hand towel or washcloth and zap it in the microwave until it's warm and steamy. Be careful not to overheat.

If your knees feel swollen after a busy day, cool them down with ice. Here are some quick solutions for an instant ice pack.

★   Grab a bag of frozen peas from your freezer.

★   Place unpopped popcorn kernels into a zip-lock freezer bag and keep in the freezer.

★   Fill an uninflated balloon or a disposable rubber glove with water and freeze.

★   Wet a clean sock, stick it in a zip-lock bag, and freeze.

Osteoporosis

Slash your risk for unexpected fractures

Postmenopausal women get osteoporosis more often than any other group. But millions of other adults have this bone-thinning disease and don't realize it — even when they break a bone because of it. Read on to see if you're on the "at-risk" list and how you can avoid suffering an unexpected fracture.

Don't assume you have strong bones. It may sound strange, but you can crack a bone in your foot without dropping something heavy on it or hitting it against a hard surface. And if that happens, it could be a sign you have osteoporosis. Researchers at Ohio State University studied 21 cases where people suffered unexplained fractures.

"Each foot fracture had been caused by normal weight bearing — some patients were walking when they felt their bones break," says Rodney Tomczak, co-author of the study.

And these were not just older people. In fact the average age for men was 35, and for women, 54. Twenty of the 21 participants had at least early signs of osteoporosis, although none was aware of it.

Such unexplained fractures are often the first sign of osteoporosis in many people, says Tomczak. He recommends having a bone density test if you suffer a fracture for no apparent reason.

Beware if you're a delicate woman. This is one time where extra weight may be a plus. Having some meat on your bones may actually protect them, a large-scale Minnesota study found. Among the 8,000 women studied, lower-weight women had lower bone density and twice the risk of hip, pelvis, and rib fractures of heavier women. This wasn't true for breaks to arms, wrists, ankles, and other bones.

Of course, you don't want to gain weight just to help your bones. But if you are thin, it's a reminder you need to work even harder to keep them strong.

Don't count on ethnic background for protection. White women 65 or older break twice as many bones as black women. But one out of 10 black women over 50 has osteoporosis, and another 30 percent have low bone density that puts them at risk of developing the disease. Asian women tend to be even more at risk than black and Hispanic women. Although certain racial groups are more likely to get osteoporosis, no one should assume that race alone will protect their bones.

The bottom line — as a woman, you will have a hard time avoiding this disease unless you actively work to protect yourself throughout your life.

Watch out if you're an older man. It's true that men start with larger, stronger bones that weaken more slowly than women's. But after age 70, they are more likely than women to get this brittle-bone disease. And men in general get about a third of the hip fractures associated with osteoporosis.

So even though it's harder to exercise as you get older, this shows that for men, too, it's more important than ever to keep up with such activities as walking and weight training.

Think twice about vitamin A. If you take supplements of vitamin A, or retinol, you may raise your chances of getting a hip fracture by 40 percent. Your risk also goes up when you eat foods fortified with this vitamin.

Fortunately, there's a safe way to get the vitamin A your body needs and still protect your bones. Beta carotene — found in red and yellow fruits and vegetables — converts to vitamin A in your body, but doesn't seem to increase your risk of fractures. So try to eat lots of carrots, sweet potatoes, apricots, and mangoes.

Be careful if you exercise and take the pill. A surprising two-year study at Purdue University suggests women who exercise and use oral contraceptives may be at greater risk for bone fractures later in life than inactive women on the pill. So what's a committed exerciser to do?

Well, first of all, don't stop exercising. It's too important for overall health. The study showed only the spine and hip were affected and, then, only if people didn't get enough calcium. So this bone-building mineral seems to be the key.

"You either need to get calcium through foods — and that could be dairy or fortified foods, such as juices or cereals — or you need to supplement," advises researcher Connie Weaver, a Purdue professor of foods and nutrition.

Try to get 1,000 milligrams (mg) a day if you're between the ages of 19 and 50. If you're older, you need 1,200 mg a day. Also, if you take oral contraceptives, ask your doctor to test your bone density just to be on the safe side.

A bone density test is a good idea for anyone who thinks she may be at risk for osteoporosis. And here are some steps you can take — in addition to diet and exercise — to slow or stop bone loss.

★ Stop smoking, and drink alcohol in moderation, if at all. Both these habits have been associated with osteoporosis.

★ Deal with depression. Scientists are not sure exactly why, but depression seems to increase your chances of osteoporosis. It could be related to too much of the hormone cortisol or lack of attention to diet and exercise. If you are taking a medication for depression, talk to your doctor about the possibility that bone loss may be a side effect.

★ Ask your doctor if hormone replacement therapy (HRT) will help your condition. HRT has been the most commonly prescribed treatment for osteoporosis, but new research shows greater health risks — breast cancer, heart disease, heart attacks, strokes, and blood clots — than previously believed. The Food and Drug Administration (FDA) advises doctors to prescribe estrogen only when benefits clearly outweigh the risks, just long enough for successful treatment, and at the lowest effective dose. Be sure you discuss all the risks and benefits of HRT with your doctor first.

Shake, don't break, your bones

Take your pick — bone-building medication for the rest of your life or 20 minutes a day of shaking gently on a platform. If you have osteoporosis, that may someday be your choice — thanks to a group of "shimmying" sheep who found that's all it took to strengthen their bones.

When you don't use your bones, they get smaller and lighter, while physical activity makes them grow thicker and stronger. That's one reason you need to exercise. But what if you could trick your bones into thinking they are working hard without even breaking a sweat?

Researchers believe that may be what happened when they put sheep on a gently vibrating platform for 20 minutes a day, five days a week. At the end of a year, the bones in their hind legs were 34 percent more solid compared to a control group of unshaken sheep.

Now researchers are testing to see how vibration affects the bones of postmenopausal women. One thing's for sure, you'll be trembling with delight if they find that you, like the sheep, can build your bones while you "shimmy like your sister Kate."

Diet do's and don'ts for better bones

The right foods and supplements can help you build better bones, but the choices may not be as simple as you think. Let these suggestions take away some of the mystery about bone builders and bone losers.

Count calcium to boost bones. Calcium is probably the most important nutrient for strong bones at all ages, not just during childhood.

★ Do get a minimum of 1,200 milligrams a day, preferably from foods like low-fat milk and yogurt, fortified orange juice, kale, almonds, and sardines with bones.

★ Don't stop taking calcium. Any gain in bone strength is lost within a year if you don't keep getting enough.

★ Do take calcium supplements if you aren't sure you are getting plenty from your diet.

★ Don't overdo it. Try to calculate how much you get from your diet, and add only enough in supplements to reach the recommended dose.

★ Do take small amounts throughout the day for better absorption. Or use the chewable kind, which breaks down more easily in your system.

★ Don't let a fear of kidney stones scare you away from calcium. Two recent Harvard studies suggest calcium-rich foods protect against stones. In one study, men with a history of kidney stones had a lower risk of osteoporosis if they drank milk.

Soak up the sunshine vitamin. Your body needs vitamin D to help it absorb and use calcium.

★ Do get out in the sunlight to help your body make vitamin D naturally.

★ Don't count on the sun alone, especially if you live in a cloudy climate or can't get outdoors for some reason.

★ Do get extra vitamin D in fortified milk and breakfast cereals, or ask your doctor about taking supplements to get the recommended amount — 10-15 micrograms.

★ Don't take too much. If you overdo it, vitamin D can cause the amount of calcium in your blood to get too high. Side effects include headache, nausea, and diarrhea.

Help bones and heart with other vital vitamins. High cholesterol is bad for your bones as well as your heart. But colorful vegetables, full of antioxidant vitamins C, E, and beta carotene, will help you keep it under control. And vitamin K affects your bones more directly, helping lower your risk of hip fracture.

★ Do toss together a bone-healthy salad. Begin with iceberg lettuce, parsley, and cauliflower for vitamin K. Add dark leafy greens and tomatoes for vitamin C and carrots for beta carotene. Sprinkle with sunflower seed for vitamin E.

★ Don't shake on a lot of salt. While your body is flushing it out of your system, calcium can go right with it. Herbs, onions, and garlic, on the other hand, will spice up your salad and add vitamins, too.

Fight fractures with minerals. Potassium and magnesium make it possible for your bones to use calcium.

★ Do eat lots of bananas, avocados, fish, prunes, and dried figs for potassium; and oranges, nuts, dark leafy vegetables, and beans for magnesium.

★ Don't take potassium or magnesium supplements without your doctor's recommendation. Too much of these can be dangerous.

Pick your proteins to prevent breaks. Knowing how much and what kind of protein to eat may be confusing. Some studies find people who eat the lowest amount of protein have the weakest bones. But others suggest eating less meat — a main source of protein for many people — will help prevent broken bones.

★ Do be sure to get enough protein through a variety of sources, like lean meats, eggs, and low-fat dairy products as well as beans, grains, and other plant foods.

★ Don't overdo the meat, eggs, and dairy foods. One study found more hip fractures — almost four times the risk — in older women who ate the highest amounts of animal protein compared to plant protein.

Keep your frame fit with fiber. Roughage is another important way to help your bones by controlling cholesterol.

★ Do start your day with a bowl of high-fiber cereal. And eat other foods the American Heart Association recommends — like apples, beans, barley, oat and rice bran, and strawberries.

★ Don't forget to have milk with your breakfast cereal and perhaps a second helping of kale at lunch. You need the extra calcium because high-fiber foods can cause you to lose this mineral.

Sip some bone-building beverages. What you drink can help or harm your bones.

★ Do drink low-fat or fat-free milk, a good source of calcium.

★ Don't drink a lot of carbonated colas. Not only do they take the place of milk in your diet, they may leech calcium from your bones.

★ Do drink tea, a surprisingly nutritious beverage with flavonoids that may deserve credit for strengthening your bones.

★ Don't drink more than 32 ounces of tea a day to avoid getting too much caffeine, which can weaken your bones. And limit yourself to no more than 16 ounces a day of caffeinated coffee, which doesn't have the beneficial nutrients found in tea.

★ Do drink the local water if it's fortified with fluoride. Together with calcium and vitamin D, fluoride builds bones and lowers the risk of backbone fractures.

★ Don't drink a lot of alcohol. Over time, that may also contribute to weaker bones.

Checklist for stairway safety

Falls on stairs — going down, especially — can lead to serious injuries. And for one out of 10 people, they can be fatal. But you can avoid bumps, bruises, and breaks by using these tips to safety-proof your stairway.

★ Light the entire stairway, including landings, and put on-and-off switches at both the top and bottom. Use same-watt bulbs for even lighting, and promptly replace any that burn out.

★ Install a banister, or handrail, that is about 2 inches in diameter. When you grasp it, your thumb and index finger should form a C that goes about three-fourths of the way around the rail.

★ Extend the handrail a foot beyond the top stair. Before coming down, you will get a visual reminder that stairs are ahead.

★ Paint stairs in one non-glare color, or install a solid-pattern carpet. Add a strip in a contrasting color of paint or carpet on the inch or two closest to the edge.

★ Don't use loose rugs, and be sure carpet is tacked down securely.

★ Keep stairways clear. Never use them for storage, even temporarily.

★ Make sure wood, tile, or other smooth surfaces are dry before stepping on them.

'Hedge' your bets against osteoporosis

Walking may be the best exercise for your heart and lungs. But when it comes to toughening and protecting your bones, you need something more.

Weight-training exercises made a big difference for one group of postmenopausal women. They strengthened their bones so much with twice-a-week workouts that in just one year they were functioning like people 15 to 20 years younger. But you don't have to go to the gym and use barbells to whip your bones into shape. There are other ways — and some fun ones, at that — to get the same results at home.

Dig for better bones. Researchers at the University of Arkansas found yard work was as effective as weight training when it came to building up your bones. Both of them outscored even bicycling and jogging. So if you love puttering around in your garden, you're already ahead of the game.

"We hadn't expected yard work to be significant," says lead researcher Lori Turner. "It's taken for such a dainty activity. But there's a lot of weight-bearing motion going on in the garden — digging holes, pulling weeds, pushing a mower."

While you may choose an exercise because it's good for your bones, you also want one you will stick with. "The best thing about yard work is that so many people are willing to do it," Turner says. "They take pride in a beautiful yard and pleasure in being outdoors. They'll probably continue to do it as long as they're able."

Hop to help your hips. Jumping up and down is something you probably haven't done since childhood. But it may be one of the best ways to thicken your hipbones and prevent fractures, says Dr. Christine Snow, a leading authority on exercise and osteoporosis. At the Bone Research Laboratory at Oregon State University, she and her colleagues developed a fitness program that not only slowed bone loss in post-menopausal women, it actually helped grow new bone in the part of the hip most likely to break.

Before you try jumping, Snow recommends spending at least four months developing strength in your lower body. "It's best to perform exercises like squats, lunges, stepping up and down, and chair raises to reduce falls and improve lower body strength and balance," she explains. (Chair raises involve repeatedly standing and sitting, preferably without using the arms.)

You should check with your doctor before you start jumping to be sure your bones and joints can handle it. Then, the key to doing it safely, says Snow, "is to jump comfortably in the air — probably no more than 4 or 5 inches — and land flat footed, with knees slightly bent." Participants in her study jumped three times a week at least 50 times each and sometimes wore weighted vests to increase the resistance.

Snow's program isn't a quick fix, so don't get discouraged if you don't notice improvements right away. It took about five years for the benefits to show up in Snow's study, but the results were impressive. Women who continued to jump and perform other resistance exercises lost no bone mass at their hips, while those who did not exercise during the same period lost almost 4.5 percent. That means as long as you keep up your weight-bearing exercises, your bones will not weaken and may even grow stronger.

So spend some time working in your yard every day, and consider adding jumps to your workout routine. The results just may have you jumping for joy!

---

10 top backyard bone boosters

Build sturdy bones while beautifying your yard. These activities are sure to bring about great results.

- Pull stubborn weeds.
- Dig deep holes for trees and shrubs.
- Push a loaded wheelbarrow or a lawn mower.
- Lift and carry pots, bags of potting soil, and stones.
- Shovel soil into a flowerbed.
- Squeeze handles of hedge clippers to shape shrubbery.
- Rake, bag, and haul away leaves.
- Hammer nails to repair a fence or build a bird feeder.
- Hoist containers of soil for hanging flowerpots.
- Drag dead branches to the compost heap.

Terrific tips for climbing stairs safely

Climbing stairs can be a problem as you get older. You tend to lose strength, agility, good eyesight, and sharp attention — all the things you need to make it safely to the top.

But you won't always find an elevator when you need one, so it's important to maintain your stair-climbing skills. And all that up-and-down action has a positive side — it will help keep your bones strong. So follow these safety tips, then try using your stairs for a simple "step" exercise.

★ Wear sturdy, well-fitting shoes with non-skid soles. Never climb in loose footwear — like slippers — and, please, no stocking feet.

★ Don't wear flowing nightgowns or other long, loose clothing you might trip on.

★ Avoid carrying anything heavy or bulky. To keep hands free, wear clothing with pockets — or perhaps a carpenter's apron — for small, lightweight items.

★ Use the handrails, holding on with both hands. Consider asking for help on stairways without banisters.

★ Watch where you step. Be especially careful if you wear eyeglasses with bifocal or trifocal lenses that might distort your vision.

★ Face the rail and place your foot sideways on the stair rather than stepping with your toes pointed straight ahead.

★ Put both feet on one step before going to the next.

★ Don't talk or let other people or things distract you.

★ In public places, keep to the right-hand side to avoid collisions.

Once you feel comfortable on the stairs, try this simple step exercise. Choose a low stair, 4 to 6 inches high, to protect your knees from too much pressure. Face the stairs, holding on to the handrail.

★ Step up with your right foot, and then bring up your left foot. Your weight will rest equally on both feet, which will now be on the step.

★ Step down to the floor with your right foot and then down with your left.

★ Do the steps again, but start with the left foot this time.

★ Do this set of steps five times, rest, and then do them five more times.

★ Gradually increase the number of steps until you can complete three sets of 10 repetitions.

Parkinson's Disease

Take control with simple self-help

Parkinson's disease (PD) is a disorder in which your brain cells, or neurons, break down. These neurons produce a chemical called dopamine. Without this chemical, your brain can't direct your muscles, and you gradually lose control of your movements.

The early symptoms of PD are easy to overlook. At first, you may simply feel weak and tired, and your hands might tremble at rest. Eventually, your muscles can begin to feel stiff, and you could have trouble walking or keeping your balance.

Although experts aren't sure why some people get this muscle-weakening condition, many think it could be inherited or caused by environmental chemicals, like pesticides.

PD usually affects people over the age of 50, but it sometimes strikes people in their 20s. It's a little more common in men than in women.

While there isn't a cure for PD yet, if you're diagnosed with the disease, you can take these steps to help control it naturally.

Get moving to stay moving. If you've always been an active person, keep up your normal activities as long as you can. If you're a more sedentary person, now is a good time to start getting your muscles in shape. Exercises, like strength training and mild aerobics, are beneficial, but just taking a walk every day will loosen stiff muscles and keep them strong.

Eliminate constipation. About 80 percent of people with PD also suffer from constipation. To stay regular, get plenty of fiber — about 20 to 35 grams a day. Whole grain foods, vegetables, and fruits are packed with fiber. Just be sure to add them to your diet gradually, or you could make your constipation worse. Finally, drink at least eight glasses of water a day to help your body process the fiber.

Beware of protein. Surprisingly, eating too much protein can make some PD symptoms worse, especially if you take the drug levodopa, or L-dopa. Researchers think protein can affect the way your body absorbs this medication. You can short cut this side effect by taking your medication 30 to 45 minutes before you eat and eating most of your protein in the evening when the medicine doesn't have to work as well. You could also cut back on the protein in your diet, but be sure to replace those lost calories with other healthy foods.

Find supportive friends. People who have experienced first hand what you're going through can offer good advice and help you overcome loneliness and depression. Consider joining a support group and sharing your worries and frustrations with other people who have PD. Contact the American Parkinson Disease Association and ask if they have a chapter near you. Call the national headquarters at 1-800-223-2732 or visit them on the Internet at <http://apdaparkinson.com>.

Getting PD doesn't have to mean losing your independence. Work with your doctor and invest time in your physical and mental well-being so you can live life to the fullest.

Foil Parkinson's with food do's and don'ts

You are what you eat when it comes to Parkinson's disease (PD). Some scientists think nutrition can influence your chances of getting PD, especially once you're over 50.

Knowing which foods to eat and which to avoid can even your odds against this mysterious illness.

Sip a cup of green tea. This ancient drink contains powerful antioxidants that can help protect the nerve cells that make dopamine. Experts aren't sure how much green tea you should drink for the most benefit — too much could actually damage these important cells. So aim for moderation by only drinking a cup or two a day.

Get your greens and grains. Folate, one of the B vitamins, helps maintain your memory, and it could save you from Parkinson's as well. Researchers think the amino acid homocysteine damages the cells that produce dopamine, putting you at risk for PD. Folate rides to the rescue by lowering your homocysteine levels. Spinach, asparagus, and other green, leafy vegetables are natural folate powerhouses, while fortified flours, grains, and cereals are blockbuster sources for added folate.

Zap the fat. A recent study found that eating too many high-fat foods could contribute to PD. While researchers confirm the findings, you might want to eat less fat, especially saturated fat, which is found in meat, egg yolks, dairy products, and hydrogenated vegetable shortenings. That's because saturated fat can raise your cholesterol level. Researchers point the finger at a high-cholesterol diet as another risk factor for PD.

So give PD the one-two punch. First, cut back on the total amount of fat you eat. Then, replace some of the saturated fats in your diet with "good" monounsaturated (MUFAs) or polyunsaturated fats (PUFAs). Olive oil and avocados are full of MUFAs, while fish such as tuna and salmon are packed with the PUFA omega-3.

You can also lower your cholesterol by eating foods high in soluble fiber. Oat bran is a great source of soluble fiber, as are beans, barley, apples, and other fruits and vegetables.

Don't pick the pawpaws. Children sing about "picking up pawpaws, and putting them in your pocket," but bite into one and you may get more than you bargained for. Scientists found that people in the French West Indies who ate pawpaw fruits and custard apples, or drank teas made from them, were more likely to develop forms of PD that the drug levodopa can't treat. You may not get Parkinson's from snacking on them, but until more tests are conducted, maybe you should skip the pawpaw patch.

Although good nutrition can help ward off some diseases, if you notice signs of Parkinson's disease such as weakness, uncontrollable trembling, or difficulty walking, see your doctor immediately. He can diagnose your symptoms and set you on a proven course of treatment.

The latest buzz on tai chi

Tai chi may be the newest weapon in the fight against Parkinson's disease (PD). Scientists at Emory University in Atlanta think tai chi exercises might help you build and maintain the muscle control that PD slowly steals away.

Tai chi is a "soft" Chinese martial art form. Instead of focusing on speed and power, it improves your balance and flexibility. The slow, steady movements of tai chi have made it a popular exercise among older adults — and a candidate for helping people with PD control their muscles.

Dr. Steven Wolf, a professor of Rehabilitation Medicine at Emory University, has found that seniors who practice tai chi have better balance and fewer falls. Wolf and Dr. Jorge Juncos, a neurology professor at Emory, are currently studying the benefits of tai chi for PD sufferers. Although the results are not in, the researchers are hopeful that tai chi will improve the quality of life for people with PD.

Talk with your doctor about the health benefits of tai chi. Many fitness clubs, recreation centers, colleges, and hospitals offer tai chi classes.

New hope for women with Parkinson's

Being a woman could have a startling benefit. Women have less chance of getting Parkinson's disease (PD) than men. In fact, many experts think estrogen can make a difference in preventing and treating this illness.

Researchers at the Mayo Clinic found that women who had lost their natural estrogen due to early menopause or a total hysterectomy had a higher risk of developing PD. But out of this group, the women who received estrogen replacement therapy (ERT) reduced their risk by 50 percent.

This hormone could even help women who already have PD. In another study, postmenopausal women with PD took low doses of estrogen along with their regular PD medication. Amazingly, adding the hormone helped them control their movements better than drugs alone.

ERT isn't for everyone. New research shows it may increase your risk of heart disease, stroke, breast cancer, and blood clots. You need to talk to your doctor and discuss all the pros and cons.

Top 5 natural alternatives to pesticides

Spraying pesticides around your home and garden might raise your chances of developing Parkinson's disease, and the longer you use these dangerous chemicals, the higher your risk.

The best solution may be to avoid pesticides altogether. Instead, try these five natural alternatives to protect yourself and the environment.

- ✪ Sprinkle peppermint oil or leaves around the places in your house where mice, ants, and other pests creep in.

- ✪ Squeeze four lemons into a half-gallon of water, toss in the rinds, and mop the floor with this mixture to wipe out roaches and fleas.

- ✪ Repel cockroaches by combining cucumber skins with chopped bay leaves. Sprinkle the mixture wherever roaches like to hang out.

- ✪ Steep the stems and leaves of a stinging nettle plant in a bucket of water for 24 hours. Take out the nettle, and spray the mixture on your plants to kill aphids and mites.

- ✪ Splash vinegar around door and window frames, under appliances, and anywhere else you've noticed ants marching.

Prostate Cancer

Take a load off your prostate

Losing your love handles could make all the difference in the world to your prostate — and here's why. The latest research shows being overweight increases your odds of suffering a more aggressive type of prostate cancer, as well as having the cancer spread to other organs.

And body fat is being blamed because it stores hormones and other factors that encourage prostate cancer growth. On top of that, excess body fat could interfere with your immune system and its anti-tumor defenses.

The findings of a recent study at the University of California – Los Angeles (UCLA) provide good evidence. In this study, 13 overweight men made simple lifestyle changes, like eating a low-fat, high-fiber diet and exercising.

After only 11 days, researchers were amazed at the results. The men not only lost weight, blood tests showed a favorable change in hormones and growth factor levels, which appeared to slow cancer cell growth by 30 percent in a test-tube experiment.

Now that you're convinced it's time to lose a few pounds, why not make these other healthy changes in your life, too.

Eat more fish. If you eat fish instead of red meat, you'll be cutting back on harmful saturated fat and getting omega-3 fatty acids. These "good" fats seem to protect against cancer. Men who frequently eat fish are up to three times less likely to get prostate cancer than men who eat little or no fish. Fatty fish rich in omega-3 fatty acids, like salmon, herring, and mackerel, seem to take the biggest bite out of cancer.

NSAIDs join prostate cancer battle

At just a few dollars a bottle, nonsteroidal anti-inflammatory drugs (NSAIDs) — like aspirin and ibuprofen — may be the latest and greatest weapons to protect older men from prostate cancer.

According to cutting-edge research from the Mayo Clinic, a daily dose of an NSAID could halve your prostate cancer risk. Men ages 70 to 79 seem to benefit the most simply because they tend to use more NSAIDs over a longer period of time.

NSAIDs shut down your body's COX-2 enzyme. This natural chemical causes inflammation, but it could also lead to cancer. By deactivating it, NSAIDs appear to slow tumor growth, force cancer cells to self-destruct, and boost your body's anti-cancer defenses.

Researchers aren't sure about the dose, and they don't know if you need to take NSAIDs every day to get protection. Also, they warn these pain relievers can have serious side effects, like stomach or liver damage.

Although further studies are needed to confirm these results, men already taking aspirin to prevent a heart attack could also be protecting their prostate.

Learn to love healthy fats. Experts have known monounsaturated fatty acids (MUFAs) are good for your heart, but now they believe MUFAs also protect your prostate. In one recent study, subjects who consumed at least one teaspoon of olive, canola, or peanut oil a day — all good sources of MUFAs — had a 50-percent lower risk of prostate cancer than the people who didn't get MUFAs in their diet. Eating peanuts and avocados is another great way to increase your MUFA intake.

Think like a vegetarian. According to a recent study, strict vegetarians had less of a protein called insulin-like growth factor (IGF-I) than meat eaters. Researchers believe high levels of IGF-I could play a role in causing prostate cancer.

If avoiding meat and dairy products doesn't sound like much fun, at least do what the men in the UCLA study did — eat fewer fatty foods and more fruits, vegetables, and whole grains. These natural wonders are loaded with fiber and powerful anti-cancer phytochemicals, like indoles, carotenoids, and flavonoids.

Take a walk. You don't have to slave away in a gym or run a marathon to get a great workout. In the UCLA study, the men walked briskly for 30 to 60 minutes four to five days a week, then at a slower pace for 40 to 60 minutes once or twice a week.

It's not as difficult as you think to squeeze exercise into your schedule — just be creative and have fun.

Dairy foods linked to cancer risk

Swapping a big bowl of ice cream for a tangy tangerine might protect you from prostate cancer. According to Harvard researchers, eating more than two-and-a-half servings of dairy foods a day could raise your risk of prostate cancer by 32 percent. And it's easy to eat that much — one serving equals a scoop of ice cream, an 8-ounce glass of milk, or a slice of cheese.

Surprisingly, it looks like calcium could be to blame. This bone-building mineral seems to overpower the most-active form of vitamin D, which may protect against prostate cancer.

But don't pour your glass of skim milk down the drain just yet. The calcium issue is far from over and research continues. Instead of dropping dairy foods from your diet, eat them in moderation. And just to be on the safe side, talk with your doctor before taking calcium supplements.

But don't stop there. The next time you're at the grocery store, load your cart with these powerful cancer fighters.

Tangerines. Out of all the citrus fruits — tangerines, lemons, grapefruit, and oranges — tangerines have the most pectin. Pectin is already a celebrity for lowering cholesterol and blood sugar levels. Now, experts believe, this complex carbohydrate may also stop normal prostate cells from becoming cancerous. Healthy cells, researchers say, communicate with each other. When this communication breaks down, it can lead to cancer. Pectin seems to keep prostate cells "talking." To get this benefit, eat the pectin-rich cords between the fruit slices, too.

Tomato sauce. You've probably heard about lycopene and its cancer-preventing powers. But did you know it could also come to your rescue if you already have prostate cancer? In a recent study, men with newly diagnosed cancer who ate three-fourths of a cup of tomato sauce a day for three weeks had lower prostate specific antigen (PSA) scores and less DNA damage to their prostate cancer cells and white blood cells. DNA damage increases cancer risk.

Besides the usual suspects — tomato-based soups and sauces, fresh tomatoes, pink grapefruits, and watermelon — be on the lookout for the autumn olive berry. By weight, it has 17 times more lycopene than a raw tomato. Someday soon, this tiny berry may end up as an ingredient in processed foods. So keep an eye out.

Broccoli. Eating broccoli and other cruciferous vegetables at least three times a week could lower your risk of prostate cancer by 41 percent, compared with men eating less than one serving a week. Cruciferous vegetables have secret weapons called isothiocyanates. These compounds activate enzymes that detoxify cancer-causing substances.

To get these cancer-fighting benefits, eat broccoli raw or lightly cooked, or try one of its cousins — cauliflower, cabbage, brussels sprouts, or kohlrabi.

Warning — recall of herbal supplement

Taking the herbal supplement known as PC-SPES could be hazardous to your health, warns the FDA.

For years, this blend of eight Chinese herbs lifted the hopes of both prostate cancer victims and health researchers. In scientific studies, PC-SPES seemed to cause tumor cells to self-destruct, while reducing prostate pain and inflammation.

Top 7 remedies for prostate problems

Odds are, you'll face a prostate problem some time in your life. It could be benign prostatic hyperplasia (BPH), a noncancerous condition that causes problems when you urinate. Or it could be prostatitis, an inflammation of the prostate that brings on excruciating pain. Let your doctor make the diagnosis, then try one of these remedies for relief.

Eat an apple. Quercetin, a compound in apples, onions, and tea, seems to take a bite out of the swelling and pain of prostatitis.

Pray for help. Join the flocks of people who fight off stress through prayer. Taming tension may relieve an inflamed prostate.

Sit in a sitz bath. To relieve discomfort, sit in your bathtub for 15 minutes, three times a day, in 8 inches of warm water.

Take charge with Kegel exercises. Try squeezing the muscles you use to stop urinating. Hold them tight for about 10 seconds, and then relax them for 10 seconds. Do this 10 times a day.

Cut out spicy food. They can irritate your prostate. Also, cut out alcohol, coffee, chocolate, and tomatoes if they are causing problems for your prostate.

Guzzle some cranberry juice. It can sweep away bacteria to help prevent infections in your bladder and prostate.

Crack open a crab. Shellfish are loaded with zinc, a mineral that's essential for prostate health.

However, PC-SPES has a dark side. Researchers have warned it can cause dangerous blood clots, sexual problems, leg cramps, breast enlargement, and hot flashes, as well as diarrhea and nausea. Now add uncontrollable bleeding to this list.

Scientists recently discovered traces of the prescription drug Warfarin in the herbal concoction. Warfarin is a blood thinner that can be dangerous in large doses. In fact, the *New England Journal of Medicine* reported a case in which PC-SPES caused internal bleeding.

Responding to these findings, the manufacturer, BotanicLab-SPES, recalled all of its PC-SPES supply as of February 8, 2002.

If you have questions about this supplement, you can contact the California Department of Public Health at 800-495-3232. Remember to always check with your doctor before taking any herbal prostate remedy.

2 simple tests that could save your life

Your odds of getting prostate cancer during your lifetime are one in six. They're even higher if you are black or have a family history of the disease. These two tests could detect a tumor in the knick of time, while the cancer is still treatable.

★ Digital rectal exam (DRE). In this test, your doctor physically examines your prostate with his finger. A healthy prostate feels firm and elastic to the touch. Soft and tender areas could indicate an infection. Hard lumps could suggest cancer.

★ Prostate specific antigen (PSA) screening. This test measures the amount of PSA in your blood. All men normally have some of this prostate protein in their bloodstream, but higher than normal levels could indicate you're at risk for cancer or another prostate problem. You and your doctor would then decide if further tests are needed.

For all its potential to do good, the PSA screening is fraught with controversy. Many experts disagree how often you should have one, while others wonder if you should have one at all. According to the National Prostate Cancer Coalition and its panel of scientists and cancer survivors, the arguments for the PSA test outweigh the complaints against it.

Opponents say it's inaccurate, nabbing only the harmless tumors and letting the serious ones sneak by. The facts say otherwise. After PSA and DRE screening became a regular practice, three out of four men diagnosed with prostate cancer had tumors that were still treatable. Before the tests, three out of four men discovered their cancer when it was too late.

It's up to you and your doctor to decide how often to test for prostate cancer. You must weigh your risk of cancer against the inconvenience, worry, and discomfort that testing may cause. Your peace of mind and your health are worth this serious consideration.

Rheumatoid Arthritis

Vanquish RA with vegan diet

A simple thing like changing your diet may bring about a pleasant change in your rheumatoid arthritis (RA) symptoms.

Veg out. A recent Swedish study found that a vegan, gluten-free diet might help ease your RA pain. Vegan diets are strict vegetarian diets that eliminate all animal products, including milk and cheese. Gluten is a protein found in wheat, rye, oats, and barley.

In the small, one-year study, about 40 percent of the people eating the vegan, gluten-free diet improved, compared to only 4 percent of those eating a normal, well-balanced diet.

These results support the theory that certain foods can aggravate — or even help cause — rheumatoid arthritis.

Ditch problem foods. No scientific studies prove a connection between food and RA — but eliminating certain foods has helped in some cases.

Protein-free, or elemental, diets have succeeded in the past. Cutting out milk and dairy products has helped, too. Gluten-free diets, essential for celiac disease, have also improved RA symptoms. In fact, RA frequently occurs along with celiac disease.

Cereals and legumes contain plant proteins called lectins, which could increase your risk for RA. Lectins can spur your immune system to attack your body's own joints, leading to inflammation.

Not everyone with RA has this sensitivity to food. So modifying your diet may not do anything for you — but it also might be worth a try.

Fill up on folate. While you're eliminating foods, you may want to add some as well.

Dutch researchers recently discovered folate supplements reduced the risk of liver damage caused by methotrexate, a drug commonly prescribed for rheumatoid arthritis. This allowed people to continue taking the drug for longer periods.

If you take methotrexate for your RA, you may want to get more folate in your diet. Good food sources of this B vitamin include spinach, asparagus, beets, and avocados.

One word of caution, though. People in the Dutch study who took supplemental folate needed to take even more methotrexate to get the benefits. Besides liver damage, other possible side effects of methotrexate include upset stomach, fever, dizziness, and diarrhea.

What you eat — or don't eat — may mean the difference between RA pain and relief. But keep in mind that managing RA through your diet is neither a proven nor widely accepted strategy. Talk to your doctor before drastically changing your diet.

Beware of unexpected risks for RA

Imagine rheumatoid arthritis as a mystery. Something must cause the swelling, tenderness, and inflammation in your joints — but no one knows for sure what it is.

Scientists act as detectives, trying to find out what triggers this painful condition. So far, they haven't solved the mystery of RA. But like any good detective, they've uncovered some surprising clues.

You'll be amazed by these unusual risk factors. However, by making some lifestyle changes, you just may lower your chances of getting rheumatoid arthritis.

★ **Hair dye.** Women who've been dyeing or bleaching their hair for 20 years or more are almost twice as likely to develop RA, according to a recent Swedish study. Researchers aren't sure why but suspect chemicals in the dye may damage the immune system and trigger the disease. If you color your hair frequently, you may want to consider taking a break and going a natural gray.

★ **Farm animals.** In the same study, men who worked around farm animals tripled their risk for RA. So did men who used a private well. This lends some support to the idea that bacteria might cause RA. If you live in the country, be aware it could affect your joint health later on. You may decide it's time to give up the rural life and move to town.

★ **Mold.** Watch out for mold in your home. It can quadruple your risk of getting rheumatoid arthritis. Keep your windows closed, and use an air conditioner and dehumidifier to keep your home cool and dry.

★ **Decaf coffee.** Women who drink four or more cups of decaf coffee a day more than double their risk for rheumatoid arthritis, according to a University of Alabama-Birmingham study. Regular coffee has previously been linked to RA. The solution is simple — drink less coffee or switch to a different hot beverage. Women who drink three or more cups of tea each day actually cut their risk by 60 percent.

★ **Diabetes.** Having type 1 diabetes — where your body produces little or no insulin — may put you at greater risk for RA. Women who took insulin were a whopping 10 times more likely to develop RA in the Swedish study.

★ **Being female.** There's not much you can do about this one. Just be aware that RA strikes three times as many women as men. Experts suspect female hormones might play a role.

★ **Smoking.** On the other hand, you can lower your risk by kicking this habit. Both men and women who smoke boost their risk of developing RA later in life. Your risk increases with every year and every cigarette you smoke.

Keep in mind that many of these risk factors have no concrete explanation. As the investigation of RA continues, they may even be ruled out as suspects. But they might also provide the key to cracking the mysterious case of rheumatoid arthritis.

Popular painkillers linked to heart problems

COX-2 inhibitors can end your arthritis pain and lower your risk of stomach ulcers. But such popular painkillers as Celebrex and Vioxx may also double your risk for a life-threatening heart problem.

According to a new report in *The Journal of the American Medical Association*, these nonsteroidal anti-inflammatory drugs (NSAIDs) could cause blood clots, a heart attack, or another serious heart condition. They seem to block a natural compound in your body that helps your blood vessels stay open and flow smoothly.

This finding is still controversial, though. Critics say rheumatoid arthritis sufferers are more at risk for heart problems to begin with. Also, some other risk factor could be to blame instead. More research will help determine if these medications are responsible for heart complications.

In the meantime, talk with your doctor about the pros and cons of COX-2 inhibitors. They may not be a smart idea if you suffer from a kidney condition, high blood pressure, congestive heart failure, or liver problems, or if you are on a salt-restricted diet or diuretic therapy.

However, they could be the right choice if you are age 75 or older and at a high risk for ulcers or stomach bleeding.

Overcome disheartening odds

Your joints aren't the only things in danger when you have rheumatoid arthritis. You're also much more likely to suffer a heart attack or stroke. But take heart — you can take steps to lower your risk. Read on to discover how.

Realize your risk. First, you have to understand what you're up against.

Researchers at the University of Texas Health Science Center in San Antonio recently studied how often people with RA had heart problems. They found people with RA are more than three times as likely to suffer a cardiovascular problem like a heart attack or stroke.

Scientists arrived at that scary statistic after adjusting for traditional risk factors, such as obesity or smoking. In other words, they made sure the risk comes from RA and not from some other lifestyle factor.

Why the increased risk? Experts still aren't sure, but they have some good ideas. People with RA often have high cholesterol and high triglyceride levels, which increase your heart disease risk. The inflammation that comes with RA might also damage your heart.

Help your heart. Just because you're more likely to have heart problems doesn't mean you're powerless to prevent them. Start by focusing on the positive things you can do to offset your higher risk. Remember these basic steps to good heart health.

- ★ Eat a low-fat diet
- ★ Exercise regularly
- ★ Lose weight
- ★ Quit smoking

This simple action plan will maximize your chances of avoiding a heart attack or stroke. Your doctor can help by checking your cholesterol and triglyceride levels regularly and prescribing medication if necessary.

Reel in relief. For an easy — and tasty — way to fight both heart disease and rheumatoid arthritis, eat fish.

The omega-3 fatty acids in fish have anti-inflammatory powers that soothe your stiff, achy joints and protect your heart. They also zap triglycerides and may even lower blood pressure. No wonder both the American Heart Association and the Arthritis Foundation recommend eating fish twice a week.

You get the most omega-3 from fatty fish such as salmon, tuna, or mackerel. Serve your fish with dark, leafy, vitamin-E filled greens for even more relief. Promising new research on mice shows that combining fish oil with vitamin E reduces inflammation and makes it easier to move.

Even if you don't have RA, you can benefit from a fishy diet. Eating just one to two servings of broiled or baked fish a week might slash your risk of developing RA in the first place.

Heart attacks, strokes, and other cardiovascular problems often accompany rheumatoid arthritis. But if you take care of your heart and feast on fish, you can beat the odds.

Guard your gums if you have RA

Rheumatoid arthritis hasn't kept you from smiling. Unfortunately, your smile may reveal fewer teeth.

That's because people with RA often develop gum disease, too. A recent Australian study found that people with rheumatoid arthritis had more missing teeth from periodontal disease than a non-arthritis group. Periodontal disease is a more advanced form of gingivitis that affects not only your gums, but also the bones and other structures that support your teeth.

It's unclear why this link exists. Perhaps chronic inflammation and a faulty immune system contribute to both conditions. Or maybe it's because RA limits your range of motion, making it hard to brush and floss thoroughly. However, this did not seem to be a factor in the recent study.

Stifle swelling with balanced food plan

Painful joints? You may find real pain relief naturally just by balancing these two nutrients found in eggs, meat, milk, and fish.

Omega-3 fatty acids, found mostly in fish, decrease the enzymes in your body that promote inflammation. Omega-6 fatty acids, found in vegetable oils, meats, milk, and eggs, encourage your body to make more.

To make sure omega-3 wins this tug-of-war, you'll probably need to change your diet. Most people get 10 to 25 times more omega-6 than omega-3. By lowering the ratio to between 2-to-1 and 4-to-1, you should feel better and need fewer anti-inflammatory drugs.

Eat cold-water, fatty fish like salmon, mackerel, albacore tuna, and herring for the biggest boost of omega-3. Between seafood suppers, try cooking with canola oil and making salad dressings with flaxseed oil.

Trim omega-6 from your diet by cutting back on meats, processed and fast foods, and vegetable oils like safflower, corn, and soybean.

Whatever the reason for the link, you can take steps to prevent gum disease and protect your smile.

Search for signs. Look in the mirror for hints you might have periodontal disease. Check for red, swollen gums that bleed easily. If you detect the condition early, it's easier to treat. Other possible signs include chronic bad breath and a bad taste in your mouth.

Brush up on oral hygiene. Taking good care of your mouth helps stop the spread of gum disease. Make sure to brush your teeth and tongue and floss regularly. Schedule regular dental checkups.

Focus on nutrition. About 65 percent of gum specialists think a well-balanced diet can help prevent gum disease. Most also recommend vitamin C and calcium, which strengthen your teeth and immune system. You can find calcium in milk, cheese, and yogurt, and vitamin C in fruits and vegetables like oranges, strawberries, and tomatoes.

Remember, eat right, practice good oral hygiene, and watch for early signs of gum disease. And keep smiling.

Say a prayer to soothe your pain

If you're looking for alternatives to traditional rheumatoid arthritis treatments, your prayers have been answered.

Exercise, rest, hot and cold compresses, and nonsteroidal anti-inflammatory drugs (NSAIDs) remain trusty ways to manage your RA. But they only focus on the body. New scientific research reveals how the mind and spirit can overcome the physical pain of rheumatoid arthritis.

Pray away pain. Do you believe in the power of prayer to heal? Medical experts are gaining faith in old-time religion as a new treatment for rheumatoid arthritis.

A recent study in Florida examined the effect of direct-contact prayer. Ministers experienced in healing visited 40 RA patients at a private clinic. Over a three-day period, they spent six hours praying aloud for each patient and laying hands on their affected joints.

The results were dramatic — and long lasting. One year later, the people with RA showed remarkable improvement. In fact, prayer was about as effective as methotrexate, a powerful disease-modifying anti-rheumatic drug (DMARD), in reducing the number of swollen and tender joints.

Because the study involved older, devoutly Christian women, the results may not apply to everyone. But it does provide hope that prayer can help the treatment process.

Stay spiritually strong. You don't need a faith healer to make your rheumatoid arthritis more bearable. You just need faith.

When researchers examined the diaries of 35 people with RA, they realized spirituality played an important role in dealing with rheumatoid arthritis. The people who had daily spiritual experiences — such as feeling moved by the beauty of creation or wanting to be closer to God — were in better moods and had much less joint pain. They were also more likely to have a support group to help them when things got rough.

Just the thought of some spiritual support can be helpful. In the Florida prayer study, people being prayed for from a distance didn't show any additional improvement — but those who believed someone was praying for them were more likely to improve.

Beat the blues. You've heard the expression "mind over matter." When it comes to managing rheumatoid arthritis, your state of mind certainly does matter.

Arizona State University researchers explored the links between depression, stress, and RA. When you're depressed, you experience more stress. When you're stressed or depressed, you feel more pain. In other words, your mood and your response to stress make a huge difference in your physical well-being.

Try these tips to break the cycle of depression, stress, and pain.

★ Take control of your stress. Simple stress-busting techniques such as listening to music, working a puzzle, or watching fish in an aquarium can calm you down and brighten your day.

★ Eat more fish. The omega-3 fatty acids in fish help boost your mood and soothe your aching joints. So you're fighting both depression and RA. Aim for fatty fish like salmon, tuna, or mackerel. You can also take fish oil supplements.

★ Seek professional help. Sometimes self-help isn't enough. If you feel completely overwhelmed by depression, don't be afraid to see a therapist.

Just because your body aches doesn't mean it should get all the attention. Remember to focus on your mental, emotional, and spiritual health as well. Your entire body will feel better.

Top tips for traveling with arthritis

Traveling can be a real pain — especially when you have arthritis. Make sure you're "PACKED" for a successful trip.

P-ack light. Don't bring more clothes than you need. You'll only make your suitcase heavier. Bring garments you can mix and match.

A-sk for help. A porter can carry your bags, and a flight attendant can put your carry-on in the overhead compartment. Request an aisle seat on the plane or a handicapped-accessible hotel room.

C-arry some relief. Carry some oils or lotions for a massage. Tote a pillow and heating pad to ease flare-ups.

K-eep to your schedule. If you travel out of your time zone, keep your watch set to home time so you'll know when to take your medication.

E-xercise on the way. Get up and walk around the plane's cabin. If you're driving, stop and stretch once in a while. While sitting, stretch your legs, shrug your shoulders, or flex your ankles.

D-ress comfortably. Wear loose, comfortable clothing. Elastic waistbands and roomy sleeves make items easier to put on and take off.

Rosacea

Keep cool to keep your face clear

For months, people stared at former President Bill Clinton's face and wondered. Then the media finally asked the obvious: Why did his nose seem to get larger and redder each day?

The answer is rosacea. This little understood disorder usually begins in middle age or later and affects three times as many men as women. Men are also more likely to develop a symptom called rhinophyma — a condition in which the nose becomes red and swollen. President Clinton is a perfect example, as was the famous comedian W.C. Fields.

Treatment with topical antibiotics often improves rosacea, so don't delay seeking medical help. However, anything that causes your face to get hot and red can worsen it. Steer around common triggers with the following tips.

Skip the suntan. Everyone knows the sun can make your skin red. With rosacea, though, your reaction to a little sun can be severe. Stay out of those harmful rays as much as possible. If you must be outside, cover up with sun block containing a Sun Protection Factor (SPF) of at least 15. When the mercury rises, wear a large-brimmed hat to shade your face and sunglasses to protect your eyes. If humidity aggravates your skin, invest in an air conditioner, and use it during the summer months.

Watch out for Old Man Winter. Winter weather can be equally hard on rosacea sufferers. Cold can make your face redden, and icy winds can chap your skin. So cover up. Use a good moisturizer, and wrap a scarf around your face when you go outside.

Say no to saunas. They feel great, but a sauna raises your body temperature and expands blood vessels in your skin. That's the last thing you need.

Cool your emotions. If you "see red" easily, you might be seeing more of it in your mirror. Anger can cause a red face, as can embarrassment or even excitement. Try to get your emotions under control. Relaxation, breathing exercises, or biofeedback might help to keep your face cool. But don't just ignore your feelings. Talk about what bothers you so you don't keep emotions bottled up.

Focus on food. Many people with rosacea can't eat spicy foods. Pay attention to any dishes that cause your face to flush, and avoid them. Sometimes hot soups or drinks can cause the same problem. Let them cool to room temperature before indulging.

Assess alcohol. If having a glass of red wine makes you look like you have a fever, try white instead. If all alcohol bothers you, choose non-alcoholic drinks.

Exercise restraint. Rosacea is the perfect excuse for needing help with heavy housework. Straining to lift sends blood rushing to your head, turning your skin red. Obviously, that means weight lifting is out. Avoid swimming in heated pools, too.

Mind your meds. Some drugs, such as corticosteroids, can cause a type of rosacea. If you have symptoms of the disorder while taking steroids, report it to your doctor immediately. He may be able to switch you to something else. Certain other drugs called vasodilators relax your blood vessels. Prescribed for heart and circulation problems, they allow better blood flow. But that could be a problem for your face. Ask your doctor if any medicine you take is a vasodilator.

Fighting rosacea early could prevent scarring and other skin damage in the future. So keep a cool head for a clear face.

Secrets to soothing sensitive skin

You could easily mistake rosacea for adult acne. But if you treat it with over-the-counter acne scrubs, you can actually make it worse. Gentle cleansing is the secret to caring for your delicate skin.

Avoid irritants. Unlike acne, rosacea can worsen with skin toners and alcohol-based astringents designed for oily skin. Also, avoid cleansers with grainy particles, salicylic acid, and witch hazel. Steer clear of oils and fragrances, too. If any skin product causes stinging, stop using it immediately.

Don't scrub. Wash with a gentle, water-soluble facial cleanser, and carefully smooth it on with clean fingers or a soft sponge. Then rinse completely with lukewarm water. Don't use washcloths as they can "rough up" your already ruddy face.

Skip the towel. Let your skin dry slowly and naturally without using a towel, which might contain traces of laundry detergent or fabric softener. Wait at least half an hour before applying makeup.

Block those rays. Protect your face with sunscreen every day. Even on cloudy days, ultraviolet rays that can cause redness and damage attack your skin. Use a sun block with Sun Protection Factor (SPF) of at least 15.

Invest in special cosmetics. Like most rosacea sufferers, you're probably anxious to cover your inflamed skin with makeup. Just be sure to use extra gentle products that have been approved by a dermatologist, such as those made by Clinique. The Clinique line of cosmetics includes a foundation with SPF 15 built in.

To cover redness, use tinted color correctors in green or yellow shades. Avoid makeup with pink or orange tones, which can make you look even more flushed. Choose neutral or yellow instead.

Visit your dermatologist regularly. Find a dermatologist you trust, and don't skip appointments. Dermatologists can prescribe medicine for your rosacea, either as creams or pills. Antibiotics often help, but you might have to take them for a long time. If you've already developed scarring or broken blood vessels, a trained skin doctor can enhance your appearance with outpatient procedures such as dermabrasion or laser surgery.

In treating your rosacea, patience and gentle care of your skin is key. Although improvement often comes slowly, the payoff of a clear face is well worth the extra effort.

When rosy cheeks aren't healthy

Your face looks like you have a severe sunburn — and you haven't been out in the sun. Alarm bells should be going off in your head.

Rosacea usually begins with patchy, red areas on your nose, chin, or cheeks that can spread to your entire face. You may develop bumps and pimples that leave pockmarks, along with a web of spider veins all over your face. Swollen, red eyelids and burning eyes may add to the discomfort.

Before this disease catches you by surprise, check to see if you're at risk. Certain people are more likely than others to get rosacea. In fact, the disorder can even run in families. Your risk is higher if you:

★ are fair skinned.

★ have Irish, English, Scottish, Scandinavian, or East European ancestry.

★ flush easily.

★ have trouble expressing emotions.

★ are undergoing hormonal changes.

★ have sensitive skin.

Because rosacea typically comes and goes in cycles, you may think you can just ignore it. Don't. Without treatment, it tends to worsen over time. If you suspect you have this condition, see your doctor right away for an evaluation.

Shingles

9 ways to survive a shingles attack

Health experts estimate that 50 percent of people who live to be 80 will have an attack of the herpes zoster virus, which you probably know as shingles. The virus — a version of the one that gave you chickenpox as a child — hides in your body, sometimes for 50 years or more, until something provokes it. Experts say a weak immune system, an illness, or even stress can activate it.

An attack of shingles begins with a fever, chills, and a tingling sensation along a nerve pathway in your body. The tingling eventually becomes a burning or shooting pain. As if that's not enough misery for one person, a few days later a blistery, itchy rash breaks out, much like the one you had with chickenpox. But this time the rash follows the line of the affected nerves. After a few days, the sores form a crust, but symptoms can last anywhere from 10 days to five weeks. The virus is contagious during the blistering stage, but once the rash has scabbed over, you can't spread it.

You're most likely to get the blisters somewhere on your midsection, but occasionally they appear on the face, arms, or shoulders. Getting the rash near your eyes or ears can sometimes damage your sight or hearing. Consult your doctor if this happens to you.

Although there isn't a cure for this painful virus yet, researchers hope the new immunization for chickenpox might spare future generations from this outbreak. In the meantime, you can get relief from the misery of shingles with the following remedies.

Climb into your tub. Pour one to two cups of finely ground (colloidal) oatmeal in a tub of warm water and soak for 20 minutes. Or try one-half to one cup of baking soda or a cup of cornstarch. These skin treatments can help with the itching.

Dry it up. Remember calamine lotion? Your mom probably swabbed it on your poison ivy. Dab it on your blisters for relief. Some people prefer aloe vera gel, apple cider vinegar, or hydrogen peroxide.

Don't scratch. Although the itching may be unbearable, try not to scratch. If you break open a blister, you could spread the rash even more. Keep your nails trimmed, and if you think you might scratch in your sleep, wear a pair of lightweight, cotton gloves to bed.

Take care of your mouth. Gargle with saltwater if you develop sores in your mouth. Eat soft, bland foods until they heal, and brush your teeth carefully with a child-size toothbrush.

Temper itching with temperature. Use warm or cool compresses, whichever feels most soothing on the sores. Moisten them first for best results.

Dodge that draft. Stay away from cold air blowing from an air conditioner or an open window. Shivering can make your skin feel more sensitive.

Keep it uncovered. Your blisters will heal faster if you leave them unbandaged. That's because circulating air helps them dry out faster.

Hit pain with a pill. Aspirin, ibuprofen, or acetaminophen can help with pain. Nonprescription antihistamines can dry up the blisters and help you get a good night's sleep.

Distract yourself. If you lay on the couch all day, you'll feel sick. In addition, blankets and the weight of your body can irritate your rash. Keep your hands busy with a project, like arranging pictures in a photo album or straightening out a closet. Soon your mind will be off your discomfort, if only for a few minutes at a time.

If the itching and pain of shingles is too much for you, don't be afraid to ask your doctor for help. Just remember, shingles will eventually clear up like any other virus, and soon you'll be back to your old self.

Zap long-term nerve pain

When a young person develops shingles, there are rarely complications. But if you're past 60 years of age, the herpes zoster virus can keep you down a long time. In addition, you're at risk for a condition called postherpetic neuralgia (PHN), the medical term for nerve pain that lingers after the virus.

PHN pain can range from tenderness to a constant burning or throbbing in a nerve. Some people become so sensitive to any sensation that even a breeze can cause pain.

If you suffer from PHN, you are not alone. It affects millions of adults. Don't suffer in silence. Ask your doctor about the following treatments.

Lidocaine patch. The lidocaine patch is one of the newest treatments for PHN. Lidocaine is an ingredient often found in products that relieve sunburn and other skin pain. Now researchers have developed large, lidocaine-filled patches that penetrate your skin to numb nerve pain. Although some people report skin reactions, like a rash, others have found significant pain relief with the patches.

Capsaicin. This over-the-counter cream is made from hot red peppers. It sounds strange, but applying the hot pepper cream to your skin actually makes the area less sensitive to heat and pain. Wait until blisters have healed completely before using the cream. Keep in mind that capsaicin can cause allergic reactions in some people.

Antidepressants. You might feel better on a low-dose antidepressant, which can limit pain signals to your brain. Several trials of antidepressant use in elderly individuals with PHN showed moderate to good pain relief in 44 to 67 percent of the people. Experts recommend at least four weeks of therapy. If it helps, you should continue it for three to six months.

Alternative therapies. You might find help with acupuncture or biofeedback. Look into these alternate therapies to see if one suits you.

Positive thinking. Why is it that people who expect to get well usually do? Doctors say it's the power of positive thinking. Use visualization to picture yourself doing activities without pain. Imagine your nerves growing stronger and healthier every day. Harness positive talk as well. Tell yourself that your body is slowly repairing damage caused by the virus. Focus on the times you feel good and expect to feel increasingly better.

Your doctor can prescribe powerful pain medicine if you need it. Talk to her about your discomfort and speak up if any treatment is not working.

Researchers hope to develop new therapies in the near future and maybe even a vaccine to prevent PHN. With a little luck, nerve pain after shingles could soon be a thing of the past.

Sinusitis

Super self-help strategies for your sinuses

It's one of the most commonly reported illnesses in the U.S. — with the numbers climbing every year.

Sinusitis occurs when the air-filled pockets around your eyes and nose — your sinuses — become inflamed and swollen. This prevents mucus from draining properly. Pressure inside builds, leading to a headache, stuffy nose, and pain in your face and teeth.

Acute sinusitis, which usually lasts one to three weeks, develops during or after a cold. Chronic sinusitis, which can last for months or years, is often caused by allergies. However, acute sinusitis can turn into chronic sinusitis if it's not treated properly.

Here are 10 things you can do to relieve your pain and discomfort.

Sleep tight. Get the right amount of sleep. Oversleeping or not getting enough shuteye can aggravate your condition and make your sinusitis last longer. To help your sinuses drain at night, try sleeping with your head slightly raised. If one side is stuffier than the other, sleep with that side tilted down.

Move along. Mild to vigorous exercise can open up your nasal passages so you can breathe easier. However, some find this makes their clogged sinuses worse. Give exercise a shot — it just might help.

Moisten the air. Use a humidifier to add moisture to the air so you can breathe. It will help keep your sinuses from drying out.

Get steamed. Place warm, wet towels directly over your sinuses. Or hold your face over a steaming sink. Or just breathe in the steam from a cup of hot water. The hot vapor should clear up your airways. Add some pine oil, eucalyptus, or menthol to the water for an extra boost.

Spice up your diet. Eat horseradish, garlic, and cayenne. These spicy seasonings cut through tough sinus blockages. Add them to soups or other foods for quick relief. On the other hand, certain foods might cause stuffiness. Common culprits are wheat, milk, and red wine.

Press on. Try acupressure. You might feel relief by applying a few seconds of direct pressure to the inner edges of your eyebrows, the sides of your nose, and the bones below and around your eyes.

Rinse your nose. Make a simple nasal rinse by mixing half a teaspoon of salt with 8 ounces of warm water. With a bulb syringe, squirt the solution into your nose and let it soothe and rinse your sinuses.

Drink up. To keep your mucous membranes moist, drink plenty of water. A good rule of thumb is to drink half an ounce of water for every pound you weigh. Or, if you're more active, two-thirds of an ounce per pound. For example, if you weigh 130 pounds, you'd need between eight and 13 8-ounce glasses of water each day. For variety, drink herbal teas, natural fruit juices diluted with water, and thin soups. Avoid caffeinated beverages like coffee and soda.

Eat your vitamins. Get plenty of vitamins A, C, and E to keep your mucous membranes healthy and to fend off colds, allergies, and sinusitis. Look for vitamin C in colorful fruits and vegetables like apricots, cantaloupe, strawberries, red and green peppers, kale, and broccoli. Eat carrots, sweet potatoes, mangoes, and squash for beta carotene, which your body converts to vitamin A. Find vitamin E in dark, leafy greens, vegetable oils, nuts and seeds, and wheat germ.

Have a good cry. Sinusitis might make you feel like crying. Go ahead, releasing the pent-up emotion might also relieve pressure in your sinuses.

Chances are some of these tips will help you, and some won't. Experiment, and see what works for you. But if home remedies fail and your infection gets worse, see your doctor before your sinusitis causes lasting damage.

Is it a cold or sinusitis?

Many times, people with sinusitis think they just have a hard-to-shake cold — and vice versa.

Because the symptoms are so similar, it's hard to distinguish between a cold, an allergy, and sinusitis. For example, you can have a stuffy nose and a cough with all three conditions.

Here are some ways to determine if you have sinusitis. If you suspect you do have a sinus infection, see your doctor.

★ Bend over or jump up and down for a few minutes. If the headache pain and sinus pressure get worse, you probably have sinusitis.

★ Thick green, gray, or yellow mucus is a sign of sinusitis. With a cold or allergy, the discharge is usually clear.

★ An ache in your upper jaw generally signals sinusitis.

★ Lie down. If your condition worsens, it's probably sinusitis.

Surprising risks for sinusitis

You might know breathing in smoke or fumes can trigger sinusitis. You might even know that a fungus or mold can bring on this painful condition. But you'll be amazed by what you don't know about sinusitis. Check out these little-known risk factors.

Don't blow it. When you're stuffed up with a cold, blowing your nose helps you breathe. But, according to researchers at the University of Virginia and University of Aahrus Hospital in Denmark, blowing your nose also propels mucus into your sinuses.

Along with the mucus comes viruses or bacteria, which can lead to a sinus infection. In addition, this excess fluid hampers sinus drainage, again possibly leading to sinusitis.

As tempting as it might be to blow your nose, try to resist. The researchers recommend taking antihistamines at the first sign of a cold instead.

Boost antioxidants. Cell damage caused by harmful molecules called free radicals can contribute to sinusitis. Fortunately, you have antioxidants in your nasal lining that defend against this.

Danish scientists measured levels of the antioxidants glutathione and uric acid in the mucus of people with and without sinusitis. Those with sinusitis had only half as much glutathione and significantly less uric acid than healthy people. It's likely that below normal antioxidant defenses can lead to sinusitis.

While this hasn't been proven, you might be able to guard against sinusitis by boosting your antioxidant levels. Eat foods high in glutathione and in purines, which break down in your body to form uric acid.

Good sources of glutathione include beef, potatoes, asparagus, avocado, spinach, grapefruit, oranges or orange juice, tomatoes, cantaloupe, and watermelon. Opt for fresh fruits and vegetables rather than canned ones to get the most glutathione.

Purines can be found in liver, anchovies, sardines, herring, fish, peas, beans, whole grain cereals, asparagus, cauliflower, mushrooms, and spinach. However, be careful about eating too many high-purine foods. Too much uric acid can lead to gout.

Watch out for stroke. If you have sinusitis, that might not be your only problem. This condition might also be a risk factor for ischemic stroke, the kind caused by a blocked blood vessel in your brain.

Margaret Schlosser, a licensed practical nurse at Akron City Hospital in Ohio, noticed a link between stroke and sinusitis. In fact, over a nine-month period, 12 percent of stroke patients were also diagnosed with sinusitis.

It's not clear that sinusitis by itself can lead to stroke since most patients also had at least one other known risk factor. Still, protect yourself from stroke by exercising regularly, maintaining a healthy weight, quitting smoking, and keeping high blood pressure under control.

Now that you know these unusual risks, remember them. Load up on antioxidants, protect yourself against stroke, and think before you blow your nose.

Skin Cancer

Surprising ways to beat the sun

You might think your makeup and clothing protect you from skin cancer, but they might not be protecting you as well as you thought. Fortunately, with a few small changes to your everyday armor, you can boost your immunity to the sun's rays.

Make the most of skin care products. Makeup with a sun protection factor (SPF) of at least 15 can shield your face from sun damage. But it's only effective as long as it covers all of your skin. In reality, the tiny particles of foundation migrate toward your pores and disappear in just two hours. The smooth mask that cut the sun's rays this morning can get cracked, wiped off, or smeared with sweat, leaving you unprotected by lunchtime.

Don't count on one application of makeup to shield your skin all day. Instead, increase your cover with these simple steps.

★ Wear sunscreen under your makeup, and slather some on your arms, hands, and the tops of your feet while you're at it.

★ Powder your face frequently during the day to refresh your skin coverage.

★ Check for Melasyn in the active ingredients in your makeup. Melasyn is a synthetic form of melanin, the pigment that gives hair and skin its color. Not only does it deflect damaging rays, it adjusts to your skin tone to give you a natural-looking tan.

★ Look for products with green tea extract or a combination of the hormone melatonin and vitamins E and C. Scientists are uncovering many natural additives to help skin care products shield you from the sun. Most protect you with a layer of antioxidants that halt DNA damage in its tracks.

Take advice from desert dwellers. There are many effective ways to physically cover up and shut the sun out, but wearing a light-colored shirt isn't one of them. Less than 30 percent of white cotton or linen T-shirts tested in a lab screened out enough deadly ultraviolet (UV) rays to protect you from skin cancer.

Perhaps that's why desert nomads live in dark tents and wear dark clothing. Follow their lead and make these slight changes to your wardrobe to put a damper on sun damage.

★ Wear dark colors, like blue, purple, or black. Lab tests show dark fabrics can deflect UV rays as effectively as a sunscreen with SPF 30.

★ Choose summer clothes with a high polyester or wool content. These fabrics are generally tightly woven, and the sun's rays can't break through the dense weave.

★ Shrink your shirts in the dryer. Natural shrinkage makes the holes between the threads smaller and keeps more UV rays out.

★ Add a UV blocker to your laundry. RIT makes a UV protective laundry additive called Sun Guard that blocks more than 96 percent of UV rays. Just throw a package in with your next load of laundry and enjoy the benefits for up to three months.

★ Take advantage of space-age technology. There are new lines of sports and beachwear that filter out UV rays entirely. These SPF fabrics are so effective NASA used them to make special "sun suits" for two little boys with severe allergies to light. The boys can now step outside during the day for the first time in their lives.

Scientists are concerned that the holes in the ozone layer are making the sun our enemy instead of our friend. But with proper protection from the sun's damaging rays, there is no reason to spend your life indoors when nature beckons you outside.

Top things to carry in your beach bag

Fill your beach bag with these great skin protectors to fight cancer and premature aging.

Sunscreen with SPF of 15 to 30. Slather on at least an ounce of sunscreen — that's the amount it takes to fill a shot glass — half an hour before you go out in the sun.

A timer. Set it to go off every 60 minutes to remind you to reapply your sunscreen.

A blue T-shirt. Research shows a dark blue shirt protects your skin from UV rays better than a white one.

Your favorite lipstick or lip balm. Apply it twice a day and cut your risk of developing lip cancer in half — just make sure the brand you choose contains sunscreen.

A wide-brimmed hat. It's a great way to shade your face from the sun.

A thermos of green tea. Research on mice shows drinking about three cups of green tea a day may increase your skin's ability to ward off sun damage.

A water bottle. You need to drink at least 8 ounces of water before any outdoor activity. Then continue drinking water every 15 minutes.

Take charge with self-exams

Skin cancer is one of the easiest cancers to cure if you catch it early, but don't just count on your doctor to find it for you. Recent research reveals some surprising statistics — 57 percent of people diagnosed with skin cancer detected it themselves. Doctors discovered only 16 percent of skin cancers.

Spotting skin cancer is easy once you are familiar with your own body markings. Set a monthly date to examine yourself for possible warning signs of cancer.

Know your ABCDs. Look carefully at your moles and pay attention to these four red flags:

★ **A**symmetry. Both sides of a mole should look alike. If one side bulges, have it checked out.

★ **B**orders. Safe moles have sharp, round borders. Note any blurred, jagged, or irregular outlines.

★ **C**olor. Regular moles are generally a uniform brown. A red, pink, tan, blue, or black multi-colored spot is a warning sign of melanoma.

★ **D**iameter. A doctor should inspect any mole larger than the eraser on the end of your pencil.

Investigate unwelcome guests. Take special note of small, shiny lumps that may suddenly crop up on your skin. Have a dermatologist check any red, scaly, or itchy patches that don't fade away.

Look in the mirror. Now that you know what you are looking for, search every nook and cranny of your body to spot changes on your skin.

★ Inspect your palms, the back of your hands, and the front and back of your arms.

★ Undress before a full-length mirror and check your torso, legs, genitals, and underarms. Use a hand mirror to study your neck, back, and the back of your legs.

★ With a mirror held in one hand, look closely at your face, and then part your hair and search for hidden moles. Also peek behind your ears and along your jaw line.

★ Sit down and investigate the tops and soles of your feet. Part your toes and look between them.

Rope in a partner. If your spouse comments on an unusual mole or spot, make sure you take heed. Over 10 percent of skin cancers were discovered first by a close family member.

See doctor for free. May is National Skin Cancer Screening Month. Watch for notices of free skin cancer screenings in your area and get your skin checked yearly by a dermatologist.

Skin cancer is quite common. Fortunately, you have all the resources you need to avoid it. Just stay protected in the sun and watch your moles to keep cancer from getting under your skin.

Don't get burned by psoriasis treatment

Your doctor may advise you to soak up some sun to treat your psoriasis. Tanning beds and sun tanning are often recommended because ultraviolet rays slow down the production of skin cells. Yet, these rays can damage your skin and increase your risk of skin cancer.

To cut your risks, limit your exposure to ultraviolet light; wear sunscreen, a wide-brimmed hat, and protective clothing when you're outside; and check your skin regularly for signs of cancer.

And if you have ever undergone PUVA therapy — a combination of ultraviolet light and the drug psoralen, be sure to warn your doctor before he recommends cyclosporine for your psoriasis. If you combine both treatments, you are four times more likely to get squamous cell carcinoma, a form of skin cancer. Your risk level stays high even if you take cyclosporine years after the original PUVA treatments.

Stop smoking to save your skin

Smoking doesn't just cause lung cancer. Depending on how much you smoke, you could be two to four times as likely to get squamous cell carcinoma, a common type of skin cancer, as your nonsmoking neighbor. Lighting up also increases your risk of basal cell carcinoma and melanoma — the more serious skin cancers.

Here's how smoking harms your skin:

★ It weakens your immune system, making you more vulnerable to cancer.

★ It reduces the amount of oxygen reaching your skin cells by narrowing the blood vessels, leaving your skin paper thin and fragile.

★ It raises your risk of being burned in a house fire. This sounds bizarre, but it's true. Scar tissue resulting from a burn is very sensitive to the sun and can develop skin cancer faster than normal skin.

If you smoke, check your skin regularly for signs of cancer. Better yet, quit your smoking habit. It might be difficult, but it will be worth the effort.

Slick way to outsmart sun damage

Don't panic if your skin is slightly pink even after you took extra pains to protect it from the sun. A well-known Mediterranean cooking oil might undo cancer-causing damage to your cells.

A group of scientists in Japan say applying extra virgin olive oil to your skin after coming in from the sun might protect it from damage. Research on mice suggests it may heal your skin and reduce your chances of developing skin cancer — but it has to be extra virgin olive oil. Regular virgin olive oil won't do the trick. Continue applying extra virgin olive oil daily, and it will sink into your skin and help nourish it back to health.

Stress

Learn new coping skills

Some people feel powerless when confronted with stressful events, while other people are able to rise to the occasion. These hardy folks usually maintain a cheerful attitude and good health despite stressful situations.

Scientists discovered several common characteristics among those who cope well with adversity. See if any of these apply to you.

★ You handle stress well because you view problems that come up as exciting challenges to solve, instead of dreading them.

★ You control the amount of stressful information you take in and give yourself time to gradually get used to new circumstances.

★ When major situations are out of your control, you find ways to take responsibility for those things you can control.

★ You are a good taskmaster. You break down large projects into manageable blocks and set realistic timelines.

★ You embrace deadlines, relishing the exhilaration and satisfaction of a job well done. You are deeply committed to what you do.

★ You are unafraid to bond with a friend or family member when times are tough.

If these traits don't come naturally to you, don't worry. There's help. Here are some ways you can improve your coping skills.

Is your pet stressing you out?

Did you know your dog can help you figure your taxes? The stress of a complicated mental task, like doing taxes or making an unexpected speech, can dangerously raise your blood pressure. But if you have a pet, your stress levels will drop with your blood pressure, and you will have more patience to deal with paperwork.

But like any loved one, your pet can also cause you unwanted anxiety. If you are hospitalized, worrying about your dog or cat may tempt you to leave the hospital without being released. Some pet owners have even risked their lives to get back to their beloved pooch. For your own peace of mind, give a neighbor who loves your pet a key to your house. While you are away, she can lavish it with attention and care, giving you time to take care of yourself.

Look for the silver lining. Learn to see setbacks as challenges. Looking for something good in a bad situation will reduce stress and help you cope.

Focus on today. Live your life in the moment. Don't allow guilt about the past or anxiety about the future to rob you of today.

Build strong relationships. Invest in those around you. Friendships and love are the spice of life, and they provide you with important social support in rough times. Researchers discovered that people with a strong support network weathered stress more successfully than people who had no one to turn to. But try to avoid people who are cynical or mistrustful. They are bad for your health, spiritually and physically.

Drop old grudges. Forgiving someone for something they did to you is very hard, but pent up resentment causes stress. To help you forgive someone, replay the hurtful incident in your mind, and rewrite your response to it. Instead of getting upset, find a positive way to view the situation. Once you are rid of your negative emotions, you break that person's hold on you and forgiveness comes easier.

Pen your thoughts. Write down your worries in a journal. Journaling helps you see things differently and come up with new solutions to your problems. Writing about a stressful incident may also improve your health. In one study of people with asthma or rheumatoid arthritis, participants who wrote about a traumatic event had less severe symptoms than those who wrote about everyday topics.

Put your worries to rest with prayer

When times get tough, the tough start praying. A recent study shows at least 96 percent of older adults use prayer to deal with stress.

What is it about prayer that makes it so effective? Dr. Harold Koenig, director of the Center for the Study of Religion/Spirituality and Health at Duke University, suggests prayer goes beyond physical relaxation. "The sense that God deeply cares about a person and is in control of everything that happens to them provides comfort that penetrates into all other areas of life and endures over time."

When unexpected events come your way, you may notice your heart races, your muscles tense, and your senses sharpen. This is called the stress response. If this heightened alert lasts too long, your immune system weakens and stress chemicals build up in your body.

To counteract the stress response and bring on the relaxation response, experts recommend tai chi, yoga, biofeedback, or meditation. Now many experts say prayer is just as effective. Actually, prayer and meditation have a lot in common. They both can help you:

★ **Maintain a positive attitude.** By praying or meditating, you can take the sting out of daily events that would otherwise send you into a tizzy.

★ **Live in the moment.** In Matthew 6:34, the Bible tells us not to worry about tomorrow, since it will take care of itself. Living each day as it comes is a central theme in both prayer and meditation. Since worrying about the past or the future often causes anxiety, concentrating on the present automatically knocks out a major cause of stress.

★ **Focus on one subject.** Those who meditate set their mind at ease by concentrating on something as simple as breathing. When you pray, you choose to set your eyes on God. You may wonder at his power, respect his holiness, or give thanks for his love. By focusing on one thing, the jumble of daily frustrations and events melts away, and your body can relax.

★ **Find wonder in the routine.** While meditating, you may note the simple satisfaction of everyday activities, like cleaning the house or watering the yard. Koenig says devout believers often view the changing of the seasons with awe and delight — taking pleasure in the natural world as a gift from God. When you can glory in smelling the flowers, you pay homage to every moment of life.

★ **Use reason instead of reaction.** Meditating gives you time to look at a tense situation without making snap judgments or reacting in the heat of the moment. Prayer teaches you to see your life as God sees it. With his support, you know you will have the strength to face anything that comes your way.

★ **Make peace with the past.** Forgiveness is an important key to any stress-release program. Doctors and religious leaders both agree — freeing yourself from bitterness about the past helps you develop compassion for others, as well as an inner calm.

Meditation offers you immediate and short-term relief. But, according to Koenig, the effects of prayer are much more permanent and satisfying.

"I think (prayer) is even more effective than the 'temporary' reduction in stress that meditation offers," Koenig says. "This is because prayer involves a relationship with God and a relationship with community — which involves more of a person's world-view and whole life."

So set your fears aside and turn to God in prayer, the greatest source of peace available to you any time you choose.

Prepare for a rainy day

Planning for the unexpected can give you a sense of control over your situation. It's a good idea to have an emergency plan in case you need to leave your home suddenly. Follow these suggestions for an effective plan.

★ Arrange to stay with a friend in an emergency. Also, call a family member who can let others know where you are.

★ Pack a bag with an overnight supply of clothes and personal things. Include any prescription medicine or special care items. Keep your bag with you in the car.

★ Make copies of official and important documents. Keep a copy with you, and stash a second one outside your home — in a safe deposit box or with a friend.

★ Stock a small supply of canned goods and bottled water in your basement.

Try a hands-on approach to relaxation

Touch therapy has been used for centuries to relax and invigorate. In Roman times, gladiators had a session with a masseur to loosen them up before battle. Today, practitioners use anything from traditional Swedish massage to exotic Chinese acupuncture to bring relief to stressed-out people.

When you face a stressful situation, your brain signals the release of chemicals that tighten your muscles. If the stress continues for a long time, these chemicals get trapped in your tissues and tie your muscles in knots. Sometimes these knots develop into trigger points — painful spots that send pain signals to the rest of your body. Touch therapy can relax these muscles and let the chemicals seep out. Try these relaxing techniques for yourself.

Massage. If you are wound up like a spring, try a massage. It not only relieves tension, it increases circulation and makes your muscles and joints more flexible.

To work out tension in your neck and shoulders, loosely tie two tennis balls in a clean, cotton sock. Lie down and gently position the tennis balls under your head, one on either side of the base of your skull. Rest for 20 minutes. The pressure from the balls should ease the tension all the way down to your toes.

Many health experts agree that a five-minute foot massage can lower your heart rate and slow your breathing. To pamper your toot-sies, gently knead your foot with your thumbs, rubbing around the bones in gentle, circular motions. Or roll a tennis ball under the sole of your foot while you relax on the couch.

For a soothing face massage, gently run your fingers around your eyes, tightening the circle until your fingers run along the ridge of your eyebrows. Using small, circular motions, travel down your cheekbones to your jaw and ear. To finish, run your fingers lightly from the center of your forehead, out along your cheek and jaw line. Remember to use a butterfly touch, like a caress, to pamper your face.

Acupressure. Acupressure defuses tension with simple downward pressure on specific trigger points. Practitioners believe that stress and illness come from blocks in energy pathways, called meridians, which run through your body. An acupressurist presses down on anti-fatigue points, which they say can restore the flow and replenish your energy.

To try it for yourself, experts recommend pressing down gradually on various trigger points, holding your finger at a 90-degree angle to your skin. Press until you feel a gentle pulse under your fingertip. Release your hold slowly to allow your tissues to adjust.

Common acupressure trigger points for stress are just below the two bony ridges at the base of your skull and on the inner crest of your eyebrows.

Reflexology. Similar to acupressure, reflexologists believe that your organs and limbs are connected with energy currents that end up in your hands and feet. They say pressing down on certain reflex points on your hands or feet can positively affect the health of the rest of your body.

One reflex point to relieve stress is just below the fleshy pads of mus-cle at the base of your middle fingers. Reflexologists suggest pressing down on this area with the thumb on your opposite hand. Then move the thumb in a circular motion, increasing the pressure slightly. Do this several times on each hand.

It doesn't take much time or effort to tap into the healing power of touch. Just remember — if you use finger pressure to relieve tension, make sure you press down gently, without causing yourself pain. And if you are pregnant or have a serious health problem, you should avoid massaging any trigger points.

Beat stress with these vital nutrients

Eating your way out of a stressful situation is usually a bad idea, yet some foods can help make anxiety a thing of the past. Try changing your breakfast from a doughnut and a cup of coffee to a nutritious meal of enriched cereal with strawberries, a banana, and a glass of orange juice. These delicious foods replenish your body's supply of important nutrients, which can run low in times of stress.

So the next time you're frazzled and crave a snack, pass up the chips and dip and choose foods loaded with these stress-busting vitamins and minerals.

Vitamin C. Vitamin C works together with your adrenal gland to limit the production of a tension-causing hormone called cortisol. Good sources of vitamin C include strawberries, citrus fruits, red and green peppers, cabbage, and broccoli.

B vitamins. This family of vitamins is essential because your body uses them quickly when it's stressed. Vitamin B12, vitamin B6, and folate are especially important. Avocados; potatoes; bananas; beans; seeds; spinach; meat; poultry; fish; and enriched pasta, bread, and cereal are rich in these vitamins.

Magnesium. Researchers in Yugoslavia found that people exposed to chronic stress had low levels of magnesium in their body, which only made their stress worse. To get more magnesium, eat avocados, sunflower seeds, spinach, yogurt, bran cereals, legumes, and shellfish.

Zinc, iron, and selenium. In a recent study, participants under physical and mental stress experienced a drop in zinc, iron, and selenium levels. If you are under stress, eat foods high in these minerals, such as beans, crab meat, yogurt, steak, clams, and oysters.

Poor eating habits during stressful times can weaken your body's immune system. This makes you more susceptible to illness and can increase the effects of stress. By choosing nutritious foods, you'll be giving your body the ammunition it needs to fight off the damaging effects of stress.

Popular herb might cause liver damage

Who thought soothing your mind could rattle your liver? The Federal Drug Administration (FDA) recently warned against taking too much kava to relieve stress. They say this widely used herb might cause liver damage if you regularly take large doses.

There have been numerous reported incidents of liver failure associated with its use, and a number of countries have banned the sale of kava products. Scientists recently reported that the culprit could be a compound in the peelings of the plant's leaves and stems, but more research is needed to prove a link.

While researchers continue to investigate kava and liver damage, consider this advice just to be on the safe side:

★ Don't take more than the recommended amount and only take it for a short time.

★ Don't mix kava with alcohol or sleeping pills, since it enhances their effect.

★ Don't use kava if you take blood-thinning medications or have Parkinson's disease.

If you notice any signs of liver damage, like yellow skin and brown urine, stomach pain, fatigue, or loss of appetite, see your doctor and mention that you are taking kava.

4 herbal ways to tame your tension

Look to the plant world for herbal remedies to relieve stress and tension. Sitting back and relaxing with a cup of herbal tea is the perfect way to unwind. These herbs can be found at herb shops and health food stores.

Indulge in ginseng. Many animal studies support the theory that ginseng helps the body cope more effectively with stress, and it may have a similar effect in humans. Some researchers think ginseng stops stress by indirectly recharging rundown adrenal glands, which help your body react and adapt in times of stress. When constant stress has left your adrenals run down and worn out, ginseng gets them going again. Once the adrenals are recharged, they can continue to help your body rebound from stress. Ginseng is available in several forms, including capsules, teas, soft drinks, and chewing gum.

Calm your nerves with chamomile. The flowers from this common garden weed have been used for centuries to cure anything from the common cold to indigestion. Sip a cup of warm tea for a great, natural stress reliever. Just keep in mind that chamomile and daisies are related, so try something else if you have allergies to pollen.

Turn down the heat with passionflower. The extract of passionflower is used as a mild sedative. Brew the leaves and stem of this flower into a flavorful tea, which can soothe nervous restlessness. It is especially useful when anxiety is long lasting. In medical trials, it was as effective as the anti-anxiety drug oxazepam, but it didn't have any side affects.

Drift off with valerian. Once used to flavor root beer, extracts from the root of this flowering shrub make great tea. Valerian is a popular sleeping aid that herbalists say can relax your body and mind, although few studies have been done on its effectiveness and safety. Taking too much valerian can cause tremors, headache, and heart disturbances, so only take it for short periods. And avoid it if you are also taking drugs like sedatives or tranquilizers.

Herbs and supplements should only be taken as recommended and with caution. Taking too much could cause serious side effects.

Top 12 stress busters

Hit the snooze button. According to a recent study, early birds have higher levels of the stress hormone cortisol than people who sleep in.

Skip rush hour. Plan your day so you are off the streets during peak hours for shopping and commuting.

Turn on the radio. If you get stuck in traffic, sing along with the radio. Or turn on some soft, instrumental music.

Head for the beach. Plan a relaxing vacation away from the daily grind.

Use your nose. The scent of green apples, coconut, orange, chamomile, or lavender can calm your nerves.

Stop the madness. Say "stop" when you feel your muscles tense from stress.

Prioritize your worries. Ask yourself if they will be important in five years. If not, let them go.

Find the absurd. Search for the humor in every situation.

Avoid negative people. Their cynicism will put you in a rut.

Soak up some sun. Sunshine can rejuvenate your spirit and help put things in perspective.

Tune out the tube. Turn off the news in the evening and read a book or go for a walk.

Pick up the phone. Call an old friend to relive pleasant memories before bedtime.

Stroke

Little-known triggers spell sudden danger

Don't jump out of your chair to answer that phone! If you're at risk, a sudden movement like this could trigger an ischemic stroke. It's the most common kind of stroke and occurs when a blood clot blocks the flow of blood to your brain.

Researcher Silvia Koton from Tel Aviv University in Israel studied short-term triggers for stroke in older people. Surprisingly, she found that many had strokes within two hours of a sudden movement or strong, negative emotion. Even activities you're familiar with, like a doorbell or ringing telephone, can be startling enough to act as a trigger.

"The most important finding," says Koton, "is that new risk factors may interact with conventional risk factors for ischemic stroke."

Here's how to protect yourself from these unexpected troublemakers.

Move with purpose. According to Dr. Larry Goldstein, Director of the Center for Cerebrovascular Disease at Duke University Medical Center, you should plan how you're going to change positions. Don't bound out of bed in the morning even if you're full of energy. He suggests you first dangle your legs over the edge of the bed for a few minutes. "Move slowly," he says, "rather than rapidly."

But don't be afraid to exercise — it reduces your stroke risk. Just get your doctor's approval for brisk walking, swimming, or other activities that help your circulation and don't require sudden, jerking movements.

Avoid startling noises. You can't escape every heart-quickening sound — like someone yelling for help — but you can change your doorbell.

325

Replace an ear-splitting alert with a soothing chime. It will still get your attention, but you won't jump out of your skin when it rings. The same goes for your phone. Find one with a sound that doesn't rattle you.

Control your temper. Koton also found that 13 percent of her study patients experienced strong negative emotions just hours before their stroke. In other words, a short fuse could mean serious health consequences.

Count to 10 before reacting in anger. Or take a walk when you feel negative emotions welling up. If you feel angry much of the time, visit a psychologist or counselor for help dealing constructively with your feelings.

Although she hasn't completed her study, Koton is spreading the word. "High risk populations should be aware of the potential influence of sudden, unusual exposures to familiar activities and emotions."

Be careful with chiropractors. It's rare for people younger than 45 to suffer a stroke. When it happens, doctors want to know why. Recently, Canadian researchers found that out of almost 600 people who had a stroke, those in this age group were five times more likely to have visited a chiropractor the week before their brain attack.

Experts believe it's very rare for a neck manipulation to damage an artery and block the flow of blood to your brain. However, think twice about this treatment if you have other risk factors for stroke.

Serve notice on stress. If you can remain calm in the midst of chaos, you're less likely to suffer a stroke. It's the vein-popping tension that puts extra stress on your heart and circulation.

Researchers gave over 200 men a test designed to frustrate. Those who felt stressed out during the test were more likely to have a stroke within the next decade than men who handled the pressure well.

Use humor to deflect stress whenever you can. Sometimes laughing about a situation helps put it in perspective. Or write in a journal. Put your problems down on paper and you may be able to calmly think of solutions.

Stay in motion. You're more likely to get a blood clot if you remain in the same position for many hours — like on a long airplane flight. This little-known stroke trigger is a risk even for young, healthy people.

Be sure to walk up and down the aisle or to the bathroom every few hours to help keep your blood flowing. And drink lots of water, not alcohol or coffee. Otherwise you could become dehydrated from the pressurized cabin — another risk factor for clots.

Even if you don't fly often, try not to stay in bed or in a chair for long stretches of time. Plan to exercise every day — even if it's just a walk to mail a letter.

The thought of a stroke can be scary, but don't let fear rule your life. Many people believe that even engaging in sex can trigger a stroke. The risk is actually quite low, say experts. In fact, regular sexual activity can help your heart and circulation.

Smart advice for reducing your risk

There's no guarantee you'll never have a stroke. Nevertheless, here are some things you can do to minimize the danger:

★ stop smoking

★ lose weight

★ lower your cholesterol

★ lower your blood pressure

★ control diabetes

Of course there are factors you can't change. For instance, your risk of stroke is higher than average if you've already had a heart attack or a TIA (transient ischemic attack or mini-stroke).

And while the studies on alcohol and stroke aren't quite as clear-cut, most experts agree a drink a day for a woman — two for a man — might help protect you. Consume more alcohol than that, though, and your risk could triple. Talk to your doctor about having a glass of wine with dinner. Just skip the cocktails before and the nightcap after.

Top 10 food choices to side-step stroke

Here's a sample menu packed with stroke-fighting foods. If you take the drug warfarin, check with your doctor about eating nuts and garlic.

Start with cantaloupe. It's packed with beta carotene which guards against brain attacks.

Fill your cereal bowl with whole grains. Fiber helps lower artery-clogging cholesterol.

Drain a glass of OJ. Oranges contain vitamin C, another antioxidant that fights bad cholesterol.

Grab a handful of nuts. A good source of vitamin E, nuts help keep cholesterol from sticking to artery walls.

Peel a banana. The potassium in this delicious fruit fights stroke and high blood pressure.

Hook salmon for dinner. Two servings of fatty fish each week will cut your risk of stroke in half.

Cook your fish with garlic. Ajoene is a compound in garlic that keeps blood clots from forming.

Serve lima beans. Full of folate, these legumes help neutralize the amino acid homocysteine. This natural chemical can build up to toxic levels in your blood, causing clots and hardening of the arteries.

Snack on cherries. These juicy treats contain more than 17 compounds that inhibit plaque buildup in your arteries.

Relax with ginger tea. A substance in ginger called gingerol might prevent blood clots from forming.

Get stroke savvy and save a life

Helen Miller stood up after dinner and felt dizzy. A few minutes later, things looked blurry and she was still unsteady on her feet. She wanted to go home and rest — but home alone was the last place she should be. Helen Miller just had a stroke.

Many people don't recognize the warning signs of a stroke, or what's sometimes called a brain attack. But getting to a hospital fast is crucial. Waiting too long could mean a lifetime of disability or even death. Learn what a stroke looks like so you can react quickly.

Know the symptoms. Any of these problems could be a warning sign of stroke.

★ Dizziness

★ Difficulty walking

★ Weakness on one side

★ Blurred vision

★ Trouble speaking

★ Difficulty understanding words

★ Confusion

★ Sudden, severe headache

Sometimes it's less obvious — simply not being able to do the things you used to, such as writing neatly or applying makeup.

Call for help. If you suspect someone is having a stroke, call emergency services. Stroke victims fare better when emergency medical technicians treat them. These professionals know the quickest way to the hospital and exactly what to do when they arrive. If you drive, you could get lost or waste time looking for a parking space.

Get medication. There's another reason to get to the hospital fast. A medicine called tPA can quickly dissolve clots from an ischemic stroke and drastically reduce the risk of permanent damage. However, you must take it within three hours of the first symptom. And doctors must first run tests. That means, just like a heart attack, every minute counts.

Stroke doesn't have to catch you off guard. Knowledge and action can make a huge difference for you and your loved ones.

Dangerous fish: how to stay off the hook

Certain large fish could contain a hidden health hazard — mercury.

Normally heart-healthy food choices because of their omega-3 fatty acids, some fish become polluted with mercury through the environment. Most people don't eat enough fish to be in serious danger of mercury poisoning, but this heavy metal can cause brain damage and interfere with the development of unborn and young children. The FDA has advised pregnant women and women who could become pregnant to limit the amount of shark, swordfish, King mackerel, and tilefish they eat.

Even tuna can pose a threat. Larger tunas, such as the white albacore, typically contain higher amounts than the smaller, light tuna. Experts say an average-size woman should eat no more than one can of white tuna a week, or two cans of light tuna. Young children shouldn't eat more than one tuna sandwich per week.

Don't cut fish out of your diet altogether, since you can still benefit from omega-3's. Just pick your fish wisely. Northern or Atlantic mackerel and Spanish mackerel are varieties of mackerel that are smaller and come with a much lower mercury risk. Farm-raised fish are another, safe option.

Perk up your mood and pass up a stroke

Take a minute to pull yourself out of the dumps and you'll cut your risk of stroke. It's true. Experts say you're more likely to have a stroke if you're depressed.

The blues don't directly cause a stroke, however, but the exact relationship is still a little fuzzy. Some think depression causes high blood pressure, which in turn increases your risk of stroke. Others believe negative thinking, anxiety, and other symptoms of depression relate to a chemical imbalance associated with stroke.

Whatever the reason, there's no arguing with the statistics. A history of depression means you're 73 percent more likely to have a stroke. So plan a day of mood-lifting activities to keep depression and stroke from darkening your doorway.

Let the sunshine in. As soon as you're out of bed, open drapes and blinds. Turn on lights if it's a gray day. Bright morning light increases your level of melatonin, a hormone that regulates sleep and mood.

Crank up the radio. Tune in your favorite radio station for songs that make your heart glad. Listening to enjoyable music can lower your blood pressure, which in turn lowers your stroke risk.

Eat breakfast. People who eat breakfast every day tend to be happier than those who skip this important meal. Of course, what you eat makes all the difference. Choose complex carbohydrates like oatmeal with sliced apples. Grains and fruits break down more slowly than sugary breakfast foods, giving your brain a boost of the feel-good chemical serotonin. If you like, have a steaming cup of coffee for a caffeinated pick-me-up.

Take a walk. Exercise can help lift your mood while improving your circulation. And good circulation will help you avoid blood clots that can cause a brain attack. Regular exercise may even be as effective as antidepressants. So put on your walking shoes and step lively.

Use flower power. Pick some flowers while you're out walking or stop and buy a bouquet for yourself. Experts say blossoms do more than brighten a table — they can also brighten your mood.

Have a heart-healthy meal. Grill a piece of salmon and toss a spinach salad. Omega-3 fatty acids in some seafood help maintain the proper balance of chemicals in your brain. And eat spinach to avoid a B-vitamin deficiency, thought to bring on depression. This menu is simply all-around good for your blood pressure, cholesterol, and stroke risk, too.

Phone a friend. Keep in contact with family and friends who love you, especially if you live alone. According to research, people with fewer than three social relationships were twice as likely to die from heart disease than people with more friends. Staying connected to others is vital to your mental and physical health. Like the saying goes, reach out and touch someone today.

Soak in a scented bath. Pour a few drops of lavender oil in a warm bath and plan your next great day while soaking. Lavender smells heavenly and, according to research, can make you feel more relaxed and less depressed. As a bonus, lavender can work as well as some sleeping pills, without side effects.

Sip valerian tea. This herb has been used for centuries to calm, relax, and to encourage slumber. Since a good night's sleep is front-line defense against depression, brew yourself a cup just before bed.

Turn in on time. Get to bed at a reasonable hour for a full night's rest, but don't sleep more than eight hours. Too much shut-eye can actually make depression worse — you wind up feeling grumpy and even more tired.

Make these depression-fighting activities part of every day, and you'll lift your mood while you lower your stroke risk.

Surprising secret to surviving a stroke

An ordinary chemical in green tea, called gallotannin, might wind up becoming an extraordinary means of avoiding brain damage after a stroke.

Normally, brain cells die from destructive free radicals unleashed during a stroke. But gallotannin blocks a certain chemical chain reaction and, as a result, keeps these critical cells alive.

This is just one of many exciting health benefits of green tea. In addition to gallotannin, it's also loaded with a substance that boosts your body's natural ability to fight atherosclerosis.

Researchers can't say you'll get the necessary cell-saving dose of gallotannin from a cup of tea, but this chemical may become the key ingredient in future medications.

For now, warm the teakettle and take advantage of this wonder drink. To get the most heart-saving benefit, drink two to five cups a day.

TMJ Disorder

Work out your TMJ pain

Jaw aerobics may sound bizarre, but they'll help you beat the pain of a TMJ disorder. Your temporomandibular joint (TMJ) is a hinge that connects your lower jawbone to your skull. You can feel it move if you put your finger right next to your ear. This powerful joint is a complex mass of bone, muscle, and connective tissue. Because it's so complicated, many things can go wrong — resulting in pain, clicking, difficulty opening or closing your mouth, and headaches.

Dr. Robert Uppgaard, a dentist and TMJ disorder expert from Minnesota, believes changes in daily life, work, posture, and general habits give you the power to help yourself feel better. In his book, *Taking Control of TMJ*, he talks about exercising to loosen and strengthen the muscles that keep your jaw locked in pain. He recommends these stretches as part of his Total Wellness Program.

★ Strengthen gently. Make a fist and place it under your jaw so that your chin rests between your index and second finger. Gently open your mouth against the pressure of your fist. Don't open until it hurts — you just want to stretch and strengthen your chewing muscles. Hold this stretch for 10 seconds, then release the pressure. Do this exercise 10 times twice a day.

★ Guide your jaw. Sit in front of a mirror. Grasp both sides of your chin with your three middle fingers along the line of your jaw, placing your thumbs under your chin. Gently open your jaw straight down until your mouth is about two finger widths apart. Open and close a few times, using a little resistance. Then gently shift your jaw to the left and to the right. The point of this exercise is to teach your jaw to open and close straight up and down.

★ Open wider. Don't do this exercise if your jaw clicks or pops, or if you're having extreme pain. You can, however, use ice or moist heat on your jaw while you do this. Open your mouth slightly. Put one finger in parallel to your front teeth and gently bite down on your knuckle. Hold for a minute. Open wider and stack another finger between your teeth and hold. If you can squeeze a third finger in the space between your front teeth, you have reached the maximum opening of your jaw. Hold this position for about a minute. Do this exercise twice a day.

Since you are doing these stretches to release an already aching jaw, don't push yourself to the point of pain. Just stretch as far as you can, and repeat these exercises as recommended.

Uppgaard and other experts agree posture is a major factor in TMJ disorders. Align your body correctly, they say, and you'll reduce TMJ

12 tips to turn off TMJ pain

Sleep on your back. If you lie on your side or stomach, you place extra stress on your neck and jaw.

Don't cradle the phone. Holding it between your shoulder and neck will tense your muscles.

Check your hand. If it's balled into a fist, you're probably clenching. Try to keep your entire body relaxed.

Rest your tongue on the roof of your mouth. Keep your lips together but your teeth slightly open. Practice until this position becomes natural.

Use hot and cold packs. They'll help relieve jaw pain.

Make an appointment with your dentist. He is often more familiar with TMJ disorders than a doctor.

Don't use your teeth as tools. Don't bite your nails, chew on pencils, or use them to hold or open things.

Cut thick foods into bite-size pieces. You won't have to open so wide to eat that double-decker sandwich.

Be kind to your mouth. Don't yawn, chew gum, or have long dental appointments.

Ask your dentist about a bite-guard. This will keep you from grinding your teeth or clenching while you sleep.

Take aspirin or ibuprofen. They'll help for short-term pain relief.

Don't rush into surgery. Most pain will go away with simple lifestyle changes.

pain. If you carry your head forward — over your chest — instead of keeping it tucked over your shoulders, these exercises will be especially helpful. So take a deep breath and give your posture a tune-up.

★ Tuck your chin. Gently pull your chin back until your ears are in line with the tops of your shoulders. Hold this stretch for five seconds and repeat it 10 times every hour.

★ Surrender to the stretch. Stand with your back against a wall. Bend your arms and raise them as if you're surrendering to the enemy. Press your elbows and lower back against the wall. Tuck your chin down and in, keeping your head upright. Hold this stretch for 15 seconds and repeat three times a day.

★ Float like a butterfly. Lie down on your back with your knees bent. Fold your hands behind your head as if you were getting ready to do sit-ups. As you exhale, slowly lift just your elbows and bring them together so they touch in front of your face. Gently release them back to the floor while you inhale. Do this 10 times before going to bed.

In a Texas study, improving posture through exercises like these led to a 40 percent reduction in TMJ symptoms. Talk to your doctor, dentist, or physical therapist about any exercises. If you do them incorrectly, you could make your symptoms worse.

Do-it-yourself ways to save your jaw

Don't schedule that surgery — yet. Eight out of 10 people with TMJ disorders find relief with simple lifestyle changes. Try some of these less invasive ways to rid yourself of TMJ-related pain before you take that drastic step.

Fling worry to the wind. Stress, depression, and anxiety are sneaky but significant sources of TMJ pain. You may not even notice your muscles tighten, your heart speed up, or your jaw and hand clench. But this tension strains all the tissues in your joints, causing pain and damage to your TMJ. Depression often follows stress, slowing down your immune system, and making it harder to fight off inflammation.

Practice relaxation techniques and free yourself from jaw-breaking stress.

★ Deep breathing. It's easiest to learn how to do this lying down. So pick a comfortable spot and lie on your back. Place one hand on your stomach and one on your chest. Breathe in deeply, filling your abdomen. Your chest shouldn't move. Remember what this feels like. Eventually you should be able to do this anywhere. Stop what you're doing every hour and take a few healing breaths.

★ Muscle control. Concentrate on each group of muscles in your face. Carefully tighten them and hold this position for a few seconds. Slowly relax everything as you count to 10. You'll be surprised how often you think you're relaxed when you're not.

★ Visualization. When you feel yourself tense, think of a place where you were happy and restful. Remember the sound of lapping water and the feel of sand between your toes. Or picture the colors of leaves in the fall. Keep adding details to your memory until your worry is forgotten.

★ Exercise. Take long walks to think through your day. The exercise and fresh air will restore your good attitude and help you find a new perspective.

★ Hobbies. Find something you love doing — gardening, mentoring children, woodworking, even reading — and do it often.

★ Counseling. Share your worries with a loved one or a therapist. A professional can often recommend other ways to banish stress.

Improve your odds with supplements. Your body can always use a little boost to help it fight off chronic pain and inflammation. Try these joint-friendly supplements to strengthen your jaw.

★ Collagen. This natural protein builds cartilage, muscles, tendons, and bone — in other words, everything that makes up your joints. In clinical studies, taking collagen hydrolysat as a food supplement dramatically improved TMJ disorder symptoms. Researchers tested one tablespoon with water on an empty stomach before bedtime. You can find collagen supplements in most drug and health stores. Just read the label and make sure the active ingredient is collagen hydrolysat and not hydrolyzed collagen.

★ Glucosamine. If you, or your doctor, suspect your TMJ pain is related to osteoarthritis, stock up on glucosamine and chondroiten. Both of these supplements will provide important sugars your body uses to build cartilage. They also help you retain water in your joints and reduce pain and swelling. However, if you take aspirin, blood thinners, or are diabetic, talk to your doctor before taking any supplements.

Look for help in unusual places. Ask your doctor about certified therapists who practice these alternative approaches to pain relief.

★ Biofeedback. A trained professional can use a machine to measure the temperature and electrical activity in your muscles. With their help, you gradually learn to control muscle tension in your mouth and jaw while chewing, talking, and resting.

★ Myotherapy. Also known as trigger point massage, this technique involves locating points of muscle pain in your neck and upper back, applying steady pressure for a few seconds, then stretching out the affected muscles. Surprisingly, this can release pain in your jaw.

★ Myofascial release. Many physical therapists use this gentle form of stretching. It focuses on loosening the connective tissues that join every part of your body.

★ Vibration therapy. Don't try this one at home, but find a physical therapist familiar with this treatment. According to research, a special vibrating-traction unit can help reposition the bones in your jaw.

★ Chinese traditional medicine. Try a combination of acupressure, acupuncture, and massage on sensitive points in your neck and jaw.

Think of TMJ pain as a symptom of a larger problem — one that involves your whole body. Once the body is well, your jaw will heal too.

Bite into jaw-friendly foods

If you can't chew because your jaw aches, chew on this — simple diet changes can break the cycle of pain and headaches associated with TMJ disorders.

Lock up free radicals. It's all about electrons. Certain molecules, called free radicals, are missing one, so they steal them anywhere they can. Unfortunately, by taking an electron and leaving another molecule short, they've just created a new free radical, on the prowl for a replacement — and so the chain reaction goes.

This chemical thievery, called oxidation, breaks down collagen and bone in your joints, and causes inflammation — leading to TMJ pain.

You can fend off free radical take-over by boning up on antioxidants like vitamins C, E, and selenium. These either combine with free radicals to form a harmless substance or give up an electron, making the free radical stable.

Citrus fruits, strawberries, spinach, broccoli, cauliflower, and green and red peppers are all great sources of vitamin C. Vitamin E is abundant in wheat germ, avocados, and canola oil. Selenium not only locks up raging radicals, it also helps you create collagen, one of the building blocks of cartilage. Selenium is plentiful in mushrooms, seafood, and unprocessed grains.

Sidestep muscle exciters. Sugar and caffeine are great pick-me-ups when you need a sudden burst of energy. But stimulating muscles that are already strained is a recipe for irritation and pain. So step away from that pastry puff, cup of coffee, or can of cola. Instead, drink plenty of water. It's a key ingredient in cartilage and cushions your joints.

Mind your minerals. Experts also think the pH levels in your body affect cartilage and bone damage. You won't know what your pH levels are, but your doctor or dentist can check them. If yours are low and you're experiencing TMJ pain, get enough calcium, magnesium, and zinc. You need the proper balance of these minerals to maintain a stable pH.

Yogurt, cottage cheese, sardines, broccoli, and beans will give you natural calcium. And good sources of magnesium are wheat germ, spinach, beans, and avocados. Zinc is in shellfish, whole grains, and beans. Talk to your doctor before taking supplements.

In addition, avoid alcohol, sugar, and caffeine, which leach calcium and magnesium from your body.

Be gentle with your jaw. It's not just what you eat, but how you eat that can make the difference.

While crunchy or hard foods will irritate muscles that are already sore and inflamed, they may also be part of a larger problem. Something called mechanical stress can create those pesky free radicals. Experts believe your jaw is under this kind of stress when you bite down hard.

So steer clear of crunchy foods that push your jaw into overdrive, like carrots, bagels, celery, and steak. And stop chewing gum, which has no nutritional value anyway. Pad your diet with soft foods like soups, cottage cheese, certain fruits, yogurt, and rice.

Pamper your jaw and switch to a healthier diet. If your TMJ pain persists, have your doctor check for underlying conditions like osteoarthritis or fibromyalgia.

Brighten your smile for free

Why pay for expensive dental care when you can get it for free? Here's how to tap into a program near you.

★ Join a clinical trial and get free cutting-edge dental work while helping science at the same time. Browse the listings in the Mouth and Tooth Diseases section on the <ClinicalTrials.gov> Web site for ongoing research in your area.

★ Dental schools around the country may offer free care if you are willing to be seen by a dental student supervised by a licensed dentist. To get a list of the dental schools in your state, contact the American Dental Association (ADA) at 312-440-2593. You can also check their Web site at <www.ada.org> or write:

211 E. Chicago Ave.
Chicago, IL 60611

★ A lot of dentists volunteer time at free dental clinics. Contact your state's Dental Association or the Department of Public Health to request a list of programs in your area. Don't forget to ask about discounted or free denture services as well as TMJ disorder specialists.

Ulcers

Save your stomach from NSAID disasters

Nonsteroidal anti-inflammatory drugs (NSAIDs) are a dream come true if you suffer from pain. But they can be a nightmare if they give you an ulcer. Taking the right precautions, though, can keep your mind — and your stomach — at ease.

On average, all NSAIDs quadruple your risk of ulcers and stomach bleeding. That's because they block enzymes in your body which normally protect the lining of your gut. Without this shield, the lining can wear away.

You may be in more danger if you have a history of ulcers, or if you:

★ are age 75 or older.

★ use corticosteroids.

★ take a blood thinning medication.

★ suffer from other serious health problems.

If you match one or more on this list, it's important you follow these stomach-saving tips.

Exterminate the bugs first. It's no wonder experts recommend you get tested for *Helicobacter pylori* before you take a round of NSAIDs. This bacteria and the painkillers independently can cause ulcers. But your chances of stomach problems are much worse if you take NSAIDs while infected with *H. pylori*.

If you do have an *H. pylori* infection, one short round of antibiotics may solve the problem, according to a recent study in the prestigious medical journal *The Lancet*. NSAID-users in the study got fewer and smaller ulcers when they treated the infection first.

Pick an alternative. Another way to sidestep the side effects of NSAIDs is to avoid these painkillers altogether. Herbal remedies may be safe alternatives. Willow bark extract, for instance, is proven to relieve back pain — without any serious stomach side effects. Cramp bark and valerian are also possible stand-ins. Remember to talk with your doctor before taking any herbs.

Acetaminophen, on the other hand, may not be a good substitute. Taking two or more grams of acetaminophen a day, according to new research, appears to increase your odds of stomach bleeding and ulcers. Just like NSAIDs, acetaminophen shuts down the enzymes that guard your stomach lining.

Lower your dose. If you decide to stick with NSAIDs, talk with your doctor about a lower dose. Or ask about less irritating types like the new COX-2 inhibitors.

Coat your stomach. Take your painkiller of choice with food or a glass of milk to cut down on stomach irritation. Don't count on so-called "safety coatings" to do the job for you. Manufacturers claim these enteric coatings make NSAIDs easier on your stomach. But recent research shows they have the same risk as regular NSAIDs.

Be cautious with combos. It's also smart to be careful when taking two or more different kinds of pain relievers. Low-dose aspirin combined with another NSAID, for example, could be enough to send you to the emergency room. Talk with your doctor before mixing medicines.

Ultimately, you must weigh the pros and cons of taking NSAIDs over the long-term. Remember — they are serious medicines.

Super snacks sock it to stomach problems

These common foods can perform an uncommon feat. They battle the bacteria *Helicobacter pylori* and help prevent ulcers, gastritis, and stomach cancer.

Cranberry juice. It keeps *H. pylori* from hanging onto the tissues in your digestive system. The bacteria is swept away before it can do damage.

Garlic. Garlic is packed with allicin, a natural bacteria-killing chemical.

Green tea. Drinking green tea regularly could ease stomach inflammation and prevent cancer.

Honey. Antibacterial compounds make honey a great stomach soother.

Milk. Milk also stops the bug from setting up shop in your stomach. On top of that, it's a great source of vitamin A, which protects your mucous membranes and builds new cells.

Spinach. With its carotenoids and fiber, spinach may be your stomach's best friend. Research proves, the more carotenoids in your system, the lower your risk of stomach problems like gastritis. And fiber encourages the growth of the mucous layer that protects your stomach from digestive acids.

Sunflower seeds. Thanks to polyunsaturated fats, sunflower seeds may keep the infamous stomach bug at bay.

Yogurt. The good bacteria in this dairy treat destroy the bad bacteria in your belly.

Stomach cancer: a hidden hazard of *H. pylori*

Protect yourself from ulcer-causing *Helicobacter pylori* and you may slam the door on stomach cancer, as well.

According to results from an 8-year study, stomach cancer develops in about 5 percent of those people infected with *H. pylori*, but not in any without the bacteria. It may be that this type of cancer develops more readily when there is already damage to your gastrointestinal system. As it turns out, there are very few people with stomach cancer who are not infected with *H. pylori*.

The wisest course of action, obviously, is to get rid of *H. pylori* infection. In the research follow-up, no one that did so developed stomach cancer.

Begin with C-rich foods. One top-notch nutrient, vitamin C, is an invaluable weapon in this fight. Not only can vitamin C kill *H. pylori*, but it also sweeps away the bacteria's toxic byproducts as it boosts your body's immune system.

Eating foods rich in vitamin C is one of the best ways to get these triple-powered benefits. In fact, without enough C in your diet you increase your cancer risk.

One problem, however, is the acidity in high-C foods like oranges and grapefruits — these may bother your belly if you have an ulcer. You can try gentler sources of vitamin C such as strawberries, broccoli, cantaloupe, sweet peppers, and brussels sprouts.

Slip in some supplements. Even if you eat these foods, *H. pylori* could block your body's ability to absorb and get the benefits from the vitamin C. Experts say you can overcome this obstacle with two 500-milligram supplements. Taken every day, that amount seems to punch up vitamin C levels enough to help protect your stomach lining.

Finish off with antibiotics. Your best bet to skirt stomach cancer is to annihilate *H. pylori* with medicine. Antibiotics appear to kill the bacteria in three out of four people. And according to research, once they're gone, ulcers, precancerous sores, and other effects of the bacteria usually go with them.

Stomach cancer is the second most common fatal cancer in the world. Talk to your doctor about how you can prevent it by wiping out *H. pylori*.

3 easy steps to an ulcer-free life

Look around you. One out of two people has the *Helicobacter pylori* bacteria alive and well in his digestive system. But not all of those infected will get an ulcer. The difference — healthy lifestyle choices.

Say goodnight to ulcers. Give your tummy a good night's rest, and it'll fix itself. That's because your body has its own "repairmen," proteins called TFF2. Experts believe these natural compounds patch up everyday wear-and-tear in your gut. Otherwise, those tiny bits of damage you get from ordinary food and drink could, over time, grow into ulcers.

While there's some TFF2 in your stomach most of the time, the amount seems to increase — up to 300 percent — during normal sleep. So make sure you're snoozing from at least 1 a.m. to 5 a.m. That way you'll get the best natural repair to your stomach lining.

Walk away every day. A daily walk could cut your ulcer risk in half, according to a 20-year study of more than 11,000 people. Exercise may fight ulcers by boosting your immune system, reducing stress, or by lowering the acid level in your gut.

The researchers believe moderate exercise could benefit anyone, though in their study it seemed to protect against duodenal ulcers — those in the upper intestine — and only work for men. To maximize your stomach protection, they suggest you walk or jog at least a mile and a half every day. Any kind of regular exercise, though, could do the trick.

Duke it out with diet. Eat seven servings of fruits and vegetables every day and the Harvard School of Public Health says you'll have fewer ulcers. Fiber-rich choices like carrots, celery, apples, and beans are particularly protective.

Make sure you get a healthy dose of vitamin A, too. It seems to increase the protective mucus in your stomach and intestines.

These three positive lifestyle changes can make your stomach happy and healthy. But to be sure it stays that way, drop those negative habits, like smoking and overindulging in alcohol.

Beware of B12 deficiency from bacteria

Depression, numbness, and dizziness could mean something surprising — you have a *Helicobacter pylori* infection.

While these symptoms don't have anything to do with ulcers, they are signs of a vitamin B12 deficiency that can lead to anemia. And the bug that causes ulcers can cause this condition, too.

By damaging your stomach lining, *H. pylori* reduces your ability to absorb B12 from your diet. If you're a senior, you compound the problem because, as you age, you naturally produce less of the stomach acid that helps you absorb B12.

You can look forward to a lifetime of B12 booster shots unless you treat the *H. pylori* first.

Take the *H. pylori* test. If you're positive for the bacteria, a round of antibiotics could solve your problem. In a recent study, treating the infection corrected the B12 deficiency in nearly half the people.

Fortify your diet. Compensate for your low levels of B12 by eating breakfast cereals and other fortified foods. With low stomach acid, you can more easily absorb the vitamin from these sources. Still eat enough meat, fish, and chicken, and talk to your doctor about B12 supplements.

Urinary Incontinence

Triumph over urinary incontinence

There's no need to suffer in silence if you have a leaky bladder. Talk with your doctor. Urinary incontinence (UI) can be a sign of a serious medical condition, such as multiple sclerosis or Parkinson's disease. Fortunately, for most people, a simple treatment can greatly improve the problem.

When a group of elderly women with UI followed a new home-treatment program, they saw the severity of their condition decrease by 61 percent. Yet, a similar group of women who did not follow the program experienced a 184-percent increase in the severity of their UI in the same two-year period. Designed by researchers at the University of North Carolina, Chapel Hill, the program involved bladder training, keeping a journal, and pelvic muscle exercises.

Although nurses helped the women in the study, researchers said the improvements were mostly due to self-monitoring and bladder training — things you can do at home. Here's how.

Set a goal. Do you want to be able to make it three hours without visiting a restroom? Maybe you'd like to find out if there's a trigger for your "overactive bladder." Have a goal in mind so you have something specific to strive for.

Visit the bathroom regularly. Start using the bathroom at regular intervals, such as every hour and a half, even if you don't feel the urge. Gradually increase the time until you can make it at least two and a half hours, but not longer than four hours. It might take you as long as eight weeks to achieve this goal, but the results will be worth the effort.

Keep a journal. Record the time of day and each item you eat or drink for two weeks. Also, write down every time you urinate and any accidents you have. After two weeks, analyze the journal. You might see a pattern of certain foods that irritate your bladder and trigger accidents. Caffeine, carbonated drinks, and spicy foods are frequent culprits.

Find out how much liquid you're drinking on an average day. Are you drinking fluids past 6 p.m.? That's a no-no. So is waiting longer than four hours to empty your bladder.

Make a note of any bowel problems, like constipation, that can contribute to UI. If you notice that constipation is linked to your problem, eat foods high in fiber, like whole grains, fruits, and vegetables. If that doesn't help, talk with your doctor.

Tone up pelvic muscles. Pelvic muscle exercises, such as Kegel exercises, can help restore control to weak muscles around your bladder. Give this amazing remedy a try.

* Identify the pelvic muscles that need exercising. You can do this by stopping and starting the flow of urine several times when using the bathroom.

* Tighten the muscles a little at a time. Contract your muscles slowly, hold for a count of 10, and relax the muscles slowly.

* Repeat these exercises for the anal pelvic muscles. To find these muscles, imagine you're trying to hold back a bowel movement, without tensing your legs, stomach, or buttock muscles.

* Practice tightening all the pelvic muscles together, moving from back to front.

* Start by repeating each exercise five times, three to five times a day. Gradually work up to 20 or 30 repetitions.

Drink more water. Don't deprive yourself of water in an attempt to stay dry. Your body needs it, and it keeps your urine diluted and less irritating to your urinary tract.

Although some women will still need medication or surgery to correct their incontinence, many more will improve with these simple lifestyle changes. So get with the program, and get back to your life.

Do's and don'ts to keep you dry

You can do more than Kegel exercises to fight urinary incontinence (UI). Certain foods, drinks, and habits can either help you stay dry or send you running for a restroom.

Do ...

★ Drink water. It helps keep your urine diluted, which makes it less irritating to your urinary tract.

★ Choose cranberry juice. Although it can't prevent UI, it can stop some urinary tract infections, which UI can cause.

★ Eat more fiber. Constipation can contribute to UI. Enjoy fruits and vegetables, high-fiber cereals, whole wheat and rye breads, and brown rice.

★ Stay at your ideal weight. Excess weight can prompt an overactive bladder.

Don't ...

★ Smoke. Women who smoke have a higher risk of UI because substances in cigarettes can cause problems for the bladder and urethra.

★ Eat asparagus. This vegetable can cause bad-smelling urine. Avoid it so any accidental leaking can be your secret.

★ Eat spicy foods. Some spices can irritate your urinary tract and lead to incontinence.

★ Drink carbonated drinks. The carbonation is troublesome for some people.

★ Drink coffee. Caffeine might be a trigger for you. Also avoid teas, colas, and chocolate.

How to prevent a leaky bladder

Urinary incontinence (UI) causes interrupted sleep, sexual problems, rashes, and infections for 10 to 20 million people. It's also a major reason why many people move to a nursing home. Besides the physical problems, it can wreak havoc on your social life, making you feel isolated and depressed.

Women develop UI twice as often as men do. But in many cases, you can head off this embarrassing condition before it starts.

Tone up after baby. Giving birth can weaken the muscles around your bladder, which makes you more vulnerable to a type of UI called stress incontinence. This kind of leakage happens when you laugh, cough, sneeze, or exercise.

But you can slash your odds of developing stress incontinence with Kegel exercises. (See "Tone up pelvic muscles" in this chapter.) Unlike most exercise, you can do these almost anywhere, and you won't even break a sweat. Research shows they can even help young, childless women avoid UI later in life. As a bonus, many women claim the exercises make sex more satisfying.

Pay attention at midlife. In your 40s and 50s, you go through many changes, including the big one — menopause. The end of menstruation means less estrogen, which causes thinning of skin and membranes in your urinary tract. Your urethra, the canal that leads from your bladder to the outside, can become irritated more easily, and it may not seal itself off properly between trips to the bathroom. This often leads to a type of UI called urge incontinence. Maybe you've seen commercials calling it "overactive bladder." You suddenly get the urge to urinate, but your bladder doesn't always give you enough time to find a toilet.

Also common in older women is mixed incontinence, which includes symptoms of both the stress and urge types.

If these types of UI plague you, a trip to the doctor is in order. Ask about estrogen therapy, which can help reverse some of the problems caused by lower hormone levels. Your doctor can also prescribe medicine for an overactive bladder.

As a last resort, some people require surgery to restore bladder control. But these women are the exception, not the rule.

Hesitate on hysterectomy. Many women are relieved when their doctor suggests a hysterectomy, believing it will end all their female problems. But surgery to remove your uterus can create new problems. One study found that middle-age women who undergo a hysterectomy have a 60 percent higher chance of having UI by age 60. The researchers suggest doctors discuss this possible side effect with women before the operation. Ask your doctor about your options, and talk with him about this possible complication.

By paying attention to changes in your body throughout life, you can help keep your bladder under control. That can mean fewer medical problems, an unhindered social life, and perhaps best of all — independence.

Urinary Tract Infections

Look to your kitchen for a cure

You probably associate urinary tract infections (UTIs) with your bathroom. But maybe you should keep your kitchen in mind. You just might find some surprising home remedies in your refrigerator.

Much more common in women than men, urinary tract infections occur when bacteria multiply in your urethra, bladder, or kidneys. This can lead to swelling, infection, and other problems.

You might not have any symptoms with a urinary tract infection, but you'll most likely experience some of these.

★ frequent urge to urinate

★ painful burning sensation during urination

★ ability to pass only small amounts of strong-smelling, cloudy urine

★ sense that your bladder is not completely empty, even after going to the bathroom

Fortunately, what you eat and drink can help prevent — or even treat — urinary tract infections. Sample the following foods to help keep your urinary tract healthy.

Cranberry juice. One of the oldest, and best, remedies for urinary tract infections is drinking cranberry juice. Recently, scientists have confirmed what grandmothers knew all along.

In one of the more recent studies, Finnish researchers examined women who recently had a urinary tract infection. Those who drank cranberry juice slashed their risk for another UTI by 20 percent.

An added bonus of drinking cranberry juice is that it provides a safer, cheaper alternative to antibiotics, which your doctor might prescribe to clear up UTIs.

Experts used to think cranberry juice worked by making your urine too acidic for bacteria to live. But now they believe cranberries contain powerful substances called flavonoids that prevent bacteria from clinging to the cells that line your urinary tract.

Just one glass of cranberry juice a day should be enough to protect you from a UTI. In fact, many retirement homes serve a daily glass of cranberry juice to their elderly residents for just that reason.

Blueberries. Chock-full of flavonoids that stop bacteria from sticking to your urinary tract, blueberries do the same thing as cranberries. Enjoy a bowl of these tasty berries and send UTIs packing.

Citrus fruits. Let bacteria know they aren't welcome. Citrus fruits and juices with lots of vitamin C, like orange or grapefruit juice, make your urine more acidic. That makes it tougher for bacteria to survive.

Water. Drink plenty of water to flush the bacteria from your body. Aim for 10 to14 glasses a day.

Parsley. This decorative herb is a great source of vitamin C. It's also a diuretic, which means it makes you urinate. Urinating more often helps get rid of bacteria in your urinary tract.

In addition to eating more foods that help, avoid those that hurt. Foods that might irritate your bladder include coffee, tea, alcohol, carbonated beverages, and spicy foods.

Although urinary tract infections often clear up on their own, some untreated infections can spread to the kidneys and cause serious damage. Symptoms of a kidney infection include back pain, chills, fever, nausea, and vomiting.

Your diet can help prevent and treat urinary tract infections — but sometimes you still need a doctor's help. Make sure to see a doctor if symptoms last more than two days.

Top ways to prevent UTIs

No one wants a urinary tract infection. Take these precautions, and you probably won't get one.

Heed nature's call. Don't resist the urge to urinate. The longer urine sits in your bladder, the more likely it is to stagnate and allow bacteria to grow.

Wipe wisely. If you're a woman, wipe from front to back. Otherwise, you might drag bacteria from your anus toward your urethra.

Urinate before and after sex. This washes bacteria out of your urethra. Washing your genital area also lessens the chance of spreading infection to your partner.

Discard the diaphragm. Diaphragms press against your bladder and prevent it from emptying completely. This increases your risk of infection.

Take showers, not baths. Soaking in a tub gives bacteria a better chance to enter your urethra.

Quit smoking. Here's yet another reason to kick the habit — smoking increases your risk for UTIs

Shun douches and sprays. They might smell good, but they can also irritate your urethra

Rethink your wardrobe. Wear cotton panties instead of nylon ones, avoid tight pants, and wear thigh-high stockings instead of pantyhose.

Weight Control

Weight loss strategies that work

Fad diets may help you lose weight — but you almost always gain it back. Taking it off and keeping it off, on the other hand, requires a sensible long-term plan.

Check out these weight-loss strategies that work for a lifetime.

Strive for five. How do you go about cutting fat from your diet? Penn State researchers recently examined the strategies of 65 successful dieters. All were at least 50 years old and had stuck to their fat-busting diets for at least five years. Here are their top five secrets to success.

- ★ Savor summer fruit. Eat more cantaloupes, watermelon, peaches, plums, and nectarines.

- ★ Eat more vegetables and grains. Make room for sweet potatoes, squash, beans, cooked greens, mixed salads, broccoli, rice, and noodles.

- ★ Cut back on recreational foods. Say goodbye to cookies, chocolate candy, chips, crackers, doughnuts, and ice cream, and say hello to low-fat pizza and desserts.

- ★ Decrease cooking fat. Eat less cream or meat sauces, butter, margarine, oil, cream soups, ground meat, cheese, pizza, fried chicken, french fries, and mayonnaise-based salads. Pop popcorn without oil, and eat tuna without mayonnaise.

- ★ Use fat-modified foods. Stock up on low-fat dressing, mayonnaise, and spreads. Remove the skin from chicken, and trim the fat from beef. Drink low-fat milk.

These simple strategies allowed the dieters to slash their fat intake nearly in half. But it didn't happen overnight. In most cases, these life-long weight watchers made changes to their diets gradually.

Set goals. Think of losing weight as a journey between where you are now and where you want to be. Wandering aimlessly and hoping to reach your destination probably won't work. You need a map.

Track your progress by setting short-term goals and monitoring yourself. When you reach one goal, set another and work towards that. Your journey won't seem so long with all these pit stops.

This approach worked for students at the Brooklyn College of the City University of New York who aimed to eat more fiber. Those who set short-term goals, such as boosting their fiber intake by 5 grams a week, ate 91 percent more fiber than the students who did not set goals.

Be reasonable. The key is to set realistic, reachable goals. If you try to lose 50 pounds by next Tuesday, you're going to be disappointed.

Remember, if you trim 10 percent from your body weight, you've completed a successful weight-loss program. But University of Pennsylvania researchers recently discovered that obese people often aim for weight losses 2 to 3 times greater than that. No wonder they often get discouraged and give up.

Successful weight loss is a marathon, not a sprint. Slow and steady wins the race.

Chew some fat. Face it — low-fat diets are no fun. But you don't need to lose taste to lose waist.

A Harvard study found that people on a moderate-fat, Mediterranean diet fared better than people on a strict low-fat diet. Why? They had tastier food options. For example, they could sauté vegetables in a bit of olive oil rather than steam them or use nonfat cooking spray.

After 18 months, only 20 percent of the low-fat dieters were still on the program, while more than half of the moderate-fat eaters were still going strong. What's more, the Mediterranean group lost an average of 9 pounds, while the low-fat group actually gained 6 pounds.

The low-fat group limited their fat to 20 percent of their total calories, while the Mediterranean group upped it to 35 percent. Adding just a bit more fat might help you subtract more weight in the long run.

You can lose weight and keep it off. Just make a few changes in your diet, set reasonable, short-term goals, and keep your meals interesting. Sure beats eating nothing but grapefruit for weeks, doesn't it?

---

8 foods that 'force' weight loss

Fiber-rich foods fill you up so you don't overeat or snack between meals. Check out these eight secret foods that "force" your body to lose weight.

Potatoes. Boiled potatoes are the most filling food you can eat. A baked potato in the skin is a higher-fiber option than mashed potatoes.

Beans and lentils. Your body takes a long time to absorb these high-fiber foods, so you feel fuller longer.

Whole-grain bread. It's 50 percent more filling than white bread.

Popcorn. This healthy snack makes you feel twice as full as a candy bar.

Apples. Bite into an unpeeled apple or make applesauce from unpeeled apples for a tastier, more filling alternative to regular applesauce.

Oranges. They'll fill you up more than bananas, and provide more fiber than orange juice.

Porridge. For breakfast, this hearty dish beats cold cereal every time.

Brown rice. Cook this instead of white rice to get more fiber.

High-protein diets bring high risks

Eat a juicy burger for lunch and a sizzling steak for dinner — and still lose weight. That's the undeniable appeal of high-protein diets.

These popular diets let you load up on meat, cheese, eggs, and other usual dieting outlaws while severely limiting carbohydrates, such as fruits, vegetables, and bread.

Weight-loss programs like the Atkins Diet or the Zone Diet may help you lose weight in the short term, but they raise some health concerns. In fact, the American Heart Association (AHA) recently issued a warning about high-protein, low-carbohydrate diets.

The following possible side effects suggest a high-protein diet is not a safe, long-term solution.

★ **High cholesterol.** With all that meat comes a lot of saturated fat, the kind that causes cholesterol buildup in your arteries. You may lose weight but increase your risk for heart disease and stroke.

★ **High blood pressure.** When you limit foods like fruits, vegetables, and whole grains, you're eliminating good, natural ways to lower your blood pressure.

★ **Gout.** Foods high in protein are often high in purines, which are converted into uric acid. This can build up and cause gout.

★ **Osteoporosis.** Overloading on protein causes your body to get rid of more calcium, leaving your bones weak and brittle.

★ **Cancer.** Fewer fruits, vegetables, and whole grains mean fewer cancer-fighting weapons.

★ **Diabetic renal disease.** Too much protein can put a strain on your kidneys making a high-protein diet especially dangerous for diabetics.

★ **Vitamin and mineral deficiencies.** The lack of healthy foods in your diet means you're not getting all the nutrients you need. This can lead to health problems down the road.

★ **Fatigue and muscle loss.** Carbohydrates are your main source of energy. If you cut them out, you can become fatigued after exercising. Get fewer than 100 grams of carbohydrates a day, and your body will resort to burning muscle tissue for energy.

Health issues aside, high-protein diets are generally boring and hard to stick to. You need some variety and excitement in any meal plan.

The secret to weight loss does not lie with some specific proportion of nutrients or the magic powers of protein. It lies with burning more calories than you take in. In fact, experts say it's the reduced calories, not the additional protein, that helps you lose weight on high-protein diets.

Your body does need protein to function properly. The current recommended dietary allowance (RDA) of protein is .36 grams per pound you weigh. For example, if you weigh 150 pounds, you should get 54 grams of protein a day. Recent studies suggest older people may need slightly more.

But don't go overboard. Your best bet is to eat a balanced diet. The AHA recommends getting about 55 percent of each day's calories from carbohydrates, 30 percent from fat, and just 15 percent from protein.

If you decide you want to try a high-protein diet, make sure you talk to your doctor first.

Nix the nighttime munchies

A late-night, candlelit dinner sounds romantic, but it might add pounds instead of romance. Here are some ways to avoid dimming your diet plan along with the lights.

Flip the switch. Low light removes your inhibitions, according to professor Joseph Kasof of the University of California at Irvine. This might be great for your love life but not so great for your diet. In fact, Kasof found "night people" were more likely to overindulge.

"Darkness provides a high-risk environment for binge-eating for certain people," Kasof says. "People who spend more waking hours in darkness may be more susceptible, especially if they feel a strong need to diet. But people who prefer to eat in a darkened room may find they lose their inhibitions against eating."

Try to eat earlier, while there's still some daylight. If you prefer to dine later, make sure you turn up the lights.

Spread out your calories. Overeating late at night can have a carry-over effect. The next morning, you may not be too hungry. So you skip breakfast and possibly even lunch. Then you make up for it with another big meal at night.

Many times you're not just eating a lot of food, but a lot of the wrong food. Nighttime eaters tend to get more calories from fat, protein, and alcohol than people who spread their calories out over the day. Perhaps by the time they finally eat, they're too hungry to think about nutrition.

Fight this tendency by not skipping meals, starting with breakfast. Adults who eat breakfast every day tend to weigh less than those who skip the day's first meal.

Spread out your calories over four small meals rather than three large ones. Giving your body fuel at regular intervals helps it burn calories more efficiently. Pay attention to portion sizes, fat grams, and calories — no matter what time you're eating.

Get help. For some people, nighttime eating is more than an unhealthy habit — it's an eating disorder. People with night eating syndrome eat little or nothing during the day, then splurge at night. Often, they have trouble sleeping, then wake up and raid the refrigerator.

New research suggests there might be a biological explanation for night eating syndrome. It involves disturbances in your hypothalamic-pituitary-adrenal (HPA) axis, a mechanism that controls several of your body's functions.

Because of this disturbance, your body doesn't respond properly to stress, affecting your appetite and sleep pattern. Several other disorders, such as insomnia, depression, anorexia, bulimia, and chronic fatigue syndrome have also been linked to disturbances in the HPA axis.

If you develop an unusual eating pattern that's affecting your life, ask your doctor for help.

When dieting is dangerous

It seems everyone wants to lose a few pounds — but not everyone should.

Researchers at the University of Pittsburgh recently made an alarming discovery. In a three-year study of 4,714 people 65 and older, they found even a small weight loss posed a great danger.

People who lost 5 percent or more of their body weight boosted their risk of dying by a whopping 67 percent. It didn't matter how they lost the weight — whether they dieted or had a serious illness, their risks were similarly high.

If you're 65 or older, try to keep your weight stable. Talk to your doctor before starting any weight-loss programs.

Another risk of weight loss is anorexia. Spanish researchers recently reported two cases of obese women who developed an intense, obsessive fear of gaining weight after they had lost a number of pounds, either through dieting or stomach surgery.

Although this happens rarely, it might be a good idea to look for anorexic symptoms in loved ones who've recently lost a lot of weight.

Fight flab with fiber

If dietary fiber didn't already exist, some genius would be working overtime in the laboratory trying to invent it.

This natural substance, found in a variety of fruits, vegetables, and whole grains, not only helps prevent disease, lower cholesterol, and keep you regular — it also helps you lose weight. Read on to discover how fiber zaps away pounds.

Blocks calories. Good news — you can eat as much fiber as your body can handle and add absolutely no calories to your diet. What's more, your body needs fiber to function at its peak.

Many of fiber's calories don't count because fiber can't be digested. It just passes through your system, taking waste with it. Fiber can also block the absorption of some of the fat and protein you eat. One study found that people who ate 48 grams of fiber a day absorbed 8 percent fewer calories than those who got a daily dose of 20 grams.

Just boosting your fiber intake — without changing the number of calories you eat — could mean losing a couple of pounds a month. But make sure to add fiber to your diet gradually. Too much too fast can cause uncomfortable gas and bloating.

Fills you up. Like Doug Henning or David Copperfield, fiber is a skilled illusionist. Even though it isn't digested, it still fills you up.

High-fiber foods trick your stomach into feeling full with fewer calories than you would normally eat. You also stay full longer, meaning you won't feel the urge to snack between meals.

Drink plenty of water as you add more fiber to your diet. Fiber absorbs water and swells, giving you that satisfied, full feeling.

Gets results. The main thing is, fiber works. A recent review of diets found that people eating a low-fat, high-fiber diet lost more than three times as much weight as people on a low-fat diet alone.

And fiber has another secret benefit. It allows you to eat well without clogging your arteries. Your body has a harder time converting high-fiber foods into fat. So your heart, as well as your mirror, will thank you.

Remember to add this super substance to your diet when you're watching your weight. Fiber blocks the absorption of fat, fills you up so you don't overeat, and helps you take off extra pounds. Eureka! What a magnificent invention.

CLA: magic pill for weight control?

The popular supplement CLA stands for "conjugated linoleic acid," but it could just as well stand for "conquer large abdomens."

This easy-to-find pill banishes abdominal fat, the most dangerous kind, and helps you keep weight off once you lose it. Could CLA be the next great breakthrough in the battle of the bulge?

Examine the evidence. Recent studies suggest CLA, a natural fatty acid, may help with weight control.

University of Wisconsin professor Michael Pariza, Ph.D., led a six-month study of 80 overweight people. They dieted, exercised, and lost weight. But, when they stopped their diets, many regained some of the weight they had lost.

The people who did not take CLA added pounds at a typical ratio of 75 percent fat to 25 percent muscle. For the people taking CLA, however, the results were pleasantly different.

"The ratio was more like 50:50 — 50 percent fat and 50 percent muscle," Pariza says. "That is very significant. It leads to the idea that CLA could be useful in weight management. Our results also showed that CLA made it easier for people to stay on their diets."

Pariza's study isn't the only one that gives dieters hope. Two smaller studies also support CLA. A four-week Swedish study of 25 people found that CLA decreases abdominal fat, or the fat around your middle. And a 12-week Norwegian study of 47 people showed that CLA reduces body fat. In all three studies, people took about 3 to 4 grams of CLA a day.

Wait and see. While CLA seems generally safe, more studies are needed. For example, no one knows the long-term effects of taking CLA.

No one knows for sure that it works, either. CLA produced all sorts of amazing results in animal studies, but not all human studies showed the same effects. It might depend on what form of CLA you take — and you can't always tell what form you're getting by reading the supplement's label.

Consider the cons. Possible side effects include nausea, upset stomach, and fatigue. To combat nausea, some experts recommend taking CLA with milk. And while some experts claim CLA may improve insulin levels in diabetics, others do not recommend it for people with type 2 diabetes, liver disease, or insulin resistance.

If you don't want to take a supplement, you can also find CLA in whole foods, such as beef, dairy products, poultry, and eggs. But you'd have to eat an awful lot of these foods to match the amount you get in a supplement — and that wouldn't exactly help you lose weight.

Remember, CLA is not a miracle pill. It seems promising, but it's not 100 percent proven yet. Before you start popping "magic" pills, ask your doctor about CLA.

Shake off stress to stay slim

Do you stress out because of your weight? Or do you gain weight because of your stress?

Turns out both may be true. Stress can have a tremendous effect on your diet, and vice versa. By counting every calorie and obsessing over your food, you could sabotage your weight-loss efforts. Here are some of the links between stress and weight, and what you can do to protect yourself.

Loosen up. Just trying to stick to your diet can be stressful. A recent study showed that women on a restricted diet were under more stress. They had more cortisol, a stress hormone, in their bodies than women who didn't limit what they ate. This is potentially dangerous because high levels of cortisol can lead to weak, brittle bones.

Instead of counting calories and fat grams, adopt a generally healthy diet featuring plenty of fruits, vegetables, and whole grains. You'll lose weight without the stress.

Banish your belly. Studies show stress may add to the fat around your middle. Abdominal fat raises your risk for health problems, such as heart disease and diabetes. And this is true even if the rest of your body is lean. In one study of 59 women aged 30 to 46, the thin women with potbellies seemed more vulnerable to stress than the heavier women.

A great way to cope with stress — and shed some fat — is to exercise regularly. Other good stress-busters include getting a massage, listening to music, taking deep breaths, gardening, laughing, and talking about your troubles with a friend.

Switch snacks. People who eat to cope with stress usually don't make the best food choices. They reach for comfort foods like pizza, sausage, hamburgers, and chocolate — and also drink more alcohol. Single, divorced, and unemployed men often fall into this trap, as do women who feel they don't get enough emotional support.

If stress gives you the urge to snack, try one of the stress-busting techniques mentioned earlier instead. And if you absolutely need a snack, reach for an apple or some celery sticks.

Learn to cope. Because of unrest in the world, crime, and natural disasters, many people feel constantly stressed and uneasy. Your body responds to this long-term stress by creating fat stores for energy and breaking down muscles to help fight infection.

According to University of Georgia nutrition expert Carolyn Berdanier, eating slightly more polyunsaturated fat and protein can help your body cope with long-term stress. The fat lets your body know it has some energy available, and the protein helps keep your muscles intact. Exercise helps, too.

Whether you modify your diet, your approach to stress, or both, you should be pleasantly surprised the next time you step on the scale.

Move it and lose it

Focusing on which foods to eat or avoid makes it easy to overlook the other key part of any successful weight-loss program. But if you want to shed pounds, you not only have to take in fewer calories, you also have to burn more. That means exercising.

Regular exercise does so much more than help you lose weight. You can reduce blood pressure and cholesterol, relieve chronic pain and anxiety, and lower your medical bills all with one simple self-help method. So get moving.

Step lively. Don't worry. Exercising doesn't have to include heavy weights, long runs, or fancy machines. A brisk 30-minute walk every day will help. So will everyday activities, such as raking, gardening, or cleaning up around the house. Anything that gives you a workout counts as exercise.

Spread it out. If you can't spend 30 minutes exercising, split your exercise time into three 10-minute sessions or two 15-minute ones. Short bursts of exercise work just as well as one longer session when it comes to burning calories and losing weight.

Try something new. Looking for a change? Try tai chi. This traditional Chinese exercise program is perfect for older people. It improves your balance, cardiovascular fitness, and your ability to walk, lift things, and even run. Chances are you can find an instructor in your area.

Other good exercises include swimming, tennis, bicycling, golf, and stair walking. Make sure you talk to your doctor before you begin a new exercise program.

Visualize your workout. If the results of a recent study hold up, you may not have to exercise at all. Researchers at the Cleveland Clinic Foundation recently discovered you could improve your strength just by imagining you're exercising a certain muscle.

They think this "virtual" workout may help stroke victims and those suffering from spinal cord injuries. But healthy people probably would benefit more from real activities. Until more is known about this technique, keep working out the traditional way.

Eating right is important, of course. But don't forget, if you truly want to lose weight and improve your health, you must stay active. The more you move, the more you'll lose.

How to find the perfect exercise machine

You're a lean, mean, exercising machine — or at least you plan to become one. You just need a little help.

An exercise machine can help put you on the road to fitness and weight loss. But what machine is right for you? Check out the nuts and bolts of some of the more popular items according to *Consumer Reports*.

Try a treadmill. The best-selling home exercise machines, treadmills burn the most calories. They're also the least likely to sit unused. You can walk or run on them, change speeds, and pick different landscapes — both hilly and flat — to walk on. Before you buy one, check for the following features.

- ★ Easy-to-find controls, including a large stop button

- ★ Easy-to-read displays with large numbers and letters

- ★ Enough horsepower (at least 2 hp) if you have a heavy build

- ★ Thick deck (at least 3/4 of an inch) that absorbs shocks well and lies flat at the lowest setting

- ★ Monitors that track your heart rate and number of calories burned

- ★ Wide range of speeds and workouts

- ★ Gradual start and stop so you don't lose your balance

Ease onto an elliptical exerciser. If you're over 55 or have knee problems, this pedaling machine might be for you. A cross between a stair climber and a cross-country ski machine, the elliptical exerciser is easier on your joints than a treadmill. Make sure your machine is:

- ★ Easy to use. Elliptical exercisers have fewer settings than a treadmill, but watch out for knobs and hard-to-read monitors.

- ★ Right for your body. Make sure you can easily get on the machine and that the pedals are wide enough.

★ Stable. Stay away from machines that sway or twist when you use them.

Work out with a home gym. Strength-training devices come in a variety of styles with the same basic idea — to give your entire body a workout in the privacy of your own home.

Therefore, your home becomes an important factor. If you have the space, you might choose a sturdy, Nautilus-type weight stack machine, the kind where you use a pin to determine how much weight you lift. If not, you might opt for a lighter device, like a Bowflex-style rod or rubber band system that you can assemble and move more easily.

No matter what model you choose, look for the following features.

★ Low, middle, and high pulleys

★ Leg-extension and leg-curl station

★ Vertical-butterfly station

★ Bench with adjustable incline

★ Pull-down bar

★ Curl bar

★ Hand grips

★ Ankle strap

Before you buy, find out what works for you. Spend some time at a health club or gym to see what equipment you like. Or ask if you can try out your friend's home exercise machine. Do some research. Don't just jump at the first TV offer you see.

Just as important as finding the right machine is finding the right price. Exercise machines aren't cheap. Shop around to find the best deal. You might even find a good deal on used equipment. A previous owner who never found time to exercise might be willing to make a deal to get rid of a barely used machine.

Of course, you might not need a machine at all. Free weights, like barbells and dumbbells, can work just as well. But they can be tough to use if you're unfamiliar with them, and you need someone to spot you for certain exercises.

Whether you choose a treadmill, elliptical exerciser, a home gym, or free weights, remember one thing — even the best equipment is worthless unless you actually use it.

Add 10 extra years to your life

Living healthy means living longer. Need proof? Just take a look at Seventh-Day Adventists in California.

Researchers from Loma Linda University tracked more than 34,000 members of this religious group for 12 years. They found that Adventist men can expect to live more than seven years longer than the average Californian, while Adventist women can tack on an extra four and a half years.

Learn the three big secrets of these people who live longer and do it in picture-perfect health.

Eat vegetarian. In the study, Adventists who never ate meat or ate it less than once a month lived even longer. Vegetarian Adventists also needed less medication and had fewer overnight hospital stays, surgeries, and X-ray tests. In other words, their quality of life — as well as its quantity — was higher than most.

Exercise regularly. About 40 percent of Adventists in the study exercised vigorously for 15 minutes at least three times a week. Exercise, of course, helps keep your weight down and gives your heart and lungs a healthy workout.

Do not smoke. Virtually no Adventists smoked. That means they automatically slashed their risk for heart disease, stroke, cancer, and other health problems.

These healthy folks, who outlive even the notoriously long-living Japanese, also eat nuts frequently and have a medium body mass index (BMI). Body mass index measures your weight in relation to your height. Nuts can be a good source of protein in a vegetarian diet, and a healthy diet and regular exercise help keep your weight under control.

Of course, not all Adventists live perfectly healthy lives. But an Adventist who eats a vegetarian diet, exercises regularly, eats nuts more than five times a week, has a medium BMI and doesn't smoke will live about 10 years longer than an Adventist who does none of those things.

There's no reason why the Seventh-Day Adventists in California should be the only ones to benefit from their healthy lifestyle. Add an extra 10 active years to your life by following the Seventh-Day Adventist model for healthy living. It's the most powerful treatment for reducing your risk of heart attack or stroke. It improves the quality of your life — and gives you more life to improve.

Index

A